MEN OF THE DESERT AIR FORCE

MEN OF THE
DESERT AIR FORCE
1940 – 1943

Chaz Bowyer

WILLIAM KIMBER · LONDON

First published in 1984 by
WILLIAM KIMBER & CO. LIMITED
100 Jermyn Street, London SW1Y 6EE

ISBN 0 7183 0539 6

Photoset in North Wales by
Derek Doyle & Associates, Mold, Clwyd
and printed in Great Britain by
Redwood Burn Limited, Trowbridge, Wiltshire

Contents

List of Illustrations

Introduction

Following the prime theme of my *Bomber Barons* and *Fighter Pilots of the RAF, 1939-45*, in this volume I have selected a relatively few individuals and certain facets of the air war fought in North Africa (mainly) during the years 1940-43, attempting to portray the widely diverse character of those men individually, and to offer in certain cases a modicum of long overdue public recognition of their courage and sacrifices. They came from many different lands willingly to help Britain's struggle against the evil ambitions of the Nazi and Italian dictatorships, then blended together readily in the common cause; a true 'commonwealth' of men dedicated to the cause of human freedom. It is my sincere hope that the handful of men described herein will be representative to some degree of their very many colleagues in the desert air forces, and will illustrate the multi-national nature of those airmen who fought – and too often died – in the alien skies of North Africa and the Mediterranean theatre. The 'Desert Air Force' – to give it its popular title – was an astonishing amalgam of men of differing races and creeds whose easy cohesion produced an air arm which demonstrated conclusively the importance not only of air power over any land or sea battle but the efficacy and vital necessity for true inter-Services liaison and interdependence.

My choice of the years 1940-43 in the Middle East overall war has been deliberate. That war commenced in East Africa and North Africa and *had* to be won in North Africa before the Allied commanders could realistically plan the further conquest of Italy and, ultimately, attack Hitler's Reich in its southern boundaries, thereby joining the Allied western and eastern 'pincers' in northern Europe. Had the North African campaign been lost to the Axis, the consequences might – indeed, would – have been disastrous for the Allied cause. Also deliberate on my part is the larger emphasis upon men who flew fighter aircraft over the desert, primarily to reflect the simple fact that there was a higher proportion of fighter units than other types of aircraft squadrons throughout the North African campaign. However, it is *not* my intention thereby to imply that the men of the bombers, maritime, photo-recce, torpedo-bombers, Tac R, or other facets of the Middle East aerial conflict were a jot less vital in their endeavours. It cannot be said too often that the ultimate victory in North Africa was due to the *total* cohesive efforts of *all* members of the Middle East air arm, in close liaison with the other Services.

Chaz Bowyer
Norwich, 1984

CHAPTER ONE

Background

The title 'Desert War' has become a popular misnomer for a
protracted conflict by land, sea, and air during 1939-45, the
boundaries of which in fact stretched eventually to almost every
shore of the Mediterranean Sea and lands far beyond the desert
wastelands. Commencing in East Africa, the struggle between the
Allied and Axis Powers was then fought along the northern fringes
of the vast desert areas of North Africa, but quickly embraced
territories in Egypt, Libya, Greece, Yugoslavia, the Aegean,
Palestine, Persia, the Balkans, West Africa, Aden, Tunisia, Italy, and
many other bordering lands and seas. Nevertheless, once the Italian
colonial grip of Somaliland and East Africa had been loosened, then
broken, the premier combat area was the coastal strip of North
Africa. Here the Allies faced, fought, and defeated the Axis' bid to
capture the most vital Middle East zones. From here were then
launched the invasions of Sicily, Italy, and southern France *et al*
which, in pincer-conjunction with the Allied forces in northern and
eastern Europe, ultimately closed an unbreakable ring of steel
around the remnants of Hitler's Nazi Empire and reduced his
'1000-years Reich' to a state of utter devastation and abject
surrender.

The North Africa campaigns of 1940-43 also gave birth to a form
of tri-Service liaison and fighting co-operation which not only
proved to be the key to success but inaugurated a pattern for
inter-Services intimate 'partnership' which became embellished to
high degrees in the subsequent India-Burma and northern
European campaigns of 1943-45. That interdependence of air, land,
and sea forces became the major factor in the Allies' eventual
triumph over the Axis Powers; thus the Desert War can be said to
have sown the seeds of ultimate victory. It can also be claimed that
the Mediterranean war gave Britain and her Allies some of their
gravest defeats, yet paradoxically also their first 'complete' victories

over Axis forces on a global scale. Until 1943 the fortunes of the
Allies had been dismaying, even disastrous on occasion, with only
rare, isolated triumphs to sustain morale. In North Africa and
Tunisia the 'desert' forces provided a base-rock foundation for an
upsurge in hope. Though those forces were yet to fight their way
grimly and slowly from Sicily along the entire length of Italy and
into the heart of Europe, ultimate victory was now unquestioned.

To the men who formed the RAF's 'presence' in the Middle East
zones in 1940, when Italy declared war against the Allies, the
inevitability of final victory must have been, to say the least,
problematical. While morale among the RAF air and ground crews
was high from the outset, the status of their equipment and facilities
for waging modern warfare was hardly strong or adequate to match
that of their new enemies, at least on paper. The AOC-in-C, Middle
East Command at that time was Air Chief Marshal Sir Arthur
Longmore, who had at his immediate disposal just 29 squadrons –
some 300 firstline aircraft, plus nearly 300 others in reserve, of all
types – with which to 'control' a geographical area greater than the
United States of America. Of his 14 bomber squadrons, nine were
equipped with Bristol Blenheims, while his five fighter squadrons
were all still flying Gloster Gladiator biplanes. The remaining air
'strength', apart from two Sunderland flying boat units, presented a
melancholy array of obsolete biplanes barely worthy of the
description 'operational'. Notwithstanding such a state of affairs,
the RAF pursued a constant policy of the offensive from the outset,
and at dawn on 11 June 1940, within hours of Italy's formal
declaration of war, a force of 26 Blenheims drawn from Nos 45, 55,
and 113 Squadrons bombed and strafed the Italian air base at El
Adem, doing great damage though losing two bombers to the
defences.

At that stage Longmore's prospects for increasing the strength of
his air arm were minimal. The Battle of Britain was already entering
its first phase and aircraft, especially modern fighters, and trained
air crews were necessarily being husbanded for the vital defence of
the United Kingdom after the disastrous losses incurred in the
French campaign of May-June 1940. For the moment, Longmore's
forces had just Italian opponents to contend with in Africa and the
Mediterranean – ostensibly tough enough opposition – but it could

Gladiators of 112 Squadron at
Ismailia, Egypt, mid-1939

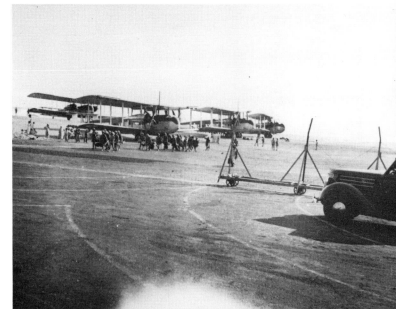

Vickers Valentias of 70
Squadron at Amriya, early
1940

Martin Maryland of No. 24
Squadron SAAF

Gladiator pilots of 112 Squadron, Greece, 1941

80 Squadron 'operations room' in the desert, 1941

be only a matter of time before Hitler despatched German reinforcements for his Axis partner. Mastery of the Mediterranean area would provide Hitler with key strategic bases and access to the oil-rich resources of the Middle East, apart from strangling the Allied supply routes to the Far East. Another major worry for Longmore in mid-1940 was the immediate threat of Italian forces in Italian Somaliland, Abyssinia, and Eritrea, menacing the Allied southern supply route via the Cape and the Gulf of Aden and the Red Sea. In view of an Italo-French armistice signed on 24 June, this southern supply line became crucial, since any reinforcements via the Mediterranean now meant running the gauntlet of the Italian navy. Then, in September 1940 Italian land forces under Marshal Graziani in North Africa advanced into Egypt, forcing the Allied armies to retreat.

While the Allied forces consolidated their new defensive positions and began to re-strengthen, several events occurred within the next few months which stretched Longmore's desert squadrons to their limits. On 28 October Italy invaded Greece, causing the British government to order Longmore to send RAF squadrons to Greece, and thereby diluting RAF strength in Egypt (eventually) by five squadrons. In December 1940 General Wavell launched a 'reconnaissance in strength' (*sic*) across the Egyptian-Libyan border which rapidly developed into a full-scale Allied advance westwards, driving the Italian colonial forces back across Cyrenaica to the border of Tripolitania. Full available air support was given to this advance, but when the Allied armies finally paused to regroup and replenish, Longmore was again ordered by Churchill's government to bolster the hopeless Greek situation, and was also 'required' to provide '10 to 15 squadrons' (*sic*) for transfer to bases in Turkey as part of Churchill's hope of intimidating Hitler from intervening in Greece, Bulgaria, and/or Turkey. Fortuitously, the Turkish government declined to permit any RAF presence within its territories. In March 1941 German troops with strong Luftwaffe support were flung into the Italo-Greek conflict and by late April the heroic Greek and RAF defenders had been overwhelmed; survivors of the decimated RAF squadrons being evacuated in piecemeal fashion via Crete *et al* to Egypt.

The bloody tragedies of Greece and Crete were only the start of a series of diversions for Arthur Longmore's already thinly-stretched air strength. In May 1941 came an Axis-supported Iraqi uprising, followed in June by the 'desirability' of occupying a hostile Vichy French-dominated Syria; each of these 'side-shows' draining further RAF units and resources. In addition to these many problems Longmore needed to provide some form of air defences for the strategically key island of Malta, which by the spring of 1941 had become the daily target for an aerial 'siege' by German and Italian bombers and fighters from Sicilian bases. The only bright spots in an otherwise depressing set of circumstances for Longmore were the cessation of the Italian East Africa campaign with an Allied victory, thereby releasing a number of air units for service in North Africa; while long-awaited reinforcement with fresh aircraft, including American designs, had gradually begun to flow to Egypt, mainly via West African ports, but occasionally from RN aircraft carriers risking the hazardous Mediterranean sea route.

Even before the Greek debacle, German troops to bolster the Italian armies in North Africa had entered the struggle, and in March 1941, under the command of Erwin Rommel, had forced the Allied armies back to the Egyptian border again. By mid-June, however, a fresh Allied offensive, code-named *Battleaxe*, had been launched, only to be heavily repulsed by Rommel's tanks, troops, and aircraft resulting in serious Allied losses. By then command of the RAF in the Middle East had passed into the capable hands of Air Marshal Arthur Tedder, Longmore's deputy. Longmore, after a long period of coping with crisis after crisis with inadequate material strength and virtually a total lack of support or understanding from his political masters in Whitehall, had been quietly transferred to England in April 1941; the latest of a select company of commanders such as Hugh Dowding, Keith Park, Wavell, and others who had incurred Churchill's displeasure (politically-speaking) by being technically responsible for defeats, or at best insufficiently dramatic victories. Tedder's succession to the reins coincided with the first steps taken in forming the Middle East RAF into a true tactical air force*, and in July 1941 the first Wing,

---

* In essence 'No 1 Tactical Air Force (TAF)', hence the subsequent titling of the Allied air formation accompanying the Allied invasion of Normandy in June 1944 as 2nd TAF.

No 253, was formed experimentally for army close support roles. Shortly after three fighter Wings were freshly formed; Nos 258 and 269, tasked initially with operations over the front line, and No 262, responsible for defence of the Nile Delta zone.

For the period July-October 1941 the North African war became relatively static as both Axis and Allied commanders built up strength for the next clash of arms. In the event the British and Commonwealth forces struck first, launching *Operation Crusader* on 18 November with a total of 28 squadrons as aerial support over the fighting areas. The ensuing battles were fought fiercely with high casualties on both sides, but the Axis forces were compelled to retreat westwards and, by mid-April 1942, the Allies had regained all the ground lost a year before. Rommel's response was a near-immediate counter-attack which succeeded in forcing the Allied armies back to the Gazala line, halfway across Cyrenaica, following which each side of the see-sawing struggle settled into further recoupment periods. At this crucial stage badly-needed RAF units and personnel were withdrawn from firstline operations and despatched to India in the light of the Japanese conquest of Malaya and impending assault on India via Burma; a decision which also depleted vital aircraft and crew reinforcements intended for the Middle East. Even as the RAF's desert air force was being reduced numerically, Rommel struck again at Gazala in late May 1942 and the subsequent lengthy slogging battle of attrition eventually forced the Eighth Army to retreat in June, back to prepared positions at El Alamein, some 60 miles west of Alexandria, where it dug in, grimly determined to give no more ground to Rommel's Afrika Korps. Thus, in almost exactly two years of war in northern Africa, Axis and Allied armies had returned to virtually their locations at the outset of their conflict.

For the men of the desert squadrons those two years had been a period of huge effort with insufficient resources, flying aircraft of less than required abilities for such warfare. The shifting nature of the various land campaigns had meant adapting to a roving gipsy form of existence, operating from hastily-cleared stretches of bald desert scarcely worthy of the name airfield; indeed, some of the most used strips became officially titled as merely 'Landing Grounds' (LGs) with a number. Life at the sharp end was reduced to

Hurricane IIC, en route to Egypt from Takoradi, West Africa

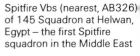

Spitfire Vbs (nearest, AB326) of 145 Squadron at Helwan, Egypt – the first Spitfire squadron in the Middle East

Hurricane II, named 'Kathleen', employed on photo-recce duties, circa 1941-42 in Middle East theatre

the bare essentials; a pup tent over a hole in the sand for individual accommodation (though even a tent was a luxury in some situations), tented offices or the back of a three-ton lorry for the Operations Room, a water ration which rarely permitted more than a face-wash, a monotonous diet of tinned bully-beef and hard-tack biscuit, washed down with captured Italian wine or German beer (*if* lucky ...) or occasional English bottled beer when the unit's local scavenging proved successful. The heat of the day contrasted vividly with the cold of night, and everywhere was sand, sand, scrub, and the omnipresent flies. All facets of a normal Service routine – working parades, inspections, smart uniform, *et al* – simply went by the board; to fly and fight was the prime purpose, and all other considerations were relegated to the pen-pushing brigade based far behind the fighting lines in the fleshpots of Cairo and Alexandria.

If the pilots' and other air crews' life was hard and basic, that of the 'Erks' – the patient ground crews – was doubly so, yet these performed minor miracles in maintenance in circumstances never envisaged in any technical air publication or manual. 'Ubendum Wemendum' became the permanent creed of the ground tradesmen, and they rarely failed in their utter dedication to keep their aircraft flying, despite a normal lack of any reasonable amenities. Improvisation was the norm, and their superb support could be summed up in the age-old cliché, 'The impossible we do today, miracles take a little longer'.

Such living and fighting conditions might have had disastrous effect on the morale of lesser men, yet the desert airmen never faltered in maintaining a constant offensive against all opponents, whether these were human, mechanical, or of raw nature. They truly exemplified Air Marshal Arthur ('Maori') Coningham's dicta 'Strip 'em of all the non-essentials, give 'em plenty of work, and they'll be a happy lot'. Even the lack of essentials on occasion failed to daunt the desert men. Long-established concepts of the perils awaiting the Englishman abroad and the 'vital' precautions necessary for protection from the mid-day sun were very quickly shattered as the war got under way in Africa, while the 'uncivilised' form of living in the desert proved surprising healthy.

Above all, perhaps, was the extraordinarily close comradeship engendered between all ranks on any fighting firstline unit; a

Wellingtons of 37 Squadron, May 1941

'Hurricane House' in Sharia Soliman Pasha, Cairo, an air crew rest centre, 1941-42

brotherhood resulting from commonly shared deprivations and a singular purpose. That such men endured totally alien conditions in strange and unfamiliar countries, and in climatic elements hitherto unknown, is all the more remarkable when it is remembered that, for the vast majority of the desert airmen, their postings to the Middle East war theatre were the first time in their lives that they had travelled beyond the coast of their native countries.

The Allied retreat from Gazala to El Alamein in late 1942 proved to be an orderly withdrawal, rather than a rout, due in no small measure to the fiercely active support of the Western Desert Air Force, whose squadrons were by then well versed in rapid deployment to fresh LGs as the land battles fluctuated, and while WDAF losses mounted alarmingly during this period it was rare for any WDAF operation to fail to fulfil its objective. Once consolidated at El Alamein the equipment of the WDAF was up-dated and the first USAAF squadrons joined the command, while many fresh combat units were added to the overall strength, particularly for coastal, bombing, and defence roles. Late in the evening of 23 October 1942 an Allied artillery barrage from the El Alamein positions commenced, of an intensity and weight not witnessed since the 1914-18 war in Europe; the prelude to an Allied ground offensive which – eventually – would prove instrumental in concluding the campaigns in North Africa.

On that date the strength of the Allied air forces in North Africa comprised almost 1,000 operational aircraft, some 60 per cent of which were fighters and 30 per cent bombers of all types. In opposition the Luftwaffe had almost 600 equivalent firstline aircraft, some 350 of these being fighters, supported by 17 *Gruppi* of the Italian Regia Aeronautica. Many of the Allied fighters, however, were by then adapted and well-practised in fighter-bomber operations in addition to their normal pure fighter roles, thereby adding yet more weight to the offensive capabilities of the Allied air efforts.

The first ten days of the Alamein offensive proved bloody in casualties for both sides of the battle, but on 3 November Rommel's army began a retreat to the Egyptian frontier, and five days later came the Allied invasion of French North Africa – *Operation Torch* – far to the west and in the rear of Rommel's Afrika Korps. By 11

November all Axis forces had left Egyptian territory and were speeding westwards to Cyrenaica and Libya, leaving only rearguard defences hopefully to delay the Allied pursuit. By the end of the month Rommel's troops had reached the El Agheila line, beyond Benghazi, where the 8th Army too paused in its advance to rebuild strength and supply lines.

The combination of *Operation Torch* and the Afrika Korps' retreat effectively ended the long-standing aerial siege of Malta as Sicilian-based German and Italian air strength was hastily transferred to bolster the North African struggle. By then Malta's defences had *claimed* a total of 915 enemy aircraft shot down throughout the entire siege – 733 by fighters and 182 by anti-aircraft guns – though enemy records later revealed combat losses of 567 German and Italian aircraft of all types in actual combat; *minimum* figures which did not include aircraft damaged but repaired, or ground losses. Towards the end of that siege, however, Allied fighter opposition over the battered island had proved too great for any further aerial onslaught, with crippling Axis casualties during intensified raids in October 1942. By November Malta could assume even greater importance as the base for aerial strangulation of Axis air and sea supply routes to North Africa. In North Africa the *Torch* forces soon became bogged down in their attempts to capture Tunisia, due in no small part to atrocious winter weather conditions, but Rommel's forces, by February 1943, were wholly within Tunisian territory, entrenched behind the formidable Mareth line. Meanwhile the Allied airmen had created huge slaughter among the many Axis transport aircraft attempting to fly in fuel, troops, armaments, and other supplies to North Africa, resulting in aircraft casualties which, in relation to the numbers employed, proved catastrophic for the Axis cause. Just one example of such Allied depredations occurred on 18 April 1943 – the so-termed 'Palm Sunday Massacre' – when RAF and USAAF fighters shot down 59 German transport Ju52s and 14 of their German and Italian fighter escorts in a single clash some six miles off Cap Bon, for the loss of six Allied fighters. The particular campaign against the Axis aerial supply formations – code-named *Operation Flax* – had officially commenced on 5 April, and its efficacy may be judged by the Allied claims to have destroyed well over 400 transport aircraft

Spitfire IX undergoing maintenance. In bkgrd a Messerschmitt Bf109G of II/JG53, fitted with underwing cannon gondolas

Douglas Boston III of 114 Sqn (Flt Lt J. Steele, DFC at controls) over 'Kings Cross' area, May 1943

within the first fortnight of *Flax* operations.

The end in Tunisia came soon after, with Generale Messe surrendering the last Axis forces in Africa on 13 May 1943. Thus almost exactly three years of unremitting battle for mastery of the North African lands were concluded. Immediate plans were put in hand for the invasion of Sicily and, ultimately, Italy, utilising Malta as a forward launching pad; projects which had been in effect anticipated even before the triumph in Tunisia with Allied heavy bombers raiding key targets in Sicily and southern Italy in increasing strength from March 1943. In the interim Allied efforts were redoubled to 'clean up' various Mediterranean islands still in Axis hands, notably Pantellaria and Sardinia; the former surrendering on 11 June 1943 after a series of incredibly severe bombardments from air and sea forces, while next day Lampedusa hurriedly surrendered before it too became subject of such punishment. Finally on 10 July 1943 *Operation Husky*, the invasion of Sicily, got underway and by 14 August the island was virtually in Allied hands. During those few weeks the Axis air forces offered desperate opposition but in the event lost well in excess of 1,000 aircraft, including many hundreds of machines destroyed or simply abandoned on the ground.

With little pause the Allies pressed forward with invasions of Italy itself, with the first elements of the 8th Army gaining a toe-hold in Calabria on 3 September, and six days later launching a larger-scale invasion force to land at Salerno. In fact, an armistice agreement had already been signed by the Italian government on 3 September at Cassibile, Sicily, though this was not made public until 8 September, and had indeed been negotiated since mid-August following the deposing and imprisonment of the Italian dictator, Benito Mussolini, in July 1943.

The subsequent bloody and prolonged slogging battles northwards along the entire length of Italy in 1943-45, though fought in the main by the former desert forces, air and land, were of a different character to the North African desert war, particularly in the context of the terrain and climatic conditions. The hard-won lessons of that desert war were to be applied and embellished to high degree, emphasising not only the vital necessity for air superiority but also the efficacy of true inter-Services' dependency and liaison. Such lessons had been learned with no small sacrifice over the sand-wastes of North Africa and provided the kernel of ultimate victory over the Axis Powers in northern Europe and the jungles of Burma in 1944-45. As General Bernard Montgomery said when addressing his 8th Army in Tripoli: 'On your behalf I have sent a special message to the Allied Air Forces that have co-operated with us. I don't suppose that any army has ever been supported by such a magnificent air striking force. I have always maintained that the 8th Army and the RAF in the Western Desert together constitute one fighting machine, and therein lies our great strength'.*

Undoubtedly, much (if not all) the success of the desert air forces had been due to the fact that *every* facet of air power came under the aegis of *one* centralised command. In Britain, for example, air power had been employed in separate packets, with each Command enjoying a great degree of autonomy and employing its strength in narrow-vision channels. In the Middle East any and every facet of air power could be (and was) used to concentrate on prime objectives as each day-to-day situation changed, ensuring maximum flexibility and striking power where most needed. Such cohesive co-operation provided the basis for all subsequent use and administration of air power.

* *The Desert Air Force* by R. Owen; Hutchinson, 1948

CHAPTER TWO

Ernest Mason

The date was 15 February 1942. The place, Gambut, a scrub-strewn desert airfield located some 60-odd miles east of Tobruk in the coastal strip of Cyrenaica, North Africa. Parked somewhat haphazardly around the landing area were a gaggle of shark-nosed Curtiss Kittyhawks of No 94 Squadron RAF. The squadron had flown in to Gambut only the day before, having spent the previous two weeks at nearby LG110 converting its crews from their former Hurricanes to these new American-designed fighters.

Also new to the squadron was its latest CO, Squadron Leader E.M. Mason, DFC, who had taken over the reins of command in January. If Mason was new to 94 Squadron, he was nevertheless a veteran of the Middle East aerial war, having served in the zone since mid-1938 and been officially credited with at least 17 air combat victories to date, apart from dozens of other enemy aircraft destroyed in daring, long-range ground-strafing sorties.

Known throughout the Middle East RAF as 'Imshi'*, Mason was already something of a legendary figure to his fellow pilots, and on this day he was to lead his latest squadron into action for the first time in their new warhorses. A wing sweep was scheduled for late afternoon, combining forces with the sharkmouth-painted Kittyhawks of No 112 Squadron based at the nearby, former Italian air base at El Adem, intending to strafe enemy airfields further west. Their primary target was an air strip at Martuba, just east of Derna, home of the élite German Jagdgeschwader 27 whose ranks included some of the top-scoring *Experten* ('aces') of the Luftwaffe in North Africa.

At 1645 hours Mason led eight of 94 Squadron's Kittyhawks off Gambut and soon linked up with twelve Kittyhawks from 112 Squadron, then set course westwards at low level. Flashing past low

* Pronounced 'Imshee', Arabic for 'Go away'.

28

Sqn Ldr E.M. 'Imshi' Mason, DFC wearing an 80 Sqn badge on his flying overalls and sporting his well-known beard

over the turrets of some Afrika Korps tanks near Bir Temrad shortly after, Mason's formation reached Martuba without opposition and swept across the landing ground firing at the parked Messerschmitt Bf109Fs of JG27.

On the ground Oberfeldwebel Otto Schulz of II/JG27 leapt into the cockpit of a recently serviced Bf109F and took off rapidly. As the leading Kittyhawks swept in for a second pass, Schulz attacked them. In quick succession – the engagement lasted less than five minutes – Schulz shot down Mason, then Pilot Officer Marshall and Sergeants Belcher and Weightman, of the first five Kittyhawks. Minutes later Schulz spotted a lone Kittyhawk flying east and quickly closed on its tail, his fire damaging the aircraft and wounding its pilot (Sergeant McQueen, 112 Squadron) before lack of ammunition forced the German to break off and return to Martuba. Otto Schulz, for whom these five *Luftsiege* had brought his victory tally to date up to 44, was awarded a Knight's Cross of the Iron Cross shortly after, then in March returned to Germany for commissioning, and rejoined the desert air war in May 1942 as an Oberleutnant.

The loss of Ernest 'Imshi' Mason was acutely felt throughout the RAF in the Middle East. The contemporary AOC-in-C during 1940-41, ACM Sir Arthur Longmore, referred to Mason as ' ... the fighter pilot *par excellence*'; while one of his junior officers remarked on 'His experience, powers of organisation, and consideration for each and every one of his men made him a leader whom we were all proud to follow'. Other tributes included such phrases as 'outstanding originality of thought', 'a fighter ace with unlimited guts', 'a most charming individual'; all facets of a man who had been born tiny in size, frail in strength, delicate in health, yet grew up to become physically tough with apparently unlimited energy.

Born in Darlington, Durham on 29 July 1913, Ernest Mitchelson Mason showed early signs of an inner determination even as a young boy, combined with a lasting interest and enthusiasm for all forms of engineering machinery; the latter being manifested by ownership of a motorcycle at age 14, and competitive dirt-track speedway riding a year later. On leaving school Mason was apprenticed to a marine engines' firm, but continued his pursuit of speed and thrills with motorcycles, then cars, with an equal enjoyment of music exemplified by his constant practice with a saxophone. His seemingly bottomless depths of restless energy led him to frequent travels around the United Kingdom, exploring, enquiring, experiencing with the personal conviction that merely being alive was not *living*. By the end of 1937 Mason had decided to join the RAF and duly applied for a Short Service Commission, meanwhile paying privately for flying lessons with a local civilian flying club. In March 1938 the RAF accepted him provisionally for pilot training, sending him to Ansty for *ab initio* instruction, then on 3 June, as an Acting Pilot Officer (on probation), Mason sailed in the SS *Ranpura* to Egypt, posted to No 4 Flying School (FTS) at Abu Sueir, which he reached on 22 June.

From June until December 1938 Mason passed through the various stages of his pilot training at Abu Sueir, flying Hawker Harts, Audaxes, Avro Ansons, and graduating with an 82 per cent overall assessment and 'Above Average' gradings in all facets of his course. Initially selected for posting to No 45 Squadron (Vickers Wellesley bombers), Mason managed to exchange his posting with a fellow graduate and went instead to No 80 Squadron, based then at Ismailia. Along with Pilot Officer John Poynton and Flying Officer Linnard*, Mason arrived on the squadron in the first week of January 1939, and was allotted to 'C' Flight, which was commanded by Pilot Officer M. St J. Pattle, a South African†. No 80 Squadron was equipped with Gloster Gladiator fighters and commanded then by Squadron Leader R.C. Jonas‡, and on 16 January the unit moved base from Ismailia to Helwan.

Once settled in to the new station Mason pursued the normal daily routine of a junior officer-pilot, mixing a variety of ground administrative duties with reasonably plentiful flying practice. As he gained experience in handling his Gladiator, Mason quickly proved to be an exceptional pilot with a natural flair for both aerobatics and marksmanship. Unlike some of his boisterous companions, Mason took great pains to keep himself in top physical condition, while his mental approach to flying a fighter was analytical. In his

* Later, Wing Commander, DFC.

† Later Squadron Leader, DFC, and killed in action in Greece on 20 April 1941.

‡ Later, Air Commodore, OBE.

own words in a letter to his mother:

> It isn't the aim to make pretty landings and flashy turns low
> down. I consider the aim is to get off and on the ground *safely* and
> *consistently* merely as a means to an end; the end being to fly
> anywhere in any weather, and to be able to shoot accurately and
> attack with ability ... but on the other hand, I throw the aircraft
> about alarmingly when at a decent height. When doing air-firing,
> for instance, I fly in a totally incorrect and violent manner
> according to the books, but it gets results and is at a safe height.
> In an aerial combat the usual methods as taught are useless, and
> one must handle the aeroplane not as an aircraft but as a *gun* with
> wings.

The outbreak of war in Europe found No 80 Squadron virtually
split, with its aircraft in Amriya but the main base still at Helwan.
Though long prepared for mobilisation for actual war, in the event
squadron routine merely continued as before professionally and
socially, with Mason and his fellow pilots continuing to enjoy the
fleshpots of Egypt in full measure. Only in June 1940, with Italy's
declaration of war against Britain, did the conflict become a reality
for the RAF in Egypt and the Middle East generally. For 'Imshi'
Mason this development was received calmly, professionally. As he
wrote to his mother on 12 June;

> I am not a fatalist, as I am paying the most minute attention to
> my aircraft, parachute, etc. I have pencils on string, cloths for
> cleaning windscreens in my overalls, map, etc. And I am also
> paying attention to gas mask, revolvers, and so on. So, if I don't
> get through, it certainly won't be my fault, unless I meet a very
> much better pilot than I am.

His comment here was devoid of mere conceit, simply an
extension of his characteristic perfectionist attitude to any task
undertaken. By July 1940 Mason had exchanged his Gladiator for
one of the few Hurricanes now arriving in the Middle East, the
initial deliveries going to No 80 Squadron, with which by 28 June
the unit was able to form a complete Hurricane Flight, commanded
by Flight Lieutenant E.G. 'Tap' Jones, and including Mason.

Gladiators of 80 Squadron, early 1940

Sqn Ldr Sidney Linnard in his Gladiator, 80 Squadron

Trio of Savoia Marchetti SM79s

Fiat CR42 downed near Buq Buq

Curtiss Tomahawk AK739 of 94 Sqn, piloted here by Sgt J.F. Edwards (later, Wg Cdr, DFC, DFM), February 1942. Squadron codes FZ were later changed to GO.

Occasional aerial combats were fought by individual pilots of the squadron, but Mason's only operational sorties during June-November were lengthy ground-strafing sorties against Italian transport columns and airfields.

On 19 August 1940 the Hurricane Flight, including Mason, joined a similar Hurricane Flight from No 33 Squadron to form No 274 Squadron, thus creating the first all-Hurricane unit in the Middle East. No 80 Squadron provided the new unit's first CO, Squadron Leader P.H. Dunn, apart from several pilots later to gain high honours and distinction, such as Peter Wykeham-Barnes* and John Lapsley†. By mid-September No 274 Squadron was flying daily operations against the Italian armies, but Mason's first head-on combat with the Italian air force did not come until 9 December, the first day of General Wavell's Libyan offensive. Shortly after mid-day 274's pilots met five Savoia-Marchetti SM79 bombers and promptly destroyed four and at least damaged the fifth. Mason's contribution was no more than a share in the general attack on these – 'I was probably too excited to aim deliberately enough' – but in the same afternoon, while patrolling the Barrani-Sofafi area, Mason was one of five Hurricane pilots who attacked a formation of 27 Fiat CR42 fighters. In Mason's later description; 'We had a lovely dogfight and I personally accounted for one (confirmed). He went down with flames coming out but not properly blazing'.

During the following few days Mason was to claim two more CR42s and an SM79, but these pure aerial combats were interspersed with many ground-strafing sorties, particularly concentrating on the retreating Italian armies' road convoys. It was an intense period of activity for the RAF's fighters especially, leaving no time between sorties for anything other than food and sleep, and Mason grew a beard ('to save shaving and water'); a personal trademark which was to become famous over the coming months.

January 1941 proved to be a particularly fruitful month for Mason in the context of operations. Many of his sorties were flown from an advanced landing ground, usually accompanied by just one other pilot, and comprised a series of daring, long-range ground

---

* Later, Air Marshal, Sir Peter Wykeham, KCB, DSO, OBE, DFC, AFC.
† Later, Air Commodore, OBE, DFC, AFC.

attacks on Italian air strips; a form of operations which Mason was not always formally detailed to carry out, but flew on his own initiative. During his two weeks' sojourn at the ALG at Sidi Barrani, Mason brought his personal tally of aerial victories up to at least ten, with two more unconfirmed by 17 January, but had also destroyed many more Italian aircraft on the ground; in one sortie alone strafing and destroying at least a dozen SM79 bombers at one airfield. On 26 January he added three more victories to his total in a single fight:

> Three of us were on patrol when we met some Italians. Patterson from Toronto chased three Fiat G.50s and I saw seven CR42s. I chased these and when they turned to attack me I had a quick dogfight with them all round me. The first one I fired at went down and crashed without burning. The second and third each turned slowly over and dived straight in and exploded. All this was over in two or three minutes. By the time the third one was down the others had disappeared, which was very fortunate as my motor cut out and I had to force-land ... unfortunately the ground was very rough and I burst a tyre and went up on my nose, wrecking the poor old aircraft with which I had got all my victories ... after I had force-landed I learnt that one of the CR42 pilots had tried to bale out but his parachute had not opened, so I had a look at him. He was about 200 yards from his still-blazing machine. I had got him in the right shoulder so he had not been able to open his 'chute. I went through his pockets and found a lot of interesting snapshots and a lot of letters. Before I left I covered him with his parachute and weighted it down with stones. After I got back I took the Magister to HQ to hand in these pictures.

A few days later Mason flew a particularly long solo sortie to Benina airfield, near Benghazi, where – instead of strafing the aerodrome – he dropped a letter written by a captured CR42 pilot to his mother in Italy; but on 30 January he scored his 14th confirmed victory on what was to be his last operational sortie with 274 Squadron. Late in the afternoon, accompanied by Patterson again, he flew back to Benina aerodrome. En route he encountered a lone Fiat CR42 and attacked it but had met a particularly tough opponent. The fight evolved into a series of head-on attacks on each other, and on the fourth confrontation the Italian kept flying and firing straight at Mason instead of breaking away. As the two aircraft closed to point-blank distance Mason pulled back on his control column to jump over his adversary, then felt a crash as the CR42 slid below him.

Mason had a fleeting glimpse of the Italian flying on, burning, but then realised he'd been hit, with a ragged hole in the cockpit wall from the impact of an explosive shell, and further damage in the wings. His right side was giving him pain and he concluded, reasonably, that he was wounded. Pressing his right hand over the painful area of his side, Mason flew his aircraft back to base with his left hand only, all the time feeling himself getting 'weaker' and finally executing a shaky landing. On evacuating his cockpit Mason gingerly examined his wound – only to discover just a few scratches where some slivers of the Italian shell had sliced through his flying clothing, scarred his skin slightly, then exited without further damage! His imagination had worked overtime during the return flight, and his gradual 'weakening' had been pure auto-suggestion ...

Awarded a DFC at the end of January, and promotion to Flying Officer, Mason was then posted to No 261 Squadron as a Flight commander. Based at Ta Kali, with a detachment at Luqa, 261 Squadron was a Hurricane unit engaged in the desperate defence of Malta, though for the first few weeks after Mason's arrival on the island there was a comparative 'lull' in the Axis' aerial siege. By April 1941, however, the Malta defences were at full stretch, and on 13 April Mason and his wing-man surprised a quartet of Messerschmitt Bf109s by attacking out of the sun. At least, Mason attacked – his No 2 failed to see his leader's wing-waggle to signify enemy aircraft and blissfully remained on patrol above! Selecting the nearest Bf109 Mason shot it down into a vertical dive. Breaking away he was then set upon by the other three Germans, each of whom made a series of beam attacks on the lone Hurricane. Their fire was deadly accurate. Cannon shells and bullets riddled the Hurricane, shattering its windscreen, pulverising Mason's instrument board, and severing control cables. One bullet ploughed through Mason's right wrist and palm, while a second pierced his left elbow, fortunately passing straight through without touching bones; splinters of shell also embedded themselves in his left leg and his skull.

Mason felt his aircraft controls go slack and the Hurricane fell headlong towards the sea. His hand had gone numb – an artery had been severed – but somehow he managed to retain some control of the Hurricane, levelled out only feet above the waves, and twisted from side to side. The engine now gave up the ghost, emitting flames along the left side of its cowling. Mason prepared to ditch, but undid his restraining webbing straps, so as the aircraft slammed into the sea Mason was thrown violently forward and broke his nose on the windscreen frame. Dazedly, Mason struggled out of his shattered cockpit and, with blood pouring out of his gloved hand, began to swim one-handed towards the nearest shore some four miles away.

Luckily his crash had been spotted and nearly an hour later a motor boat crew fished him out of the Mediterranean, tied a tourniquet on his wounded arm, then took him back to shore where an ambulance was waiting to take him to the military hospital at Imtarfa. Despite his somewhat parlous physical condition, Mason insisted that the ambulance driver first took him to the squadron mess where, in borrowed dressing gown, pyjamas, and with a stiff drink in his hand, he posed for a photograph 'for the record' ...

Mason's injuries took several months to heal completely, during which period he spent some time at the RAF HQ in Iraq. His former unit, 261 Squadron, had been disbanded on Malta in May, but on 12 July 1941 the personnel of No 127 Squadron at Habbaniyah, Iraq were redesignated as the reformed 261 Squadron, and with promotion to Squadron Leader, 'Imshi' Mason was given command of the unit. In August the squadron moved to Shaibah, primarily to protect the oil ports of Abadan and Khorramshar, but in the same month a few operational sorties were flown over Iran and Iraq, in the course of which Mason shot down a Hawker Nisr (Audax). By October 1941 the squadron's main operational work had switched westwards, with detachments at Haifa, Palestine and Nicosia, Cyprus, primarily guarding the port of Haifa.

By January 1942 the complete unit had moved to Palestine, but Mason was posted to a fresh command, that of No 94 Squadron based at Gazala 2 airfield in North Africa. It was a posting which delighted Mason because it meant a return to the 'real war' (*sic*) and in an area he knew well from his days in the first Libyan campaign. Though equipped with Hurricanes, 94 Squadron was in the process of exchanging these for Kittyhawk fighters when Mason took up his new command, and on 14 February 1942 moved to Gambut to commence Kittyhawk operations. Within 24 hours 'Imshi' Mason was dead in the flaming wreckage of his aircraft on the perimeter of Martuba airfield.

Mason's death ended a minor legend in the desert RAF's annals. Tributes to his character, prowess, and charm were profuse, including the following by Roderic Owen in his authoritative history *The Desert Air Force* (Hutchinson, 1948):

> Quiet and unassuming, 'Imshi' Mason came from Blackpool [*sic*]; his brown beard could hardly help to conceal the unusual personality that lay behind his casual, good-natured smile. Stories told of him include one to the effect that he had been accustomed in the early days of campaigning to bombard the Italians with a beer bottle, in which he corked the message, 'Come up and fight'. Great-hearted, efficient, but intensely human, popular with the men, he was representative of the new 'modern' officer, removed from his subordinates by no qualities of rank or income, but in a position of responsibility because of his ability as a leader, and because of his technical competence in flying.

His memory was later perpetuated in the RAF by the presentation by his mother of the 'Imshi' Mason Memorial Trophy for annual competition by squadrons of the Middle East RAF Command, which was first competed for in 1949.

CHAPTER THREE

Peter Wykeham

On 1 August 1940 eight Gloster Gladiators comprising 'B' Flight of No 80 Squadron RAF circled the tiny village of Sidi Barrani, some 60 miles east of the Libyan-Egyptian border, then let down to land at a satellite landing ground five miles south of the village, led in by the Flight commander, the South African 'Pat' Pattle. Within two hours of arrival Pattle was again airborne, leading three of his men on a general sweep of the forward fighting zone and eventually strafing an Italian vehicle convoy on the coastal road inside Libyan territory.

Having been detached from the squadron base at Amriya, 'B' Flight had been tasked with offensive patrols against the Italian Regia Aeronautica and general air support for Allied army units in forward locations, and on 4 August a signal was received from HQ requesting provision of four Gladiators as escort to a Westland Lysander of No 208 Squadron for the latter to carry out a reconnaissance sortie over Italian positions in the Bir Taieb el Esem area. Ever-anxious to see action Pattle decided to lead this escort and detailed Flying Officer Peter Wykeham-Barnes*, Pilot Officer H. 'Johnny' Lancaster, and Sergeant Rew to accompany him. Leaving the airstrip at 5.15 pm the four Gladiators rendezvoused with the Lysander some ten minutes later as it patiently circled at 6,000 feet. Setting course westwards, Wykeham-Barnes in Gladiator L8009 and Rew (K7908) took up position some 3,000 feet above and behind their 'charge', while Pattle (K7910) and Lancaster (K7923) flew a thousand feet higher off to starboard where they could keep the Lysander and the other Gladiators in plain view.

Crossing the front lines 20 minutes later south of Sidi Omar, the formation swung on course for Bir Taieb el Esem but as they neared

---

* He was later to drop the surname Barnes.

this a red Very light arced upwards from the Lysander – the signal for 'enemy aircraft attacking' – and it set off eastwards. Pattle and Lancaster promptly dived but, for the moment, could see no enemies, then Wykeham-Barnes' voice was heard over the R/T ordering an attack. Seven Breda Ba65 fighters from 159° Squadriglia, led by Captain Dell'Oro, were closing rapidly on the fleeing Lysander, flying in a formation of four (two pairs) and a Vic of three. Wykeham-Barnes and Rew tackled the foursome, while Pattle and Lancaster attacked the Vic of three from astern. One Breda fell away in flames under Wykeham-Barnes' fire, while Pattle sent another down to a crashlanding in the bald desert. Within seconds a flock of Fiat CR32s from 160° Squadriglia, led by Captain Duilio Fanali, descended on the four Gladiators, and in their first pass they shot Sergeant Rew down in flames.

Wykeham-Barnes managed to shoot down another fighter but was then caught in the crossfire of several CR32s and his Gladiator's rudder and elevator controls were shot away, while slivers of exploding bullets wounded him in the back. With no controls Wykeham-Barnes had no alternative but to bale out. Meanwhile Lancaster, with all his guns suffering jams, fought several CR32s before being hit in the left arm and shoulder by an explosive bullet. Wriggling somehow out of the fight, he kept his right thumb pressed over a severed artery in his left arm and, with the control column gripped between his knees, flew back to a reasonably smooth landing at base before losing consciousness.

Pattle, now alone, and having gun-jams, turned back towards the border but soon ran into five Fiat CR42s south of El Adem and fought all five, sending one down to crash before the others quit the scene. Still some 40 miles deep in enemy-occupied territory, and with only one gun still working, Pattle dropped to 1,000 feet and continued flying east. Only minutes later fresh opposition appeared – twelve CR42s and three Breda 65s. Evading their fire – his remaining gun jammed as soon as he attempted to fire – Pattle stunted for some 15 minutes before having his Gladiator's rudder controls shattered. Easing the aircraft up to 4,000 feet, Pattle took to his parachute and got his foot tangled in the pilot 'chute initially. Plummeting down, he managed to extricate his foot, the silk umbrella deployed fully, and seconds later Pattle hit the earth hard;

Wing Commander Peter Wykeham-Barnes

winded but safe. His empty Gladiator plunged head-on into the ground a short distance away and erupted in flames immediately. Both Pattle and Wykeham-Barnes spent the next 24 hours without water or food as they made their separate ways towards the Allied lines, and both were eventually picked up by detachments of the Hussars and returned to their Flight at Sidi Barrani.

In June 1941 an unofficial association – the Late Arrivals Club – came into being, membership of which was restricted to men of the desert air services who were brought down behind enemy lines but managed to walk back to friendly territory to fight again. The Club's badge was a small silver winged flying boot, and its motto; 'It's never too late to come back'. Wykeham-Barnes and Pattle, the latter posthumously, became the Club's first registered members to qualify.

*

Peter Guy Wykeham-Barnes was born in Sandhurst on 13 September 1915, and became a member of the regular RAF by enlisting as an Aircraft Apprentice at Halton in September 1932. From here he graduated on 23 July 1935 with a Cadetship, one of four only from his entry of 143 A/As to gain this distinction and *entrée* to Cranwell College. From Cranwell he was commissioned on 31 July 1937 and his first posting as a pilot was to No 80 Squadron on that date. Based at Debden under the command of Squadron Leader P.S. 'Papa' Blockey, No 80 Squadron flew Gloster Gladiators, but on 30 April 1938 the unit was embarked *en bloc* aboard HM Troopship *Lancashire* at Southampton, sailing that day to Egypt where the squadron took up its new quarters at Ismailia airfield alongside the Suez Canal, the defence of this vital waterway being the squadron's primary role. On arrival at Ismailia No 80 Squadron shared the airfield with another Gladiator unit, No 33 Squadron, which had arrived only weeks before and was in the process of working up to full fighting establishment and status. Both units were regarded as 'mobile' for operations, and it became common practice to detach complete Flights to various desert landing grounds for four to six weeks at a time to acclimatise the air and ground crews to operational conditions of living 'rough'; a mini-gipsy mode of life which was to prove invaluable experience in the years of actual war ahead.

One such detachment for 80 Squadron in August-September 1938 provided Wykeham-Barnes with his first opportunities to fire his Gladiator's machine guns in anger. The detachment comprised just Wykeham-Barnes and Pattle, plus five ground crew Erks to maintain the two Gladiators, to Samakh, Palestine. Local Arabs were fomenting rebellion against 'foreign authority' – Palestine then was a British Mandate responsibility – and the Gladiators (among other RAF aircraft and units) were to provide air support for the garrison British army units in the area.

The subsequent weeks saw both pilots engaged in a variety of duties, including reconnaissance, message-dropping to forward army posts, and a number of strafing attacks on rebel Arab positions or gatherings, usually when the rebels attacked British army convoys or troop columns. Both men suffered bullet-damage in their aircraft from sharp-shooting Arabs but no personal injuries. In late September both men were recalled to their squadron, which had moved to Amriya on 24 September, mustered to full war status, in view of the Munich Crisis in Europe. Once this crisis had abated 80 Squadron returned to Ismailia on 10 October, but on 16 January 1939 was once more on the move, this time shifting base to Helwan, some 13 miles from Cairo. By July 1939, however, the looming war in Europe had its effect throughout the RAF and on 12 July the squadron took up full residence at Amriya again, this time in preparation for war. For the following eleven months 80 Squadron continued a daily routine of practice sorties and general flying, but to all intents it remained on a peacetime footing and it was a frustrating period for most of the pilots who, understandably, itched for real action; indeed, several applied for postings to fighter squadrons in the UK, only to be ignored by RAF Middle East HQ. Then, on 10 June 1940, at midnight, Italy formally entered the war on the side of Germany.

At that date 80 Squadron possessed 22 Gladiators and one Hawker Hurricane (P2638)*, and on 17 June this Hurricane was flown by Wykeham-Barnes to Mersa Matruh for temporary attachment to No 33 Squadron. Two days later he took off in

* Only one other Hurricane, L1669, existed in North Africa at that time but this was not in operational state in June 1940.

(*Right*) Squadron Leader
Patrick Dunn in an 80 Sqn
Gladiator cockpit

(*Below*) RAF repair & salvage
personnel checking a crashed
Hurricane before its recovery

company with four of 33's Gladiators to patrol the area around Sollum and clashed with at least nine Italian Fiat CR42s and other biplanes. Wykeham-Barnes tackled the leading CR42, flown by a Sergeant Corsi, and shot it down into the sea, then destroyed a second minutes later – No 80 Squadron's first confirmed combat victories of the war. Returning to 80 Squadron on 25 June, Wykeham-Barnes' next combats came on 4 August (as related earlier), but on 8 August he extracted a modicum of revenge for being brought down on the 4th when he shot down another Italian aircraft. Then, on 17 August, while flying cover patrol for the British Fleet returning to Alexandria after bombarding Bardia, he shared in the destruction of a Cant Z501 flying boat. Two days later the Hurricane Flights of Nos 33 and 80 Squadrons were amalgamated to form a fresh unit, No 274 Squadron based at Amriya, and the CO of 80 Squadron, P.H. Dunn, was transferred to command the new, all-Hurricane* unit, taking with him Wykeham-Barnes among others.

On 29 November 1940 Peter Wykeham-Barnes was awarded a DFC, the first fighter pilot in RAF Middle East to be so decorated since the outbreak of war with Italy. Ten days later General Wavell launched an offensive against the Italian colonial armies – the first Libyan campaign had begun. Full air support that day included 274 Squadron which shortly after noon encountered five Savoia-Marchetti SM79 bombers and shot down four, damaging the fifth, Wykeham-Barnes sharing in the brief massacre. Later in the afternoon the squadron was patrolling the Sidi-Barrani-Sofafi area and flew headlong into a mass of 27 Fiat CR42s. Five Fiats were destroyed for certain, one of these by Wykeham-Barnes who also shared with P.H. Dunn in probably destroying three others.

In the following weeks 274's pilots flew several sorties each day, alternating between ground-strafing assaults on retreating Italian troops and fierce aerial combats with (mainly) Italian fighters whenever these put in an appearance over the battlefront. By 15 December all Italian forces had been driven out of Egyptian

---

* Though intended to be the first all-Hurricane squadron in the Middle East, initially its strength included some Gladiators and French Morane-Saulnier 406 fighters. The squadron only reached full establishment of 24 Hurricanes on 11 November 1940.

Hurricane pilots of 80 Squadron, 1940. Second from right is Peter Wykeham-Barnes

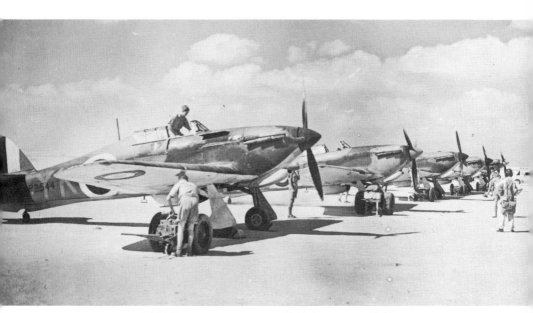

Hurricane Is of 274 Sqn, Amriya, November 1940. Nearest is P2544

Wg Cdr Peter Wykeham-Barnes (rt) & his Mosquito navigator, Fg Off Palmer, 23 Squadron

Mosquito II, DZ230, 'A-Apple' of 23 Squadron, piloted by Wg Cdr Peter Wykeham-Barnes, which arrived on Malta on 27 December 1942

territory, having already lost almost five of seven divisions, with nearly 40,000 infantrymen taken prisoner. That day 274 Squadron engaged in pure offensive patrols in the course of which Wykeham-Barnes added another CR42 destroyed to his tally.

At noon the following day 274 Squadron, reinforced by a detachment from 73 Squadron, was out in strength scouring the sky over Bardia, and near Sidi Omar encountered a formation of SM79 bombers from 9° Stormo, heavily escorted by CR42 fighters. The outcome was brief but fierce, with six SM79s being shot down, one by Wykeham-Barnes, and three others at least damaged, while two CR42s shared their fate. As the new year dawned the Allied armies continued their close offensive, storming Bardia from 3 January, and two days later 274 Squadron set out to attack the various enemy air strips in the Gambut complex, with huge success. At least seven Italian aircraft were destroyed in the air and four others damaged; Wykeham-Barnes' share in the total being one SM79 destroyed and a second probably destroyed.

Over the next two weeks 274's pilots engaged in a series of daring low-level, long-range strafing sorties against Italian airfields at Derna, Gazala, Martuba, *et al*, usually in pairs of Hurricanes, with 'Imshi' Mason and his wingman Bob Talbot particularly creating havoc among grounded Italian aircraft. On the 17th Wykeham-Barnes met an SM81 painted with Red Cross markings, but suspicious of its actual intentions he forced it down to land in the desert some ten miles west of Tobruk. His suspicions appeared to have been justified, because as soon as the aircraft rolled to a stop its crew leapt out and set fire to it before local Allied soldiers took them prisoner. Meanwhile the Allied armies were rapidly pushing their Italian opponents further westwards, occupying Tobruk on 22 January, Derna on 30 January, then on 5 February cutting off the coast road beyond Benghazi and thereby trapping the Italian 10th Army. On 6 February the 6th Australian Division entered Benghazi, and within days the Allied forward troops were taking up positions along the El Agheila front, finally halting a two-months 'dash' which had reaped 130,000 prisoners and untold quantities of material and utterly defeated the Italian armies.

On 8 February, with the land campaign apparently static, No 274 Squadron handed over its Hurricanes to No 3 Squadron RAAF, then flew the Australians' battle-weary Gladiators back to Amriya for a well-deserved break from the intense operational activities of the Libyan offensive. At Amriya the unit became part of the defences for Alexandria, while Peter Wykeham-Barnes was posted to the Sector Operations HQ at Heliopolis for a few weeks of chairborne duties. His sojourn among the fleshpots of 'Helio' was relatively brief, however, and with promotion to Squadron Leader he returned to the sharp end at the beginning of April 1941 by succeeding Squadron Leader A.D. Murray as CO of No 73 Squadron, based at El Gubbi airfield at Tobruk. By then the Allied armies were in full retreat eastwards pursued by the German General Erwin Rommel's Afrika Korps, and the vital port of Tobruk was isolated and besieged. Constant aerial attacks on Tobruk by the Luftwaffe kept 73 Squadron and its companion Hurricanes of a 6 Squadron detached Flight in unceasing action, with five or six scrambles a day becoming a virtual norm.

On 23 April the only seven serviceable Hurricanes of 73 Squadron scrambled at 10 am to meet an incoming force of 60 Messerschmitt Bf109s, Bf110s and Junkers Ju87s. In the ensuing mêlée Wykeham-Barnes shot down a Ju87 and a Bf109 but was then riddled by other German fire which set his Hurricane on fire. Baling out directly above Tobruk he delayed pulling his parachute's D-ring – Luftwaffe pilots had been known recently to fire at parachuting Allied pilots – and when he finally deployed his 'chute he hit the edge of Tobruk harbour hard, injuring a leg. Medical personnel reached him quickly and attended to his injury on the spot – using an anaesthetic which was highly successful in paralysing all movement and speech, but did nothing to kill the pain!* Next day he was back in a Hurricane cockpit but within 48 hours 73 Squadron was virtually non-existent – in his own wry comment later, 'We were down to two Hurricanes with a hundred Mes surrounding Tobruk and slowly whittling us down ...' – and in the night of 25 April the surviving pilots were airlifted out of Tobruk and flown back to Sidi Haneish.

Remaining in command of the refurbished 73 Squadron until October 1941, Wykeham-Barnes received a Bar to his DFC in

---

* Many years later he visited Tobruk where, to his chagrin, he found a German war memorial erected over the spot he had 'landed' on the harbour wall ...

August, and in October was promoted to Wing Commander Fighters, Western Desert which post he retained until January 1942. He then left the Middle East for a four months' tour of duty with the USAAF as a fighting instructor, but in April 1942 he returned to the operational scene as the latest commander of No 257 Squadron, a Hurricane unit based at Honiley, England, which shortly after converted to Hawker Typhoons and became based at High Ercall. In September, however, he joined 23 Squadron at Bradwell Bay to fly De Havilland Mosquito fighters, and when this unit left England in December 1942 it flew to Malta, with Wykeham-Barnes piloting Mosquito DZ230, 'A-Apple' as the first to land at Luqa on 27 December.

For the following four months he participated in the squadron's various depredations of enemy air bases and communications in Sicily, interspersed with sorties over the North African battle zones – all night intruder operations, which included no few contacts with the Luftwaffe. Returning to the UK in April 1943, he went to the Kenley Sector until February 1944, then joined No 140 Wing to fly Mosquito bombers in a series of long-range, daylight precision attacks against key German objectives.

In December 1944, as a Group Captain, he joined the Operations staff at No 2 Group under the dynamic leadership of Air Vice Marshal Basil Embry and finished the war in this appointment.

Peter Wykeham's post-1945 career saw him rise steadily in rank and responsibilities within the RAF, including a five-months' operational stint in the USAF's 3rd Air Force in the Korean War in late 1950 which saw him awarded a US Air Medal for gallantry, and he eventually retired from RAF service as Air Marshal Sir Peter Wykeham, KCB, DSO, OBE, DFC, AFC.

CHAPTER FOUR

Vernon Woodward

In the early morning of 14 June 1940 – just four days after Italy's intervention in the war – Italian airmen at Sidi Azeiz airfield, a few miles inland from Bardia, were preparing their aircraft for the day's operations. As they leisurely strolled in the warming sun towards their various charges, a small formation of RAF biplanes appeared over the eastern edge of the airstrip, flying low and heading directly towards the neatly parked Italian aircraft. Seconds later chaos reigned on the ground as each of the RAF Gladiators opened fire, strafing the lines of aircraft and sending the ground crews scattering hard for any form of cover from the hail of bullets.

In one Gladiator a Canadian, Vernon Woodward, selected a large civil airliner as his specific target and proceeded to riddle it from stem to stern before climbing away to rejoin his fellow pilots. Shortly before 11 am the same morning Woodward was again airborne with his Flight, flying Gladiator N5783, patrolling the sky over Fort Capuzzo, when a formation of Caproni Ca310 bombers, escorted by Fiat CR32s, crossed the Gladiators' patrol line. The ensuing dogfight was relatively brief. Woodward joined with Sergeant Craig (N5768) in sending one Ca310 hurtling down in flames, then teamed up with Flying Officer E.H. Dean (L9046)* to shoot down a pair of the CR32 escorts; Dean's victim being seen to crash into the desert, while Woodward's opponent was last seen falling vertically with smoke pouring out of its fuselage and engine.

This clash provided the RAF in the Middle East with its first fighter combat victories of World War Two, and within the following twelve months of virtually unceasing operations Vernon Woodward was to claim a total of 21 enemy aircraft destroyed in air combat, some 19 others either probably destroyed, damaged, or

* Later, Wing Commander E.H. Dean, DSO, DFC.

Wg Cdr Vernon Woodward

shared in destruction with other pilots, with uncounted numbers of other enemy aircraft destroyed or crippled during ground-strafing sorties against enemy airfields.

Such prowess might appear to indicate a fighter pilot fitting the popular lay image of an extrovert, dashing, fire-eating, ever-aggressive individual, yet Vernon Crompton Woodward was in many ways the antithesis of any such lurid conceptions. Quiet in manner, almost reserved, Woodward became widely renowned for his cool-headed judgment and invariable calm in all matters including combat, earning for himself the soubriquet 'Imperturbable Woody' – a sincere tribute by his fellow pilots to his 'unflappability', no matter how fraught the circumstances. Nevertheless, Woodward's outward quiescence masked an inner determination and depths of raw courage which manifested themselves when engaged in action.

Born on 22 December 1916 in Victoria, British Columbia, Woodward's original ambition was to be a pilot in the tiny pre-1939 RCAF, but his lack of sufficiently high educational qualifications nullified that goal. With characteristic quiet resolve Woodward sailed to England to try his luck with the RAF and was duly accepted for a Short Service Commission on 20 August 1938. On completion of pilot training at No 6 FTS, Woodward was posted to Egypt shortly before the outbreak of war in 1939, where he joined No 33 Squadron, a Gladiator fighter unit based at Ismailia and commanded by Squadron Leader H.D. McGregor*. By September 1939 the unit's base was at Mersa Matruh, but in June 1940 the squadron had moved base to Qasaba, with Flights detached to landing grounds at Sidi Barrani and Gerawla.

Having 'broken his duck' on 14 June, Woodward found plentiful action against the Italian air force during the following weeks, and on 29 June, over the Ridotto-Capuzzo area, he shot a Fiat CR32 down, then chased a second CR32 over Bardia before despatching this victim. July 1940 brought almost continuous daily action as the Italian forces were steadily strengthened in eastern Libya, but Woodward failed to add to his tally until 24 July. Flying with 'B' Flight that evening over Sollum, Woodward became embroiled with

* Later, Air Marshal Sir Hector McGregor, KCB, CBE, DSO.

18 Fiat CR42s from 10° and 13° *Gruppi*. The fight which followed saw four CR42s destroyed and a fifth claimed as probably destroyed, with Woodward claiming one confirmed and the 'probable'.

Next day, while escorting some 55 Squadron Blenheims over Bardia, Woodward's Flight was jumped by a gaggle of CR42s. Teaming up with Sergeant Slater, Woodward shot down one Fiat, saw Slater account for a second, then joined him in destroying a third CR42. Seconds later the Gladiator flown by Slater was seen spinning down, out of the fight, leaving Woodward alone, with at least six CR42s intent on killing him. The next seven or eight minutes seemed like an eternity to the cool Canadian as he outfought and outmanoeuvred his adversaries, until finally the Italians left him and flew westwards. After landing back at base Woodward made a close inspection of his Gladiator for combat damage, and found just three bullet holes in the fabric-skinned fuselage; a tribute to his superb manoeuvring skill, though equally a measure of the Italians' poor shooting abilities.

On 1 August the detached 33 Squadron Flight at Sidi Barrani was relieved by 'B' Flight of 80 Squadron, thereby allowing 33's crews to go back eastwards for rest and refurbishment of aircraft, while in September 1940 the unit's 'A' Flight began replacing their Gladiators with newly-arrived Hurricanes. In the same month, on the 13th, Italian forces advanced over the Libyan border into Egypt, forcing all Allied forces to withdraw eastwards. By the start of December, however, General Wavell was ready to launch his own offensive and this commenced on 9 December. The first three weeks of Wavell's advance brought Vernon Woodward back into frontline combat action with a vengeance, and between 9 December and 29 December the Canadian shot down five Fiat CR42s for certain, including a 'double' victory on the 18th. In the same period he probably destroyed a sixth CR42, apart from at least damaging four others. Although no further victories were claimed by Woodward throughout January 1941, his squadron was constantly engaged in close tactical support of the rapid Allied advance towards Cyrenaica, alternating between straight aerial clashes with the Regia Aeronautica, and more vital duties such as bomber escorts, groundstrafing Italian vehicle convoys and airfields, and generally assisting in dominating the skies over the forward battle zones.

Hurricane I, named 'Pamela', piloted by Flt Lt (later, Gp Capt) B.R. Pelly of No. 3 RAAF Sqn, Amriya, March 1941

Hurricane I of 260 Squadron

Then, on 15 January the squadron received an order to prepare to leave the desert and move to Greece, and on the last day of the month 33 Squadron began its journey to an airfield at Eleusis, some 15 miles west of Athens in southern Greece. A combination of this move of base to a new theatre of war, and the very recent conversion from Gladiators to Hurricanes, kept 33 Squadron virtually non-operational for a few weeks, but once its pilots had become accustomed to handling the heavier, faster Hurricanes they lost no time in tackling the Italian air force in the zone.

On 12 March the squadron received a new commander, Squadron Leader M.T.St J. Pattle, DFC and Bar, by which date it had flown north to a new airfield base, Larissa, some 15 miles south of Mount Olympus. For the first week of his new command Pattle worked his pilots hard, practising formation flying, mock combat tactics, and generally tightening up air discipline. Then, on 23 March, Pattle led 13 Hurricanes off Larissa for the first operational sorties in the early morning; an escort job for six Blenheims of 84 Squadron, assisted by eleven Gladiators from 112 Squadron. The target was Berat, which was duly bombed from relatively low level, and 33 Squadron returned to base safely, albeit with two Hurricanes damaged by anti-aircraft fire and Flying Officer C. Dyson DFC's aircraft being shot down by an Italian Fiat G50, though Dyson escaped serious injury and soon returned to his unit.

Shortly after noon the same day the squadron was detailed to ground-strafe an enemy airfield at Fieri in Albania, a base known to be heavily defended by guns and fighters. Ten Hurricanes, led by Pattle, set out on the sortie and had just reached their objective when a flock of about 20-24 Fiat G50s and Macchi 200s fell on the would-be strafers. Pattle shot one Fiat into the earth, then dived across the airfield, destroying at least three more Fiats on the ground. Vernon Woodward followed his leader's example, shooting one Fiat G50 down and probably destroying a second before making his strafing pass across Fieri airfield where his guns damaged several more aircraft. On return to Larissa Pattle tore a strip off the other eight pilots, none of whom had strafed the airfield, but been content to dogfight the Italian fighters. Only Woodward had adhered strictly to the prime purpose of the sortie – gunning Fieri despite the temptation of simply mixing it with enemy fighters – and this was yet another indication of the quiet man's resolution.

By the end of March 1941 the situation in Greece altered swiftly and dramatically when Hitler ordered his land and air forces to invade and occupy Yugoslavia and Greece. For 33 Squadron it meant an early encounter with the Luftwaffe was highly likely, and on 6 April 'Pat' Pattle led his squadron on an offensive sweep and met a formation of 20-plus Messerschmitt Bf109s in the Rupel Pass. 33's pilots promptly shot down five Bf109s without loss or damage to the Hurricanes. Woodward missed this particular triumph, being still on the ground at Larissa where his aircraft was being refuelled and armed, but as the main formation was returning to base Woodward and two other squadron pilots received warning of enemy aircraft. While Woodward waited impatiently for the armourers to fix down his Hurricane's wing gun panels, his two companions set off and intercepted five Italian Cant Z1007s over Volos and shot one Cant down in flames. By then Woodward had taken off, though only the four guns in his port wing had ammunition.

Catching up with the surviving quartet of Cants over the Gulf of Corinth, Woodward kept up a series of beam attacks and shot two down in flames, while a third disappeared into low cloud issuing thick smoke. With his ammunition spent Woodward returned to Larissa, where he was later told that his third Cant had been seen to crash in the sea. A week later, while flying a solo reconnaissance on 13 April, Woodward was attacked by three roving Bf109s. Within two minutes of engaging these the Canadian had sent one spinning down with its pilot taking to his parachute, then damaged a second severely enough for it to promptly break off and flee. The third adversary took to its heels ...

On 14 April, despite atrocious weather conditions, the bulk of 33 Squadron provided escort for Blenheims of No 11 Squadron which set out to bomb German troop convoys near Strumitsa, but Woodward teamed up with 'Dixie' Dean for a general offensive sweep of the front lines where they spotted a batch of Junkers Ju87s, escorted by Bf109s, heading towards the forward Allied infantry positions with the obvious intention of dive-bombing these. Dean and Woodward headed straight into the Ju87 formation as its Bf109 'escorts' climbed into cloud and disappeared! In less than six minutes of furious action Dean destroyed one Ju87 and damaged another, while Woodward shot two down and at least damaged another two. By then both men had used up all their ammunition, otherwise the mini-massacre might have been even greater. By that date the Allies' position in Greece had become desperate, fighting near-overwhelming odds on the ground, and no less superior numbers in the air. Moreover, the Luftwaffe in Greece now initiated a series of low-level attacks on Allied airfields in a determined attempt to wipe out all remaining aerial opposition. The morning after Woodward and Dean's 'Junkers party' three of 33 Squadron's Hurricanes were just taking off when 15 Bf110s swept across the airfield strafing. Two Hurricanes and their pilots were shot down. Later that day came an order for the squadron to evacuate Larissa and move south, back to Eleusis, and the ground crews packed all equipment onto trucks then headed out during the night through drenching rain. Next day this convoy was attacked en route by German aircraft, though 33's Hurricanes did their best to provide some air cover.

By 17 April all air and ground crews, their aircraft and equipment, had arrived safely at Eleusis, but soon found themselves under Luftwaffe attack again. On 18 April five fresh Hurricanes arrived from Egypt just before the Luftwaffe strafed Eleusis for the second time since dawn, creating damage to several Hurricanes. Throughout that night the indefatigable ground crews managed to bring five of seven damaged Hurricanes to a barely operational state – only to have these blown up in a raid by 15 Junkers Ju88s at dawn next day.

Shortly after the Ju88 attack Pattle led seven remaining Hurricanes off for an offensive sweep in the Lamia area, and after only 20 minutes' flying spotted a low-flying Henschel Hs 126 spotter aircraft. Pattle led Woodward and 'Pop' Littler down and each took his turn in riddling the Henschel, which crashed into a nearby hill aflame. Rejoining the other four Hurricanes they continued their sweep through a relatively narrow valley between some towering mountains, only to find themselves flying nose-on to a formation of nine Bf109s. The combined closing speed of the two formations left only seconds for either side to react, but Pattle and Woodward

(*Left*) Vernon Woodward in *de rigueur* issue-sun helmet

(*Below*) Lloyd Gilbert Schwab, a Canadian who served in Nos. 17, 80 and 112 Sqns, 1938-41, scoring 11 victories. Ended war as Wing Commander. Seen here at No. 1 OTU, Bagotville, Quebec on 30 November 1942

climbed and turned rapidly and attacked the rearmost Messer-schmitts. Pattle sent one yellow-nosed Bf109 into a mountainside, then climbed fast to join a milling fight at higher altitude where the remaining Bf109s and Hurricanes were now involved in fierce close-quarters combat. Spotting one Bf109 apparently leaving the fight, Pattle closed behind its tail and sank a burst into its cockpit. The 109 dived full-bore into the ground. Elsewhere Woodward, noticing a Hurricane with smoke pouring from it trying to reach safety, tried to go down to its aid but ran into two Bf109s. An accurate two-seconds' burst sent one 109 spinning earthwards in flames, and its companion climbed out of range. Back at Eleusis, when the full story emerged, 33 Squadron had lost two Hurricanes crashed, one pilot killed, and varying degrees of damage to the surviving aircraft.

Sunday, 20 April 1941, brought no respite for 33 Squadron. It was to prove a day in which the squadron was to experience its greatest triumph to date – and its worst tragedies. Starting with a dawn patrol at 5 am, the Hurricanes became embroiled early with German raiders, and had casualties throughout the various fights of the morning and early afternoon. Then, shortly after 5 pm, an air raid siren sounded across the airfield, and an announcement told of a Luftwaffe force of 'more than a hundred' bombers and fighters heading for Piraeus harbour, where Allied ships were crowded together attempting to evacuate wounded and other Allied troops. Every available Hurricane at Eleusis – a total of 15 aircraft from 33, 208 and 80 Squadrons – scrambled as fast as possible, heading for the harbour area.

It was a piecemeal take-off by individual Hurricanes, though a few managed to pair with others en route, and three of 33's pilots arrived over Piraeus just as 15 Ju88s were dive-bombing a hospital ship. Five Ju88s were shot into the water, while three others crawled away spuming smoke before the Hurricane trio left for Eleusis to re-arm. Above this scene Woodward had teamed up with Len Cottingham* in tackling the mass of Bf110 fighters escorting the bombers. Cottingham's guns set three Bf110s aflame before he was wounded and forced to bale out; while Woodward destroyed one

---

* Flight Sergeant L. Cottingham, later, Wing Commander, DFC.

Bf110 and damaged three others before his ammunition ran out and he flew back to base for replenishment.

Elsewhere in the mêlée the other Hurricane pilots were taking on fantastic odds – one pilot calmly attacking a circling formation of some 30 Junkers Ju88s on his own, and shooting two down before his ammunition was expended – but the casualties among the Hurricanes were soon mounting, and included 33's commander, 'Pat' Pattle.

One of the last to leave Eleusis – he was suffering from a high fever and had been abed when the scramble commenced – Pattle reached Piraeus at the height of the air battle, and plunged into an attack on some Bf110s which were about to close on the tail of a lone Hurricane. His fire set one Bf110 on fire, followed by a second in flames seconds later. Pattle's Hurricane was then seen to be attacked from behind by two Messerschmitts and its engine erupted in flames and dived, with the body of Pattle slumped forward against the instrument board, into Eleusis bay. The RAF's highest-scoring fighter pilot of 1939-45 had died attempting to save the life of one of his fellow pilots.

That evening the surviving pilots of 33 Squadron counted the cost of the 'Battle over Piraeus'. At least 20 German aircraft had been destroyed, and almost a dozen others severely damaged, but two Hurricane pilots had been killed and four others wounded (one dying two days later from burns). Only four Hurricanes were left in flyable condition. Hasty reinforcements plus unceasing toils by the ground crews brought the available total of Hurricanes in Greece to 23 by 23 April, but on that date some 40 Bf110s attacked, destroying 13 of these, and at dawn next day only seven Hurricanes were fit enough to fly to Crete. The air battle of Greece was over for the moment.

In Crete the remaining pilots of 33 and 80 Squadrons were merged temporarily into 'Hurricane Unit, Crete' – a title dignifying just seven Hurricanes and any available air and ground crew personnel – and the 'unit' was quickly into action. Although a handful of fresh Hurricanes were to be ferried in to the beleaguered island during April-May 1941, these merely offset daily casualties so that aircraft strength of the 'unit' never exceeded 16 Hurricanes at any given time. Facing and fighting odds of seldom less than

50-to-one in opposing Luftwaffe assaults, the outcome was inevitable and on 19 May an order was issued for the four surviving Hurricanes (and three Gladiators) to be flown back to Egypt.

From here Hurricanes continued operating over Crete, attempting to use Heraklion airfield for refuelling on occasion, but by 1 June all operations over the island officially ceased. Vernon Woodward and six other surviving pilots from the Greek evacuation were sent back to Amriya where they were attached to No 30 Squadron, and where Woodward was tardily notified of his award of a DFC granted on 9 May. By then he had been promoted to Flight Lieutenant, and on 13 June was one of seven pilots from 33 Squadron attached to No 274 Squadron at Gerawla, commanded by Squadron Leader G.E. Hawkins. A Hurricane unit – indeed, 274 had been the first squadron in the Middle East to receive a full establishment of the type – its pilots were then engaged primarily in ground-strafing sorties along the north African coastal zone, and on 17 June Woodward led his Flight in an intended attack on enemy transport near Sidi Omar. Over the objective he spotted nine Ju87s, escorted by a dozen Bf109s and Fiat G50s, and immediately swung into this formation, personally destroying one G50 and damaging a second.

Continuing in the ground attack role for the next four weeks, Woodward's next, and ultimate, aerial victory came on 12 July. With Flying Officer Crockett, he was scrambled to intercept a lone Ju88 from 2(F)/123 on a high reconnaissance of the Alexandria area, flying at some 26,000 feet. Woodward's first pass caused the Junkers to drop in a near-vertical dive but the two Hurricanes followed suit and eventually chased the Ju88 at ground level until Woodward's firing sent it down to crash about 40 miles south-west of Amriya. With this victory Vernon Woodward became the RAF's highest-scoring fighter pilot still operational in the Middle East, and was also Canada's top fighter ace of the war for the following year before George Beurling succeeded him in that status in the mid-1942 Malta battles.

By then too Vernon Woodward had been flying operationally for more than a year without respite, and through some of the most desperate aerial fighting witnessed around the Mediterranean theatres of war. Accordingly he was posted to Rhodesia for a 'rest' as an instructor at No 20 SFTS in September 1941. This 'rest' posting lasted until January 1943 when, with the rank of Squadron Leader, he returned to the North African campaign on being appointed CO of No 213 Squadron based at Misurata West. Flying cannon-armed Hurricane IICs, 213's prime role was defence of Allied merchant shipping along the coast, both by day and by night. Remaining in command of 213 Squadron until August 1943 Woodward found few opportunities to add to his tally, but on leaving the squadron for a staff appointment at HQ Middle East, he was awarded a Bar to his DFC.

For the remainder of the war Vernon Woodward continued serving in the Middle East theatre, then in 1946 he returned to England after seven years 'in the sun' to accept a permanent commission in the RAF, granted in 1948, and to serve in various flying appointments both in the UK and overseas until his ultimate retirement from service as a Wing Commander on 31 January 1963.

CHAPTER FIVE

Marmaduke Pattle

The name of Squadron Leader Marmaduke Thomas St John Pattle, DFC and Bar, now heads any list of the RAF's highest-scoring fighter pilots throughout the 1939-45 war, yet his rightful position *per se* was not to be finally acknowledged until some 25 years after his death in action. Even now full confirmation of his *actual* total of combat victories is still unresolved, due primarily to the loss or destruction of much contemporary documentation, but from those facts which can be established Pattle can faithfully be credited with (at least) a tally in excess of 40 victories, thereby placing him at the top of every tabulation of RAF fighter pilots of World War Two.

Contrary to most lay images of outstanding fighter 'aces', such prowess and fame were in direct contrast to Pattle's character. Physically small in stature, inherently modest, reticent about his achievements, Pattle at no time sought the limelight of self-publicity. He regarded his 'job' as a skilled profession and therefore applied total dedication to that profession even in the smallest details. For Pattle flying as a fighter pilot was a serious business, requiring the highest attainable standards in every facet. Though inspired in his youth by the reported exploits of the 1916-18 fighter pilots, he eschewed any suggestion of 'glamour' in his chosen role, and constantly sought to improve his – and his subordinates' – efficiency, technically, tactically, and physically. Aerial fighting for Pattle was more a deadly science than any form of game or sport.

Born on 23 July 1914 in Butterworth in the South African Transkei territory, Pattle displayed an early interest in all things mechanical, especially aeroplanes, and his ambition to fly led him to volunteer to join the tiny South African Air Force while in the later stage of his college education – only to be rejected. In early 1936 he joined the Special Service Battalion as a cadet in the hope that this

'Pat' Pattle as OC 33 Sqn at Larissa, Greece, April 1941

might provide a way in eventually to the SAAF, but was soon disillusioned on that hope. Then in March 1936 he read an RAF appeal for air crew recruits under a Short Service Commission scheme. It would mean making his own way to England, at his own expense, with no pre-guarantee of acceptance, but for Pattle it represented a golden opportunity.

Purchasing his discharge from the SSB, he set sail from South Africa in the SS *Llandovery* on 30 April 1936 and within 24 hours of arrival in London had presented himself at the Air Ministry to apply formally for an SSC in the RAF. Passing his medical examination and initial interviews without problems, Pattle, along with 27 other young hopefuls, reported to the Prestwick Civil Flying School on 29 June 1936 and soon commenced *ab initio* flying training in the school's DH Tiger Moths. Pattle's dedication and concentration became evident quickly as he consistently achieved top marks in the various progressive examinations and demonstrated piloting skill well above the average, particularly in aerobatic manoeuvring; attributes summed up in his end-of-course report with the prophecy ' ... should make an outstanding Service pilot'. Granted an SSC with effect from 24 August 1936, on the same date Pattle reported to RAF Uxbridge for the nominal two-weeks' disciplinary and administrative course prior to being promoted to Acting Pilot Officer (on probation) with effect from 8 September.

Three days prior to this 'rise' to the RAF aristocracy Pattle – by this time commonly called 'Pat' by his RAF colleagues – reported to No 10 FTS, Ternhill in Shropshire to commence his Service pilot training, along with 26 other would-be pilots, among whom were several destined to achieve fame as fighter pilots in the 1940 Battles of France and Britain, including J.R.M. Boothby* and A.W.A. Baynet†. The subsequent six months confirmed Pattle's outstanding qualities in handling aircraft with 'Exceptional' gradings in flying and navigation – rare assessments for any embryo RAF pilot – while his marksmanship during air-to-air and air-to-ground firing was summed up by his gunnery instructor as 'phenomenal'. Accordingly he was awarded a Distinguished Pass on final graduation on 24 April 1937, and received a plum posting, as a fighter pilot to No 80

---

* Later, Flight Lieutenant, DFC.
† Later, Squadron Leader, DFC.

Squadron at Henlow.

Reformed officially on 8 March 1937 at Kenley, No 80 Squadron was equipped with Gloster Gauntlets when Pattle joined it, though in May these began being replaced gradually with Gladiators. On 17 May the first appointed CO, Squadron Leader P.S. Blockey, officially took up his command, though in fact he arrived two days later, and on 9 June the squadron moved en bloc to a new base, Debden. Here the unit followed a normal peacetime routine for most RAF squadrons at that period, a leisurely existence of daily flying, formation practices, and plentiful off-duty pleasures of social life, though 'Papa' Blockey soon instituted a more energetic work programme in order to bring his men up to the highest standards of efficiency in all facets.

Pattle became the 'owner' of Gladiator K7913 and had a small armorial shield, bearing his family coat of arms and motto 'Perseverance', painted just below the left side of his cockpit, and continued his quest to achieve perfection in flying and handling his aircraft. To that end he kept himself in top physically fit state and honed his perfect vision by constant practice. In March 1938 the squadron received orders for a move overseas to Egypt and on 30 April all personnel sailed from Southampton aboard the troopship HMT *Lancashire*, finally arriving at their venue, Ismailia, alongside the Suez Canal, on 10 May 1938. Here they joined No 33 Squadron (Gladiators) which had been reconstituted, as the first RAF fighter squadron to be based in the Middle East since 1926, on 1 March 1938.

In August-September 1938 Pattle first fired his Gladiator's guns in anger when he and Peter Wykeham-Barnes were detached to Palestine to help quell a local Arab revolt, and on return to the squadron found that it had moved to its 'war station' at Amriya, near Alexandria on 24 September due to the Munich Crisis in Europe. However, the unit returned to Ismailia on 10 October, and on 29 November 'Papa' Blockey was succeeded as CO by Squadron Leader R.C. Jonas (later, Air Cmdre, OBE) who led the squadron to a fresh base, Helwan, on 16 January 1939. Its stay here, adjacent to the dubious 'delights' of Cairo, was to be relatively brief. In Europe war with Hitler's Reich had been considered almost inevitable by the British government and Service hierarchy by then, and on 12

Sidi Rezegh airfield, 1941, with abandoned Fiat G50s and Hurricanes of 260 Sqn.

Hurricane I of 80 Sqn's 'A' Flight at Gambut

July 1939 No 80 Squadron returned to Amriya, by which time Pattle had become 'B' Flight commander.

Full mobilisation for war came into being on 3 September, and on the 25th of that month 80 Squadron took delivery of Hawker Hurricane L1669 – the first example of its type to arrive in Middle East Command. All pilots took little time in trying their hand in this truly modern fighter, but it was to be many months before further Hurricanes became available. Thus, when Italy's dictator, Mussolini, dragged his country into the war on 10 June 1940, Pattle and his fellow pilots on 80 Squadron prepared to begin operations in their well-tried biplane Gladiators, though within the following few weeks 80 Squadron took on charge a total of seven more Hurricanes, only to have to give these over to a newly-forming all-Hurricane unit, No 274 Squadron, in August 1940. In the interim 80 Squadron had another commander appointed when Squadron Leader P.H. Dunn became CO on 6 July.*

Pattle's urge to get to grips with the Italian air force came to fruition on 4 August 1940 when, flying from the forward landing ground at Sidi Barrani, he led his Flight on a general sweep of the Libya-Egypt border while escorting a Lysander from 208 Squadron. In the course of the sweep he encountered a formation of Breda Ba65s of 159° Squadriglia and forced one of these to crashland. Separated from the other Gladiators, Pattle then headed for base only to run into five Fiat CR42 fighters and shot one down before escaping the attentions of its companions. Continuing his return flight he next met three Ba65s and twelve CR42s and in the ensuing dogfight was shot down, taking to his parachute. That night he set out to walk back to the Allied lines and was eventually picked up the next afternoon by an armoured vehicle of the 11th Hussars.

Four days later Pattle got his revenge for being shot down when 13 Gladiators from 80 Squadron bounced a force of 16 Fiat CR42s from 9° and 10° *Gruppi* escorting about ten Meridional Ro37 recce aircraft. By the end of the engagement Pattle had shot down two CR42s, while the other Gladiators claimed at least seven others brought down, all for the losses of two Gladiators, the pilot of one returning to the squadron on foot next day.

* Later, Air Vice-Marshal, CB, CBE.

On 22 August 1940 'Paddy' Dunn left 80 Squadron to command the new 274 Squadron and his place was taken by an Australian, Squadron Leader W.J. ('Bill') Hickey* who arrived at the same time as two fellow Australians, one of whom, Richard Cullen, soon to receive the nickname 'Ape' due to his bulky frame, came from Newcastle, New South Wales and was to earn a DFC in Greece a few months later before being killed in action on 4 March 1941; the other, G.F. Graham, eventually surviving the war as a Squadron Leader.

The next two months saw 80 Squadron seeking out but only occasionally finding Italian aircraft, though on 15 September Pattle managed to set an SM79's port engine on fire but then failed to catch the faster, fleeing bomber to administer the knockout blow. Though undoubtedly a fine aerobatic fighter, the Gladiator I biplane was outclassed in sheer speed by the Savoia-Marchetti SM79 bomber, making the latter a difficult target to destroy by normal fighter tactics. In September too 80 Squadron moved to Sidi Haneish LG but soon became increasingly bored with flying routine, uneventful patrols. In October the unit began replacing their well-worn Gladiator Is for Mk IIs, completing re-equipment in early November, but the new 'Glads' showed little real improvement in performance over their predecessors.

Meantime, on 28 October, Italy suddenly invaded Greece from Albania and the Greek government urgently requested RAF aid, resulting in several bomber squadrons being withdrawn from North Africa and despatched to Greece, where they assisted greatly in stemming the Italian advance though at a high cost in casualties to the Italian Regia Aeronautica's fighters. A further request to RAF Middle East HQ for fighters led to No 80 Squadron being detailed to move to Greece. Accordingly, Hickey led 'B' Flight to Eleusis airfield, near Athens, on 17 November, to be joined by the remainder of the squadron within the following few days. On 18 November Hickey led 'B' Flight to Trikkala further north, and that afternoon set off on the squadron's first operational patrol over Greece. Over Koritza the nine Gladiators were engaged by various formations of Fiat CR42s and G50s and in the massive dogfight

---

* Hickey, born in Sydney in 1907, won a DFC in Greece but died of wounds received in action on 21 December 1940.

which spread itself in all directions, the Gladiator pilots eventually claimed nine Italians shot down and two others probably destroyed in 'exchange' for one pilot bullet-wounded but safely returning to base.

Pattle's part in the brawl commenced with chasing one CR42, closing to within 100 yards of its tail, firing one crisp burst, and seeing the Fiat's pilot collapsed forward over his controls as the CR42 fell into the ground two miles west of Koritza. Climbing back to 15,000 feet, Pattle could see a general dogfight ensuing to the north and flew to join the mêlée, only to be attacked by five CR42s and two G50s. As these attacked head-on, Pattle turned in behind a CR42 and sank a brief burst into its cockpit area. The Fiat fell away burning fiercely. Then, with air pressure for firing his guns too low, Pattle headed back to base. En route he met a lone Fiat G50 but failed to entice the Italian into a fight.

The next two days brought torrential rain which turned the airfield into a mud quagmire, nullifying flying, but on 27 November a detachment was sent further west to Yanina airfield, a bald grass plain bereft of hangars and runways but at least dry enough for operations. Combining the move with a patrol over Koritza, the Gladiators met three SM79s being escorted by about a dozen CR42s. While one section dived at the bombers, Pattle led his section to ward off the CR42s. Diving almost vertically onto the Fiats' tails, the combined fire from 'Pat's' section sent two CR42s flaming to earth while the remainder fled as fast as possible.

The afternoon of 28 November brought 80 Squadron another resounding victory when six Gladiators, led by 'Tap' Jones*, coolly attacked a loose bunch of 20 CR42s near Delvinakion and destroyed seven of these, though one Gladiator collided with a CR42 and was last seen spinning down into the mountains nearby. Jones, who had claimed two victims, was then wounded by a bullet passing through the flesh of his neck, while his Gladiator was shredded with bullet damage, yet he returned to base.

Pattle led off six Gladiators on 29 November to escort some Blenheims of 84 Squadron raiding Tepelene, and once these were safely back in 'friendly' skies, the Gladiators set off to search for a

---

* Later, Air Vice-Marshal, CB, CBE, DSO, DFC.

missing pilot from the previous day's operations. Pattle and his No 2, Vale*, spotted six SM79s and attacked these head-on from out of the sun. Pattle's victim, the leader of the front section of the bombers, filled his sights until he could clearly see the pilot's face. He fired at pointblank range, skipped over the top of the SM79, then sank a burst into the belly of the rear section leader before turning out of a lattice-work of return fire from the Italian gunners. Looking back at the disappearing bombers – in his Gladiator there was no hope of catching them again – Pattle noted with some satisfaction that both the SM79s he had attacked were pluming trails of black smoke.

Two days of atrocious weather prevented any flying from Yanina on 30 November and 1 December, but on 2 December there were signs of better weather conditions and Pattle took off alone to check the conditions above the rain clouds. In the course of his recce he encountered an Ro37 flying a steady course over the Argyrokastron area and shot it down in flames with one burst. That afternoon he was airborne again, leading twelve Gladiators on a patrol over the Greek front lines and near Premeti spotted two more Ro37s lower down, presumably 'spotting' for Italian artillery guns. With his wingman, Pattle lined up behind these and in simultaneous bursts of fire both Ro37s fell in flames.

Since the water-logged Yanina airfield was now barely tenable 80 Squadron was ordered to move en bloc to Larissa, further east, and by 6 December the unit was completely in residence here; Pattle leading his own detachment there on 3 December. Next morning 14 Gladiators, led by the CO, Hickey, left Larissa for a patrol of the Tepelene area, seeking Italian aircraft and soon finding them – in abundance! Hickey, leading the lower section, led his own formation into an attack against a formation of 27 CR42s, while the middle section – four Gladiators from 112 Squadron – dived into another batch of CR42s nearby. Pattle, leading the top section, took his men around astern and up-sun of five CR42s, then attacked quickly, shooting one down to crash north of Delvinakion.

Climbing back swiftly, Pattle now joined the general battle being waged by Hickey and his section. Spotting one CR42 lining up

---

* Later, Squadron Leader W. Vale, DFC & Bar, credited with 24-28 victories at least.

behind Hickey, Pattle put a burst through its cockpit, setting it on fire, and its pilot rapidly took to his parachute.

Climbing through a thin cloud layer, he was then jumped by several CR42s, receiving bullets in his petrol tank which emitted a thin trail of escaping fuel. Annoyed by this, Pattle dived back into cloud cover and waited, then minutes later eased the nose of his Gladiator out of the cloud and found himself directly underneath a Fiat CR42 whose pilot was patently unaware of his presence. Pulling up below and astern of the Fiat, Pattle gave it a one-second burst. The Fiat rolled, then its pilot tumbled past the Gladiator close enough for Pattle to see the startled look on his face. Still leaking petrol the Gladiator dived back into cloud cover, then emerged again, only to find two CR42s coming in on a head attack.

Pattle refused to break away from this nose to nose confrontation and the two Italians were forced to reef outwards. In a flash Pattle turned onto the tail of one and his fire sent it spinning down pouring black smoke. Its partner then bore in, shattering one of the Gladiator's wing struts, and it was then joined by other CR42s all intent on killing the lone RAF pilot. Manoeuvring as only he could, Pattle evaded all attacking Fiats in a masterly exhibition of combat flying, then sank a burst into one Fiat which spun downwards obviously badly hit before he once more found refuge in the cloud cover, eventually returning to Yanina as the nearest safe airfield.

Although the Italian advance into Greece had been halted, and indeed had by now become a frantic retreat as the Greek forces pursued the invaders back into Albania, the Italian air force was still in plentiful evidence, and – relative to the RAF and Greek Air Force strength – greatly superior numerically. Other factors diluting the RAF's herculean efforts included the appalling weather and, by no means least, the obsolescence of the Gladiator as a fighter and the mountainous task facing the maintenance ground crews in attempting to keep a steadily depleting number of aircraft serviceable enough for operations, despite an almost total lack of proper tools and facilities, and working in literally primitive conditions. The winter weather prevented many sorties during the last weeks of December, though occasional days of relatively good weather saw flare-ups of air action in which 80 Squadron scored – and suffered – heavily.

Blenheim IV, T2177, of 113 Sqn in Greece, 1941

Stalwarts of 80 Sqn at Eleusis, Greece, early 1941. From left: Plt Off 'Keg' Dowding; Plt Off 'Ginger' Still; Sgt C.E. Casbolt; WO 'Mick' Richens; Sgt E. 'Ted' Hewett, DFM; Fg Off 'Twinstead' Flower. Both Sergeants were later commissioned and scored 34 victories between them

Early on 19 December 14 Gladiators were flown from Larissa to Yanina for operations over the frontlines, and at 11 am the CO, Hickey, led 13 of these off for an offensive sweep over the Tepelene zone. There they attacked five SM79s, destroying one before being jumped by a horde of CR42s and G50s. One Gladiator pilot was forced to bale out, only to be shot up by a CR42 as he swung below his parachute. Hickey swiftly despatched the murderous Italian, then close-circled the parachuting pilot until he reached the ground. Landing near Argyrokastron, Hickey commandeered a Greek lorry and set off to find the baled-out pilot, eventually discovering him seriously wounded in a mountain area being liberally shot up by artillery fire. Bringing the wounded man back to the nearest hospital, Hickey remained by his side all that night, but to no avail because the pilot died later the same evening.

Hickey returned to Yanina on 20 December and next day led ten Gladiators to sweep the area from Tepelene to the coast and found six Italian bombers over Argyrokastron. Leading the attack on these Hickey dived while Pattle and his section tackled some Fiat BR20s. At that moment a flock of CR42s came piling down in successive waves from higher altitude – estimated at 54 aircraft in 80's record book – and the Gladiators had to fight desperately for their lives. Hickey, almost surrounded by enemy fighters, had his engine shot to pieces and took to his parachute – only to be strafed by a CR42 as he hung in the air.

Pattle destroyed at least one CR42 in that fight, to add to a pair of Italian bombers shot down the previous day, but the continuing pace of the fighting was beginning to have its effect on most of 80's remaining pilots. The general lack of air activity during late December gave some relief to this fatigue, and gave the ground crews a chance to patch up the battle-scarred aircraft, while dense snowfalls permitted the squadron to celebrate Christmas in as near traditional Service fashion as was possible. Hickey's successor as CO was 'Tap' Jones who arrived from hospital convalescence by 28 December, and thus Pattle – until then acting CO – was able to take a ten-days leave in Cairo with some friends he knew there. On his return to the unit in January 1941 he found the squadron with Flights based at Larissa, Yanina, and Eleusis, near Athens, while in contrast to the balmy sun of Egypt, Greece was in the grip of a winter with Minus-30 degrees' temperatures and snow blizzard conditions.

Based at Yanina, Pattle like all other pilots flew few sorties during January, due directly to the weather, but on the 28th he shared in the destruction of two Italian bombers while patrolling between Kelcyre and Premeti. For the following week weather conditions again clamped down on any air activity but on 9 February, with clear skies, 'Tap' Jones led 14 Gladiators to Tepelene to keep the air clear of Italians while the Greek army made its bid to capture that key town. In the event three Gladiators, including that flown by Jones, aborted due to badly-running engines, and Pattle led the remaining eleven down onto five CR42s over Tepelene, personally following one Fiat down to rooftop level before shooting it down to crash and disintegrate in a rain of wreckage on the town outskirts despite a veritable wall of anti-aircraft fire. That same evening news came through that Pattle had been awarded a DFC. During the day the Italian air force made its first attempt in the campaign to bomb Yanina, the harbinger of a series of attacks to be launched in the next few days.

Next day the Italians returned in a succession of attempted bomb attacks on the airfield, during which Pattle claimed at least two bombers – a Cant Z1007 and a Fiat BR20 – as damaged. The attack on Yanina continued on 11 February when 20 CR42s ground-strafed the field, destroying several Greek Gladiators and causing more damage. A few days later 'Tap' Jones called Pattle to tell him that – at long last – 80 Squadron was to receive six Hurricanes and that he (Pattle) was to take charge of these as a detached Flight to be based at Paramythia alongside the Blenheim IVs of No 211 Squadron.

Paramythia – its Greek name meant 'the place of fairy tales' – lay in a valley, stony and flower-carpeted, with none of the normal buildings and amenities associated with regular airfields. Accommodation was tented and (mainly) sited on the sides of the surrounding mountain 'walls', but the morning sunrise invariably splashed a Joseph's coat of colours along the valley floor, giving it a mantle of incredible natural beauty on any fine day. For the Blenheim and Hurricane crews operating from this 'Valley of Wonders' Paramythia had great potential on a more pragmatic level

– it lay about halfway between Yanina and the Corfu island, was just south of the Albanian border, and was thus only some 30 minutes flying time for reaching the enemy frontline areas – virtually an ideal forward location for the offensively-minded air crews eager to engage the Italian aggressors.

The 80 Squadron Hurricanes arrived on 17 February where they were met by Pattle, who had flown his Gladiator from Yanina, and the next two days were spent in familiarising the pilots with the metal monoplanes in several practice flights. By 20 February, Pattle declared the new Flight operational to 'Tap' Jones, by which time Paramythia had received nine more Blenheims from 84 Squadron and a dozen Greek Air Force PZL monoplane fighters, apart from sundry Wellingtons and an ancient Junkers transport. By mid-day on the 20th further 'visitors' were a gaggle of 17 Gladiators, from 80 and 112 Squadrons, and virtually every aircraft on the crowded field set off in separate formations – the Gladiators escorting the Junkers and Wellingtons on an air-supply mission to Greek troops in the Kelcyre area, while Pattle's Hurricanes escorted 18 Blenheims from 211 and 84 Squadrons on a bombing raid against a bridge at Berat. As the Blenheims finished their bombing Pattle spotted four Fiat G50s climbing to intercept and selected the leading Fiat as his own target. His Hurricane's eight Browning guns stuttered briefly – and the Fiat exploded in mid-air. Rejoining the Blenheims, the Hurricanes then escorted these safely back to Paramythia.

The huge improvement in speed and firepower of the Hurricanes compared with their battle-weary Gladiators gave the 80 Squadron section commanded by Pattle a decided edge in their engagements with the Italian aircraft, exemplified on 27 February when Pattle's section of five Hurricanes attacked a dozen CR42s over Valona and swiftly sent seven down in flames apart from causing two more to collide and crash. Next day Pattle, in the course of two patrols, destroyed two CR42s, two BR20s, and probably shot down a third CR42, but even he was 'topped' that day by 'Ape' Cullen who destroyed five enemy aircraft in flames during a single combat lasting almost an hour. In all, 80 Squadron claimed 16 victories that day.

Four days later Cullen tackled five Cant Z1007s and shot down four of these, celebrating his DFC award notification of 2 March. On 4 March Cullen was flying as No 2 to 'Pat' Pattle on a Blenheim escort job, attacking ships of the Italian Fleet off Himara. Once the Blenheims were safely on their way home, the Hurricanes set out in pairs to hunt Italian aircraft, and Pattle and Cullen attacked a G50, with Pattle shooting it down onto a mountain top. On looking around again Pattle could not find Cullen and assumed he had set off alone to do his own hunting. Near Valona Pattle engaged another G50 and soon sent it down burning into Valona harbour, then turned behind its partner and shot it down in flames. He next ran into nine CR42s at 15,000 feet and picked off the far right-hand machine with a long burst into its cockpit. The Fiat reared, its engine poured smoke, then it fell into cloud in a vicious, uncontrolled spin and disappeared.

Back at the base Pattle learned the tragic news – 'Ape' Cullen had not returned, and his fate was to remain a complete mystery. Only days later 'Tap' Jones informed Pattle that he was to be promoted to Squadron Leader from 12 March and to take over command of No 33 Squadron, another Hurricane unit, while news arrived of Pattle being awarded a Bar to his DFC.

No 33 Squadron, based at Larissa, was already a veteran fighter unit with most of its pilots well-versed in combat over the North African desert and now Greece, but on his arrival on the squadron 'Pat' Pattle made it quite clear that he expected his pilots to fight as a closely co-ordinated team, not simply as a loose-knit collection of skilled individuals. Though no martinet, Pattle established his obvious authority from the outset and his already-high reputation as both fighter and, especially, leader lent great credence to his views. As ever, he emphasised to 33's pilots that, in his opinion, air fighting was a science which needed total dedication, skill, and discipline, and that the 1918 glamour image of the lone-wolf 'ace' had no part in any unit he commanded.

On 23 March Pattle led his squadron into action for the first time shortly after dawn – a Blenheim escort mission – and at mid-day received orders for 33 Squadron to carry out a strafing attack on the enemy airfield at Fieri situated deep in Italian-held territory. Leading ten Hurricanes, Pattle reached the objective flying at 25,000 feet and was about to begin the dive to attack the target when some 20 Fiat G50s and Macchi 200s pounced on the Hurricanes. In the ensuing sprawling dogfight 33's pilots eventually claimed five Italian fighters destroyed or probably destroyed before returning to

Hurricane I of 80 Sqn, Eleusis, Greece, 1941

(*Left*) Warrant Officer Len Cottingham of 33 Sqn, 1938-41. An ex-Aircraft Apprentice, he later rose to Wing Commander, DFC. (*Right*) Fg Off Charles Harold Dyson, DFC (Bar)

Larissa, but when Pattle came back he berated them for not obeying his briefing to attack Fieri as per orders. Only he and the Canadian Vernon Woodward had completed the prime objective – strafing Fieri – and though Pattle had shot down a Fiat G50 in flames when the first air clash had occurred, he had then strafed the airfield, destroying three grounded aircraft, and then shot down a Fiat as it came in to land; all in the midst of some of the heaviest anti-aircraft fire he had ever experienced.

His angry admonition had the desired effect – from that moment 33's pilots were wholly integrated as a fighting team, guided and inspired by Pattle's personal example, and as fresh inexperienced men joined the squadron these too became inculcated readily in the Pattle philosophy.

On Sunday, 6 April 1941, Hitler launched 15 divisions supported by at least 800 aircraft in an invasion of Yugoslavia and Greece simultaneously, and at Larissa Pattle received orders for an offensive patrol over the Rupel Pass near the Bulgarian border. Here the Hurricanes met their first Messerschmitt Bf109s in the Greek campaign – and promptly destroyed five from a formation of 20 Bf109s without loss to themselves. Two of these fell to Pattle's guns, destroyed in two brief bursts within seconds of each other. The following day, while escorting an 11 Squadron Blenheim bombing operation, Pattle destroyed a lone Fiat CR42 apparently trailing the formation. The weather during this period was hardly conducive to operational flying but the critical ground situation demanded extraordinary efforts by the RAF.

On 8 April, despite dense clouds which masked the mountain tops, 33 Squadron helped 211 Squadron's Blenheims in a strafe of Petrich airfield in Yugoslavia, while on the 9th, in even worse conditions, Pattle found a single Junkers Ju88 heading southwards and shot it down to crash. On the 10th the squadron once more escorted 11 Squadron's Blenheims, this time to raid Betjol in Yugoslavia and ran into a flock of Bf109s and Bf110s. Pattle got behind one Bf110 and swiftly sent it spinning down in flames, then chased a Bf109 and riddled it, causing its pilot to bale out. Next day he was flying alone when he received a report of enemy aircraft over Volos harbour. On investigation he found several Ju88s and Heinkel He111s in that area and quickly sent one of each type into the sea.

A slight improvement in the weather on 12 April gave 33 Squadron a busy day. In the afternoon, while leading his men along the Struma Valley hunting for enemy aircraft, Pattle spotted three SM79s being escorted by Bf109s. While the rest of the Hurricane sections tackled the Bf109s, Pattle led his own Vic of three down to intercept the trio of Italian bombers. Selecting the leading SM79, he methodically first killed its gunner, then set its fuel tanks afire. Climbing back to the dogfight with the Bf109s he then expended his remaining ammunition on one Bf109 which shed a wing panel and flopped its undercarriage down before disappearing from Pattle's sight.*

By Easter Sunday, 13 April, the German *Blitzkrieg* invasions were gaining ground, with huge air support being thrown into the conflict, and 33 Squadron's operations were now divided between bomber escorting and protection of the Anzac troops fighting north of Mount Olympus. By 14 April the Luftwaffe had realised the existence of Larissa airfield and that day made its first strafing attack with 15 yellow-nosed Bf109s sweeping in at zero height and destroying two of three Hurricanes which had only just got airborne, though not before two Bf109s had themselves been shot down by the same Hurricanes. The same day Pattle was ordered to evacuate Larissa and take his squadron further south to Eleusis in order to protect Athens. In miserable rainy weather the unit commenced its move by road that night when the ground crews and squadron equipment, accompanied by Pattle, drove in convoy through the mountainous country. By then Pattle was reaching a point of exhaustion from his unceasing efforts, a condition exacerbated by a high temperature and a shivering fever.

By 18 April the squadron was well in residence at Eleusis and became the target for a succession of Luftwaffe bombing and strafing attacks. Pattle, though obviously far from fit for flying, refused to relinquish his command and continued to operate. On 19 April he led seven Hurricanes on a general offensive sweep of the northern approach roads to Athens and shared the destruction of a Henschel Hs126 army co-operation machine en route. Continuing the sweep, Pattle led his men through a succession of mountain

* Earlier in the day he had also destroyed a Dornier bomber.

valleys and suddenly met nine Bf109s coming head-on. The two formations passed through each other before most pilots could react, but Pattle turned like a flash onto the tails of the Messerschmitts and shot one into a mountain side, then chased a second Bf109 down a valley and despatched this by killing its pilot.

In the afternoon the squadron sent off five Hurricanes on a second sweep, but this time the squadron medical officer was firm in ordering Pattle to remain on the ground, knowing only too well how ill the South African really was and how near he might be to cracking point. Pattle's protests were mollified to a degree by being allowed still to fly but only in the event of another attack on the airfield. In the event an incoming raid was reported a few hours later and Pattle took off immediately. Over the coast near Akra he caught up with a Ju88 and coolly destroyed this almost piece by piece, the wreckage finally tumbling into the sea.

On the morning of 20 April the total Hurricane strength at Eleusis comprised 15 aircraft, the surviving machines of 33, 80 and 208 Squadron. Pattle, by now fully in the grip of a high fever, lay in a swathe of blankets on a makeshift couch in the Readiness hut but when the air raid siren wailed he immediately made his way out to the nearest Hurricane, climbed in, and taxied out, despite the presence of several Bf110s attempting to strafe the airfield. All 15 Hurricanes got airborne individually, then set course for Piraeus further south, a key harbour, which was being dive-bombed relentlessly by at least 100 German bombers and fighters. Over the harbour the sky was filled with black-crossed aircraft, diving, climbing, bombing, wheeling – an awesome array to greet the 15 Hurricane pilots as they arrived on the scene in pairs and threes.

Within the next two hours the Hurricanes had destroyed 20 German aircraft for certain and at least seriously damaged six others, but their own losses were high; five Hurricanes, two pilots killed, and others wounded or injured. Several used up their ammunition, flew back to Eleusis, refuelled and re-armed, then rejoined the fight. And in the turmoil 'Pat' Pattle died.

On reaching Piraeus he found himself slightly higher than a circling ring of Bf110s and saw a lone Hurricane climbing hard to tackle these. Its pilot, unknown to Pattle, was Flight Lieutenant W.J. Woods, DFC – known inevitably to all as 'Timber' – an Irishman who had first fought the Axis in a Gladiator defending Malta in 1940. Instinctively Pattle dived straight through the wheeling Bf110s in order to team up with and protect Woods as the Messerschmitts began attacking the impudent Hurricane. One Bf110 was already on Woods' tail when Pattle arrived and quickly sent it down in flames. Climbing again Pattle was soon surrounded by vengeful Bf110s and as the Hurricane twisted and jinked through a hail of cannon shells, Pattle shot down a second Bf110 in flames as it flashed through his sights. Within seconds his aircraft was laced with cannon shells and bullets as two Bf110s got on its tail, and the Hurricane started a steepening dive, its pilot slumped forward over the control column, and flames licking back from its engine threatening to engulf the cockpit.

Pattle's plunge was witnessed by Flight Lieutenant 'Jimmy' Kettlewell of 80 Squadron* who promptly shot down one of the Bf110s still firing at Pattle. The burning Hurricane never came out of its dive and flew straight into the waters of the bay, to be joined seconds later by Kettlewell's victim.

'Pat' Pattle's death – attempting to protect a fellow pilot – was typical of the man. An advocate of 'teamwork' in the 'business' of aerial combat, Pattle had constantly emphasised the need to treat the profession of fighter pilot as a calculated science, leaving nothing to mere luck or chance. Privately he had kept a sort of combat 'diary' in which he jotted down as many technical and tactical notes as he could think of relating to the various types of enemy aircraft he had met. In setting the highest standards for himself, physically and mentally, he had inspired others to emulate him, breeding confidence in his subordinates and in his leadership. Yet in 'preaching' the doctrine of the calculated risk, Pattle had not hesitated in abandoning that principle when he saw one of his pilots in danger. In the fitting words of Chapter 15 of St John's Gospel; 'Greater love hath no man than this, that he lay down his life for his friends ...'.

---

* Later, Wing Commander G.V.W. Kettlewell, psc, cfs, RAF Retd.

CHAPTER SIX

Cretan Diary

The 'Battle of Athens' on 20 April 1941, during which 'Pat' Pattle had been killed, was virtually the final major air action of the Greek campaign, inasmuch as the hopelessness of remaining in Greece was now recognised and evacuation to Crete and Egypt of the remaining RAF units commenced almost immediately thereafter.

On 22 April the remaining 18 Hurricanes still flyable from Nos 33, 80 and 208 Squadrons moved to Argos, to be joined next day by five reinforcement Hurricanes from Egypt. Just as the latter five landed some 40 Bf110s made a surprise strafing attack on the field, destroying 13 Hurricanes on the ground, though the few Hurricane pilots who managed to get airborne claimed several Bf110s destroyed, including Sergeant G.E.C. Reynolds of 33 Squadron who shot down four alone. By the end of that day only seven Hurricanes remained capable of flying and these, along with the surviving bombers of Nos 11, 84, and 211 Squadrons, withdrew to Crete, where they were joined by five Blenheim IVF 'fighters' from 203 Squadron and the Gladiators of 112 Squadron.

Already on Crete were 30 Squadron's few Blenheims, these having been flown out of Greece on 18 April, and some Fleet Air Arm fighters of No 805 Squadron (Fulmars). Over the next few days several clashes with the Luftwaffe while defending the Allied evacuation to Crete caused further reductions on serviceable RAF fighters, though piecemeal reinforcement Hurricanes from Egypt helped to balance these losses to some extent, albeit never higher than a total of 16 Hurricanes fit for operations. By the end of April the remnants of 33 and 80 Squadrons (eight Hurricanes and eleven pilots in all) combined to form the 'Hurricane Unit, Crete', with all ground maintenance being the responsibility of 33 Squadron's 'Erks' since no 80 Squadron ground crew were available.

The subsequent 'campaign' in Crete deserves a volume unto itself if every RAF man's story is to be included, both air and ground crew, but the following extracts from daily diary notes by an unidentified 33 Squadron officer at least offer a glimpse of the daunting odds facing the RAF men – air and ground crews – in Crete in the fateful fighting and eventual evacuation of May 1941. Virtually all official documentation was either destroyed or simply lost during the Greek and Crete 'campaigns', but these notes give some witness to the courage, spirit, and dogged determination of the Crete RAF defenders, encapsulated by these references to the events experienced by 33 Squadron personnel only.

' ... From the beginning of May a normal routine was maintained of protective patrols over ships evacuating from Greece until about May 4, followed by standing patrols over Suda Bay and a number of scrambles during the following week. Two of these scrambles were successful in intercepting the enemy. Unit based now at Maleme.

'*3 May 41.* In the first of these (scrambles) F/O Woods and Sgt Genders encountered about 24 Ju88s, F/O Woods shooting down one confirmed and damaging a second, while Sgt Genders damaged four.

'*4 May 41.* In the second engagement F/O Woods and F/O Noel-Johnson encountered 12 more Ju88s, each pilot damaging at least two enemy aircraft.

'*6 May 41.* By this date our serviceability of aircraft had been reduced to six, owing to one aircraft landing with its undercarriage up and another suffering from internal engine trouble. Use was made of these to keep the other aircraft serviceable.

'*12 May 41.* On the evening of May 12 S/Ldr Howell* arrived from Egypt and took charge of the Hurricane Unit. Six other pilots of the (33) Squadron accompanied the Squadron Leader to relieve those pilots who had been in Crete since the evacuation of Greece. Six of the latter and approximately 30 airmen left Crete the same evening

* Later, Wing Commander E. Howell, OBE, DFC.

by Sunderland for Egypt. The spotter system was introduced so that airmen could carry on working although enemy aircraft could be seen overhead.

'*13 May 41*. 1100 hrs. During flying practice one Hurricane (V7800) overshot the aerodrome and crashed. 2100 hrs. Three enemy aircraft dropped bombs in the close vicinity of the aerodrome and Maleme village and machine-gunned the aerodrome surroundings, but no damage was done.

'*14 May 41*. 0600 hrs. One enemy aircraft dropped six bombs on west side of aerodrome, damaging Blenheims of 30 Squadron which were already unserviceable. 0900 hrs. A few hours after the bombing a large number of Me109s strafed the aerodrome for half an hour. Three Hurricanes took off to intercept, Sgts Ripsher and Reynish getting off before the strafing had developed. In the third machine S/Ldr Howell took off as the aerodrome was being strafed, passing 20 yards to the rear of one enemy aircraft and across the path of another, but keeping very low until he reached the hills and was able to climb safely. A few minutes later he shot down one Me109 confirmed.*

'Meanwhile Sgt Reynish was in combat with three enemy aircraft, one of which was seen to dive steeply into the hills after the Hurricane had made an astern attack. Sgt Reynish was then attacked by nine more Me109s and all disappeared behind the hills. At the same time Sgt Ripsher sighted six enemy aircraft out to sea and attacked. One enemy aircraft was seen to dive steeply towards the sea. Sgt Ripsher was also attacked and his aircraft damaged, and he was killed whilst making his approach to the aerodrome. Sgt Reynish was shot down and baled out over the sea, and succeeded in swimming a distance of two miles back to safety. In the first raid one Hurricane was burnt out on the ground, while in the evening raid a second was also destroyed, besides aircraft of other units on the aerodrome. S/Ldr Howell returned after an absence of 3½ hours, having landed at Retimo to refuel and re-arm.

'*Maleme. 14 May 41*. One Me109 exploded in mid-air above the

---

* Howell had never flown a Hurricane before this date.

aerodrome after being hit by an ack-ack shell.

'*15 May 41*. Two Hurricanes arrived from Egypt.

'*16 May 41*. A number of Ju87s and Ju88s, escorted by Me109s, attacked Suda Bay and were intercepted by S/Ldr Howell who shot down one Me109 confirmed and one Ju87 'probably'. Two further Me109s were shot down by others, the enemy aircraft crashing on Maleme beach and their pilots being taken prisoner. Sgt Reynish arrived back at camp.

'*17 May 41*. A small force of enemy aircraft bombed Suda Bay and the aerodrome causing a small petrol dump on the latter to burn up. We were unable to operate in spite of the efforts of the ground crew, who carried out extensive repairs keenly, efficiently, and quickly, considering the lack of tools and spares; their keenness and high morale largely due to the excellent work of F/Sgt Salmon.

'*18 May 41*. The aerodrome was dive-bombed and strafed at intervals throughout the day, the most serious raid taking place at 1430 hours during which one bomb scored a direct hit on a Hurricane in a pen, and another bomb burying three airmen in a slit trench, and a third burying two Greek civilians. The three airmen were quickly dug out and were still alive but suffering from shock. AC de Comeau, who was in a trench near that in which the Greeks were buried, left his own place of safety and proceeded to extricate the two Greeks while bombing and strafing were still in progress.* In the evening W/O Clarke, F/Sgt Salmon, and about 20 airmen left Crete by Sunderland for Egypt.

'*19 May 41*. Attempts were made to build more pens for our aircraft, but repeated strafing raids made this impossible. Sgt Bennett (80 Squadron) flew back our one remaining Hurricane to Egypt.'

At this point in the diary it is valid to interject with some background details in order to set the rest of the diarist's notes in a fuller context. Edward Howell, OC 33 Squadron (nominally) chose

---

* For greater details of 33 Squadron's ground crew activities in Crete, see *Operation Mercury* by M.G. Comeau; Wm Kimber, 1961.

(*Right*) Sgt G.E.C. Genders, DFM of 33 Squadron

(*Below*) Sunderland I, N9029, NM-V, of 228 Sqn in the eastern Mediterranean, early 1941

deliberately to stay with his men on Crete, rather than fly the last Hurricane back to Egypt, and with him remained several officer-pilots including Pilot Officer Dunscombe, Flight Lieutenant Vernon Woodward, and Commander Beale, OC 805 Squadron FAA among others. Next day, 20 May, saw the first waves of German airborne troops invade Crete, their prime objective to capture Maleme airfield and its surrounds for use in landing further waves of airborne infantry *et al*, and Hill 107 nearby which was held by nearly 12,000 men of the New Zealand 5 Brigade and commanded the approaches to Maleme airfield and village.

Shortly after dawn Dorniers, Heinkels, and Ju87s from KG2, II/KG26, and StG2 respectively commenced an aerial bombardment of the New Zealand positions and the airfield, followed by low-level strafing assaults by Messerschmitts from JG77 and ZG26. Behind this flying 'artillery' came the initial waves of crack German paratroops and airborne assault troops in towed gliders – some 6,000 men in this first shock 'drop' on Maleme. Elsewhere more gliders winged down intent on capturing the Cretan administrative centre at Canea. The German *Operation Mercury* had commenced.

Though repulsed decisively initially, with appalling casualties, the German airborne invasion began to bite by the evening of 20 May when troops of an assault regiment stormed to the summit of Hill 107. By the evening of 21 May Maleme airfield was a graveyard for the burned out hulks of at least 80 Junkers Ju52 troop transporter aircraft but the continuing German assaults from air and sea could not be denied indefinitely. By 28 May the full-scale evacuation of Allied personnel was under way, and was officially completed by 1 June.

'*20 May 41*. This morning began the long-awaited airborne invasion of Crete, heavy bombing and strafing by large formations of enemy aircraft heralding the arrival of hundreds of parachute troops as they dropped from Ju52s flying at only a few hundred feet above the ground, some of them towing gliders which were released over the dry river bed which ran along one side of the aerodrome. However, every man was on duty at 0415 hours standing in pre-arranged defensive positions. After the first few aerial attacks that morning all personnel were ordered to take up defensive positions with the New

Zealanders who had several gun posts in the vicinity of the camp. At 0730 hours while personnel were attempting to have some breakfast an extremely heavy bombing attack was made on the defensive positions of the hill adjoining the aerodrome, whilst the first loads of parachutists landed on the camp. The gliders, each containing about 20 men, and towed in 'trains' of four, were mostly wrecked or burnt on landing. Many landed very near our machine-gun posts, their numbers enabling them to overcome our posts almost immediately and use the guns against our own troops.

'One party of parachutists of about 30 in number landed all around a trench in which eight of our airmen were sheltering, so cutting them off from the main body of defenders. These eight men managed to maintain a regular and accurate fire which killed at least 13 of the enemy though out of the eight of our airmen three were killed and one wounded during the action. One of the killed was AC Eaton who volunteered to make a dash for his tent to replenish their dwindling supply of ammunition, but on reaching the tent he was apparently spotted because the tent was riddled with machine-gun bullets from which he could not have escaped. No more was seen of him.

'Ammunition supplies were now extremely low but fortunately 943205 AC Jones noticed a bandolier of 50 rounds hanging from the branch of a tree nearby. Though there was considerable danger of his being killed, he got out of the trench, made his way to the tree, grabbed the bandolier and returned safely to the trench, having drawn a good deal of fire from the enemy. Having used up this supply the party, now numbering only four, had to make a dash for our main body of defenders. After several hazardous adventures all four eventually succeeded in reaching our lines safely. With constant protection from Me109s and Me110s, and with the co-operation of Ju87s bombing our gun posts, the parachutists were not long in capturing our squadron HQ and that of the New Zealanders. Several attempts were made to encircle the hill, to which all airmen who were not captured or wounded had made their way to reinforce the New Zealanders, but all attacks were successfully beaten back, some at the bayonet point.

'After being taken prisoner by parachutists, one party of our airmen, together with some of 30 Squadron, was made to march up the hill towards our lines. Our forces opened fire against the enemy killing some of the 'hostages' and wounding LAC Hutchinson. Four of the RAF personnel were later able to escape. (On several occasions the similarity of the RAF Home Pattern blue uniform to that of the (German) parachutists resulted in many casualties to our men through the action of our own troops.)

'At approximately 1700 hours Ju52s made attempts to land on Maleme aerodrome but were driven off by three guns of the NZ artillery. By 1830 hours our position on the hill was becoming very bad, and after various engagements in which we used a few odd "I" tanks which were put out of action by German anti-tank guns, the position had to be evacuated. A new position was taken up about a mile further back on another hill. At 2300 hours it was decided to evacuate the casualties from the new position. After this was finished most of our airmen walked seven miles further to the rear to join the NZ Company's HQ established in a wood.' (*Author's note: This day Squadron Leader Howell was critically wounded and his subsequent story can be found in his autobiographical account Escape to Live; Longmans, Green & Co, 1947*).

'*21 May 41.* The day was spent helping the New Zealanders as best as possible. The latter had with them eight parachutists as prisoners. Strafing and bombing continued at regular intervals during the successful landings on the aerodrome. Ju87s released hundreds of small metal objects which whined during their fall causing our troops to take cover while the enemy captured more ground. At nightfall the squadron was nearly surrounded again, but Maoris managed to clear the road to Canea, leaving the squadron in a safer position.

'*22 May 41 – Between Maleme and Canea.* Little enemy activity took place during the morning. Some strafing was carried out by Me110s but enemy snipers proved almost as worrying as the enemy aircraft. At 1500 hours the squadron was ordered to take up new positions on the top of another hill and prepare for another attack. At 1730 hours the attack started but was repulsed at the bayonet point by the Maoris. Ju88s and Me110s bombed and strafed a village at the rear of our positions.

'*23 May 41*. At 0500 hours the squadron retired with a number of New Zealanders across country to HQ NZ Forces, where they met FAA personnel and more members of the squadron. All proceeded eastwards along the road to Canea, being strafed every 15 minutes for some 10 miles. On reaching Canea the RAF HQ evacuated the party to Traivoros, some 15 miles east of Suda.

'*24 May 41. Traivoros*. Party stayed in hiding all day while waves of Ju87s, Do17s (*sic*), and He111s bombed Canea, the attack lasting for six hours. A naval 12-inch gun mounted at Suda Bay shelled the aerodrome at Maleme throughout the day.

'*25 May 41*. Party still in hiding. At least three Ju88s shot down.

'*26 May 41*. Party left Traivoros packed very tightly in lorries and travelling throughout the night over a 7000 feet mountain range to the south-east of Spahkia. All transports were then systematically wrecked.

'*27 May 41*. Everyone lay in hiding in caves or wadis throughout the day.

'*28 May 41*. Army lorries and ambulances arrived with wounded and troops who were strafed all day. At night orders were given to move westwards. Most of the able-bodied men carried stretcher cases for three miles, having to cover very rough ground, being bombed at intervals. At 0300 hours Spahkia was reached where three destroyers were lying to take off survivors. At 0330 hours all three destroyers, loaded to capacity, sailed for Egypt.

'*29 May 41*. Six Ju88s attacked the ships without success, all reaching Alexandria safely at 1730 hours. The squadron (33) lost about 55 men in all, as well as S/Ldr Howell, P/O Butcher, P/O Dunscombe, and Sgts Reynish, Loveridge and Butterick. With the exception of P/O Dunscombe and Sgt Reynish all these pilots are known to be prisoners of war. The fates of the 55 airmen and the two latter pilots mentioned remain unknown'.

While the foregoing notes applied specifically to the men of No 33 Squadron, every unit involved in the Crete 'siege' had similar adventures to some degree. No 112 Squadron, later to achieve high fame in North Africa as the 'Shark Squadron', had evacuated from Argos in Greece in late April 1941 to Suda Bay where, on 29 April a coin was tossed to decide which Flight should remain in Crete and which go on to Egypt – 'A' Flight went and 'B' Flight remained. At mid-day the airmen and non-flying personnel of 'A' Flight boarded a ship and, at sunset, sailed from Crete in company with seven cargo steamers, four destroyers, and two cruisers.

'B' Flight's activities on Crete in May 1941 are now only recorded fragmentarily, most documents having been deliberately destroyed. Nevertheless, the Flight's Gladiators obviously made their presence felt, as witnessed by the few extant records. One combat report, dated 12 May, credits a Sergeant Weir with shooting down an SM79 (*sic*) over Heraklion, a victory confirmed by the army but probably a Junkers Ju52. On 14 May Pilot Officer N. Bowker attacked a Bf110 and shot it down into the sea, then at least damaged a second Bf110. Next day Pilot Officer D.F. Westenra scrambled with a Flying Officer Reeves (not of 112 Squadron) to tackle some Bf110s and shot one into the sea, though Reeves had to force-land afterwards.

The same day Flight Lieutenant C.H. Fry, an 'old' 112 hand, with four other pilots, engaged eight to ten Bf110s at 6,000 feet near Heraklion. Fry fired at one Bf110 which began to fall away but not before its rear gunner had so damaged Fry's Hurricane that he was forced to abandon aircraft. This combat had an interesting sequel. Pilot Officer Bowker, who had been taken ill on Crete, was in a field hospital when it was captured by the Germans on 20 May. In the next bed was placed a German pilot who had been forced to ditch in the sea on 15 May after being attacked by a Hurricane which was itself shot down by the German's gunner. Since Fry was the only Hurricane pilot shot down that day over Heraklion, this German would seem to have been Fry's victim. In a postwar published book, *Wir Kampften auf dem Balkan*, the crew of the Bf110 were said to be Oberleutnant Sophus Baagoe and Oberfeldwebel Daniel Bäcker; Baagoe being then credited with 14 combat victories and the award of a *Ritterkreuz* ('Knight's Cross') and serving with ZG26.

Bowker, incidentally, escaped from that German field hospital on

27 May – he simply walked out unchallenged – and joined a party of British troops, eventually reaching the coast and getting aboard HMS *Orion*. This cruiser, despite being badly damaged by dive-bombers, reached Egypt safely, and Bowker rejoined 112 Squadron on 16 June to recommence operations. On 27 December 1941 Bowker was forced to land in enemy territory while engaged in strafing enemy troops on the Agheila-Agedabia road and became a prisoner of war, by which date he had been awarded a DFC and credited with ten combat victories.

If Bowker's escape from Crete can be regarded as out of the ordinary, the affair of 'McLennan's Barge' became a minor legend in 112 Squadron's annals. Its title came from one of the squadron's engine fitters, AC1 G.R. McLennan, who with LAC Harrington and AC Malloy and several men from other units and Services discovered an abandoned invasion barge (presumably of German origin) on some rocks on the south coast of Crete. This was on 2 June – one day *after* the official evacuation had ceased – and the assorted party, which included two officers, R.J. Bennett and L.L. Bartley of 112 Squadron, managed to launch the barge, gather a

Sunderlands of 228 Sqn waiting to evacuate troops from Greece

quantity of water and rations and fuel, then set off at about 2015 hours that evening to 'sail' to Egypt.

Early in the morning of their second day out, 4 June, the barge was stopped by an Italian submarine whose commander took aboard all commissioned officers and ordered the rest of the barge's 'crew' to return to Crete. Once the submarine was out of sight the barge continued its original course and, travelling at a rate of about four knots, finally reached the Egyptian coast at Mersa Matruh some four days later where, recognising some troops on the sand beach as British, McLennan's 'crew' came ashore.

No 112 Squadron's losses in personnel in Crete amounted to at least three officers and 21 airmen. Overall, of the RAF ground staff who fought through the Cretan battles – totalling 618 men – 361 are known to have evacuated the island safely by one means or another. British aircraft losses amounted to 38 machines destroyed, but the Luftwaffe lost at least 220 destroyed and another 150 damaged, mainly transport aircraft shot down by ground defences. In view of the superb gallantry and fighting spirit shown by virtually every RAF ground crew 'Erk', Winston Churchill's post-Crete pronouncement recommending that in future every airfield should become 'a stronghold of fighting air-groundmen, not the abode of uniformed civilians in the prime of life protected by detachments of soldiers' was not only misguided but unworthy.

CHAPTER SEVEN

Boats over the Med

While the aerial struggle for North Africa and the Mediterranean was primarily a saga of fighter and bomber deeds, equally vital and courageous roles were played by the seldom-publicised crews of the relative handful of flying boat units based within RAF Middle East Command. When war came in late 1939 the RAF's best available aircraft for maritime reconnaissance was the giant Short Sunderland, which had entered squadron service first in May 1938. By 3 September 1939 only four squadrons had Sunderlands on charge, Nos 204 and 210 in the UK, 230 in the Far East, and 228 at Malta, though the latter unit returned to the UK within a week of the war declaration. During the following two years only three more squadrons were equipped with Sunderlands, Nos 95, 201, and 10 RAAF – the first of these based in West Africa and the other two in the UK. However, in May and June 1940 Nos 230 and 228 Squadron respectively became main-based at Alexandria for work in the Mediterranean zone, coincidental with Italy's entry into the European conflict. Here their prime purpose was reconnaissance over the sea, convoy protection, and U-boat surveillance, but their obvious potential for long range load-carrying and communication soon came to be used in various critical situations.

With the fall of France in the summer of 1940 Sunderlands flew a number of VIP secret flights, evacuating high-ranking Frenchmen who wished to continue the fight against the Axis, and conveying British government and Service chiefs to secret destinations. For the first nine months of the Middle East war Sunderlands became highly ubiquitous, attacking U-boats*, shadowing the Italian Fleet, bombing Axis shipping, dropping secret agents in Axis-held

---

* The Italian submarines *Argon Auta*, *Rubino*, and *Gondar* were all sunk by Sunderlands in 1940 in the Mediterranean.

territories, ferrying fresh air crews and supplies, troop-carrying to
Greece, and on no few occasions providing doughty opposition to
attacks by Italian aircraft. Then, in April 1941, came the Allied
evacuation of Greece. Both 228 and 230 Squadrons immediately
swung into action as 'mercy angels' to assist the evacuation. On 16
April, 230 Squadron sent two Sunderlands to Kotor, Yugoslavia to
retrieve 48 VIPs including members of the Yugoslav royal family,
while on the 20th Sunderland 'Y' of 230 Squadron commenced the
evacuation of Allied troops from Greece with individual sorties. On
these sorties the Sunderland skippers were given virtual autonomy
as to their 'loads' and methods.

Theoretically, a Sunderland's emergency capacity was laid down
in the book as 'no more than 30 personnel' additional to the crew,
but during the Greek (and later, Crete) evacuations most skippers
simply loaded their aircraft to physical limits of space rather than
leave men stranded to await imprisonment in Axis hands. On 23
April, for example, 228 Squadron joined the 'taxi ranks' when
Flight Lieutenant Alex Frame, a New Zealander, lifted 50 RAF men
from a Greek harbour and flew them to Suda Bay, Crete. Next day
Frame was ordered to fly to Nauplia Bay in the bay of Argos to
retrieve some more RAF personnel reported there. On arrival just
before dusk, however he was told that his intended passengers had
already moved on, so he took aboard 25 other men, including a
general, then waited for daylight before taking off in strange waters.
At dawn he found the whole bay blacked out by dense smoke from a
burning ammunition ship and a bombed troopship, but after
taxying fruitlessly in the hope of finding a clear path, Frame finally
took off blind through the smoke and reached Suda Bay safely.*

Meanwhile Sunderlands 'U' and 'V' of 230 Squadron, helped by
the BOAC C-class flying boats *Cambria* and *Coorong*, lifted 127 men
from Suda and flew them to Alexandria. Another skipper of 230
Squadron, D.K. Bednall, attempted to follow them in Sunderland
'Y' from Suda with only three engines working – the fourth's
propeller was crudely lashed-up with rope. When the rope lashing
began working loose Bednall alighted in a sheltered bay south of
Crete, had the offending starboard inner engine's propeller

---

* Later, Wing Commander A. Frame, DFC, RNZAF.

resecured and reached Alexandria without mishap.

On 25 April Alex Frame rescued a Group Captain and 50 RAF men from Kalamata while Flight Lieutenant Harry Lamond of 228 Squadron was sent to Githeron in Sunderland T9084 to lift a party of RAF men. Signalled by hand-mirrors from the shore Lamond landed and anchored about 100 yards off shore and of a party of 130 RAF personnel waiting patiently he took 52 on board and flew these back to Suda Bay. In the afternoon Lamond, still skippering T9048, was sent to Kalamata where a host of RAF and army men were waiting. Lamond checked his fuel state, then calmly took 82 of these on board in addition to his ten-men crew! T9048 took off 'like a bird' (*sic*) and his 'overload' was delivered safely.

Lamond's third trip that day actually involved a night trip to Kalamata from Suda Bay – without benefit of any flare-paths. After a hair-raising take-off dodging myriad floating obstacles Lamond reached Kalamata but could not even see the sea, despite the use of the aircraft's landing light. With fuel now too low to await daylight Lamond put T9048 down without sight of the sea surface. As the Sunderland touched it tore out its nose plates, turned turtle, ripping a wing off in the process. Only four of the crew, including Lamond, surfaced after the crash, three of them injured, and these eventually reached the beach, only to be captured by the Germans shortly after. Next day Alex Frame returned from Greece with 50 more RAF men, thereby bringing the total rescued by 228 Squadron alone to date to 339 (324 of these being RAF). For the following ten days 230 Squadron continued airlifting parties of men from various Greek inlets, then had a brief respite as the Allies dug in on Crete in preparation for the inevitable German onslaught to come.

The assault on Crete began on 20 May and ten days later the Sunderlands of 228 and 230 Squadrons were back in constant action in their rescue-ferry role for a 48-hour period, after which the airlift ceased. Throughout the whole Greek/Crete campaign Sunderlands had retrieved a total of 1,096 men, apart from hundreds of tons of vital equipment and supplies – accomplished by merely six Sunderlands.

Though the Sunderland was relatively heavily armed – six to eight machine guns in the 1939-41 version – it was realistically no match for the faster, often cannon-armed enemy fighters which it was to

Saro London II, TQ-H, of 202 Sqn at Gun Wharf, Gibraltar, 1939

Sunderland, I, N9021, of 20 Sqn at the FAA base Kalafrana, Malta in April 193

Catalina IB, AX-L, of 202 Sq airborne from Gibraltar 194

meet in any aerial combat. The most usual tactic by Sunderland skippers when encountering Axis fighters was to get down as near the sea surface as possible in order to protect the aircraft's vulnerable belly, then rely on its gunners' accuracy and the pilot's manoeuvring skills to evade destruction. Not all were lucky enough to avoid such a fate. On 6 August 1940 Squadron Leader Menzies of 228 Squadron left the unit's base at Aboukir for a routine recce of the Libyan and Cretan coastlines and came across an Italian merchant convoy. He immediately began shadowing the convoy, at the same time relaying the position and course of the ships back to base in order to have an eventual relief aircraft take over the shadowing if necessary.

Accordingly, a relief Sunderland, N9025, skippered by Flight Lieutenant Thurstan, M. Smith, DFC, was despatched within the hour. After two hours of careful shadowing of the convoy, the Sunderland was finally 'discovered' by several Fiat CR42 fighters of 10° *Gruppi* which bore in to attack. In their first onslaught they put the Sunderland's rear turret out of action, then put both midships' guns out of action in their second and third attacks. In doing so five crew members were wounded, one of these, LAC C.J.C. Jones, dying an hour later after being hit in the stomach by an explosive bullet. One of the midship gunners, Davies, was hit twice in the stomach and in his left eye. The starboard inner engine ground to a halt and the starboard main fuel tank erupted in flames. Expecting the tank to explode any second Smith put the crippled Sunderland down on the sea, despite continuing attacks by the Fiats which closed to 50 yards firing range on seeing no return fire. As soon as the flying boat had landed the Italians ceased firing and flew away to fetch an Italian destroyer with the convoy to retrieve the Sunderland's crew.

The battle had lasted some 15 minutes, and the 'victory' was credited to Capitano (later, Colonel) Monti of 10° *Gruppi*. The destroyer arrived some $2\frac{1}{2}$ hours later, by which time the Sunderland was about to sink, its tail already under water, but the RAF crew were taken aboard the destroyer and eventually taken to Tobruk. Here Italian surgeons worked for three hours on the seriously wounded Davies, removing his shattered left eye and a rib, and a week later Davies was completely on the mend to full recovery.

The sequel to this incident came many months later when an

Italian aircraft dropped a letter behind Allied lines, addressed to Wing Commander G.E. Nicholetts, DFC, OC 228 Squadron. Dated Sunday, 2 February 1941, it was written by the Sunderland's co-pilot, Flight Lieutenant D.R.S. Bevan-John* from the Italian PoW camp at Fonte d'Amore, Sulmona, and gave full details of the fight and its aftermath.

Another Sunderland which was forced down after an engagement with enemy fighters had a very different sequel. On 21 December 1941 Flight Lieutenant (later, Air Marshal, CB, CBE, AFC) S.W.R. Hughes, a New Zealand-born RAF pilot of 230 Squadron left Aboukir at 2 am in Sunderland T9071, 'M' to convey urgently needed supplies to Malta. In addition to his normal crew, Hughes had on board a Wellington crew, skipper Pilot Officer G.H. Easton, who were Malta-based but had crashed in North Africa a week earlier while bombing Benghazi, and an army Major, a friend of Hughes', who was going 'along for the ride'. The weather was unpromising, stormy, cold and bleak, and the Sunderland had to plough through an inky blackness westward, staying low and within 25-30 miles of the North African coastline. Shortly after first light, when approximately 50 miles north-east of Benghazi, Hughes spotted two Messerschmitt Bf110s higher up and slightly ahead which at first seemed not to have seen the flying boat, but as the pair had almost disappeared Hughes saw both fighters bank, turn, and begin their approach.

Hughes quickly took his aircraft down to within 200 feet of the sea and waited. The first Bf110 attacked from dead astern, closing to pointblank range with all guns and cannons blazing, only to run into the combined fire of most of the Sunderland's guns. It swiftly disappeared and was later to be claimed as probably destroyed, but its aim had been deadly accurate, having put both starboard engines out of action and shooting the starboard aileron away apart from riddling the boat's fuselage. The other Bf110 bore in from a beam, wounding two gunners and killing one of the RAF passengers, but was itself hit by return fire from the Australian gunner Sergeant Dupont and left the scene streaming black smoke.†

---

* Later, Group Captain, OBE, JP, RAF Retd.
† Both Bf110s were from ZG26 which reported no losses.

Hughes took stock of the Sunderland's damage quickly and knew there was no alternative but to land. Easing the nose into wind with some difficulty, Hughes set the crippled Sunderland down on the heavy-running sea. It ricocheted off the swell twice before finally stalling into a trough between the angry rollers, ripping off the starboard wing float but doing little other serious damage. The uninjured crew members clambered out onto the port wing to 'balance ship', rigging life-lines as they went, and the experienced Hughes set about the delicate task of 'sailing' his boat stern-first before the strong north-easterly wind towards the nearby coast, while the men still inside pumped out water and petrol leaking through the many shell holes. Using his sea-anchor drogues and some adroit rudder and controls manoeuvring, Hughes finally brought the wallowing flying boat broadside on to a reef so that the broken starboard wing would overhang rocks on the shoreline, only to have the wing tilted near-vertical by the wind and almost turn the huge aircraft over.

By various means the crew scrambled ashore, while the seriously wounded Flight Lieutenant Odhams was put in a dinghy and guided to shore by Dupont. The co-pilot, Flight Lieutenant Squires, fell off the wing and was sucked out to sea but was retrieved by Hughes who dived after him and after half an hour's struggle managed to bring Squires ashore. Apart from the dead Wellington crew man still aboard the Sunderland, the remaining 19 men finally gathered on the razor-sharp rocks and after applying rough first-aid to the wounded and injured watched helplessly as Sunderland 'M' gradually battered itself against the reef until its back was broken within the next two hours. As far as Hughes could figure it his party was now stranded about 100 miles east of Benghazi, near Cape Appolonia – it looked like being a long walk back to Allied territory.

Suddenly a group of Italian infantrymen appeared around a bluff and Hughes, knowing his men had no firearms, went forward to formally surrender his men, only to see the first Italian throw his rifle away and advance with outstretched hands! Then, shortly after, a second batch of about 80 Italians appeared led by a bumptious Lieutenant who announced that Hughes and his party were his prisoners. Meantime Hughes persuaded the Italians to let him return to the Sunderland to get some flying boots for the seriously wounded Odhams, and while doing so emptied a 100lb-weight bag of golden sovereigns intended for the Malta Exchequer into the sea. Constructing a makeshift stretcher from dinghy oars to carry Odhams, the combined assembly eventually set off along the coast through driving rainstorms with flashes of lightning crackling overhead.

By nightfall all were ordered to halt and sleep, though no fires were permitted – the Italians feared Arab snipers – and there were no rations, water, or blankets. Flight Lieutenant Odhams by then was delirious and visibly sinking, while Squires was still suffering from shock and exposure, and the British 'captives' huddled themselves around both men to offer some warmth, and massaged the two men constantly.

At dawn the party set off again only to be joined by 20 Italian officers who said that the retreating Germans had commandeered all transports, leaving the Italians stranded. These officers offered to help Hughes in exchange for favoured treatment should they be captured by the British, but before Hughes could make any such decision yet another crowd of Italians appeared, about 100 men of the 102nd Caribineri commanded by a middle-aged Italian Major.

It soon became apparent that most of the Italians had no further interest in the war and merely wanted to go home, but the Italian Major took over command of the increasingly large contingent and prepared to set off again. Hughes, however, accused the Major of commanding a rabble, pointing out that some Italian soldier had robbed the dying Odhams of his flying boots. The Major reacted by lining up every Italian, discovering the culprit, then publicly flogging the thief with a cat-o'-nine-tails. That afternoon Odhams died and at Hughes' insistence was given a full military burial with ceremony before the whole party moved off again.

During the second night's 'rest' two Senussi Arabs stealthily slipped through the Italian guards and contacted the British, offering to take a message to the nearest Allied troops, and two notes were handed to the Senussi who eventually delivered these to the British lines. Next morning the Italian Major told Hughes, after much argument, that he intended stepping up the pace of the 'march' but Hughes finally persuaded him to leave the British behind as a complete party in return for which Hughes gave the

(*Right*) Flt Lt Hughes on wing of his ditched Sunderland signalling to shore

(*Below*) The eventual wreck of Sunderland T9071, 'M'

Italian and RAF 'prisoners' on the trek to the Allied lines

The Fairchild 91, HK832, named appropriately 'Wings of Mercy'

Italian a signed statement saying that he had treated his prisoners with exceptional fairness and should be given equally favoured treatment if captured. The Italian agreed and left with his men.

Shortly after, some Senussi tribesmen from the El Hania village gave the British travellers food and coffee and provided a donkey to carry the sick men. Then, with Senussi guides, Hughes and his men set off south across the escarpment towards the last-known British forward lines. En route they by-passed several groups of resting Italians, then unexpectedly blundered into a gathering of exhausted Italians who soon proved friendly. The British left them behind, having 'acquired' a couple of rifles and some ammunition in the interim, but soon after began being joined by various scattered groups of disillusioned Italians who willingly 'surrendered' to Hughes' custody until eventually Hughes found that he was in charge of 156 Italian prisoners, mostly eager to become prisoners of war and opt out of any further fighting.

Suddenly a fusillade of shots whined over their heads and a staccato order to surrender rang out as some Indian soldiers appeared nearby advancing with fixed bayonets. Hughes' army major friend luckily recognised one of the Indian NCOs from former Service days in India and the situation became rationalised as the British and Italians were identified and separated. Shortly after the Sunderland survivors found refuge and succour in Tmimi.

The aftermath of this astonishing trek was almost comical. The Australian gunner, Dupont, was awarded a DFM, but Hughes had to face a court-martial for 'failing to take-off at the scheduled hour, thus causing his interception *et al* ...'. In the event this charge was quashed on the grounds of 'condonation' – in the interim Hughes had already been promoted to Squadron Leader and was awarded an OBE for his gallantry!

To those unfamiliar with the climatic conditions which often prevail around the Mediterranean sea it might be thought that the area was permanently bathed in the heat of a tropical sun. The men who were forced to ditch in Mediterranean waters knew better. On 29 April 1941 Sergeant (later, Squadron Leader) Les Brookes of 230 Squadron was taxying back to his moorings in Alexandria after an air test when he noticed his CO, Wing Commander G. Francis*,

---

* Later, Group Captain, DSO, DFC.

approaching his aircraft in a dinghy at high speed, waving to Brookes to slow down. Francis then sprang aboard, took over the controls without explanation, then took off. Once airborne Francis asked for a course for 50 miles due north and told Brookes that he was looking for a fighter pilot reported down in the sea.

On arrival at the 50-miles spot the Sunderland began a methodical square search outwards, spotted an oil slick, and shortly after saw a man bobbing on the surface wearing a yellow Mae West. The sea had a dangerous swell with a steady wind whipping white horses off the wave-tops as the Sunderland ran over the spot where the ditched pilot was floating, and the crew dropped some rescue gear on the first pass but too far to be of use. On the second drop they released a rolled rubber dinghy which fell near enough for the pilot to reach and cling to but the crew soon realised that he was unable to undo the straps and thus allow the dinghy to expand. Francis did not hesitate and announced that he was going to land and pick up the pilot.

As each crew member supported himself as best he could Francis set the Sunderland onto the heaving swell, bounced off at an alarming angle, touched again, bounced off again, but continued to attempt a landing. Gradually the bounces grew smaller until finally they were down. Taxying to bring the ditched man down the port side of the aircraft, the Sunderland crew managed to 'grab' him with a boat hook and haul him aboard. Brookes' own account said:

> I was shocked when I saw him. His face was the colour of an RAF uniform and his eyes just red sockets. We turned him face downwards and he got rid of some gallons of the Mediterranean. He then turned and said, 'Hello, Brookie!' He knew me!
>
> I hadn't the slightest idea who it could be as he was in such a state, and I only found out next day that it was a Pilot Officer Wilson of No 250 Squadron whom I'd known a couple of years before. He came to see me after some weeks in hospital and told me his story. He'd been scrambled in pursuit of a regular recce aircraft – the 'Shufti Kite' – which came over Alexandria. With the enemy in sight he suddenly found his oxygen supply wasn't working but nevertheless pressed on in pursuit. The next thing he remembered was being in a spin, and he finally 'woke up' in the sea, with no memory of the crash. He was only in the water for *one*

hour – which was a lesson to us all. If the Med in 'summer' could produce a man in *that* state, we needed urgently to brush up on our Air-Sea Rescue drills and equipment ...

While the Short Sunderland flying boat tends to dominate the maritime-air aspect of the Mediterranean air war, it was by no means the only RAF flying boat design to see action in the theatre. No 202 Squadron, based at Kalafrana, Malta, on 3 September 1939, was equipped with the biplane Saro London II flying boats, and moved base to Gibraltar by 10 September as a guard for the vital entrance waters to the Mediterranean, carrying out the unit's first operational patrol the following day. The squadron was to remain as 'The Rock's' resident flying boat unit for the next five years, during which extended period it was commanded by a succession of veteran 'boat skippers, including Wing Commanders E.A. Blake, MM, A.D. Rogers, AFC, T.Q. Horner, L.F. Brown, A.A. Case, B.E. Dobb, and G.P. Harger, DFC; all but one of whom were to reach Group Captain or Air rank in later years.

Initially the unit flew routine recces, anti-submarine patrols, and general convoy protection sorties, often using French ports and harbours as 'advanced landing' bases. In the main such sorties proved boringly uneventful in the context of direct engagement with any enemy ship, submarine, or aircraft, though an occasional clash with Italian aircraft began to break the monotony once Italy entered the active war in June 1940. The constant searching for submarines was now given even higher priority but the only Saro Londons to become involved in a successful conclusion to an anti-submarine operation were K5909 and K5913, skippered respectively by Flight Lieutenants N.F. Eagleton and Hatfield. These came upon the Italian submarine *Durbo* on 18 October 1940, promptly depth-charged it, then called up some RN destroyers to complete its capture.

In the same month the squadron took on charge some Fairey Swordfish torpedo-bombers from No 2 AACU to form 'B' Flight for short-range patrolling, but in April 1941 began exchanging its outmoded biplanes for Consolidated Catalina Ib flying boats.

The 'Cats' immediately offered greater range in operations and in June alone three U-boats were attacked, one being destroyed by RN destroyers called to the scene. Convoy protection became a prime role and in December 1941 several Sunderland IIs were added to the unit's strength, complemented a few months later by some Sunderland IIIs. Air combats became occasional hazards with resulting casualties, as on 18 May 1942 when Flight Lieutenant Bradley's AJ158 was brought down onto the sea by a Vichy French Dewoitine D520, though the crew were safely retrieved by a naval vessel later. Sunderlands remained with 202 Squadron until September 1942, in which month Flight Lieutenant E.P. Walshe, RAAF, skippering Sunderland W6002, 'R', sank the submarine *Alabastro* on the 14th near Algiers, leaving some 40 surviving submariners floating in the water.

In November 1942 the squadron, much strengthened in men and aircraft attached from UK squadrons, became heavily involved in the Allied *Operation Torch* – the Anglo-US invasion of Algiers *et al* – with an intense schedule of convoy protection sorties during which three Catalinas were lost (one of these to the guns of the convoy it was protecting …!), and in February 1943 an increase in U-boat forays saw 202's crews make six positive attacks during the month, including the sinking of *U-620* on 13 February 1943 by Flight Lieutenant Sheardown and his crew in Catalina FP114. Thereafter the squadron found little activity beyond routine sea patrols but remained based at Gibraltar until ordered to move back to the UK on 3 September 1944.

Any record of 'maritime' aircraft associated with the desert air war cannot fail to include mention, albeit briefly, of the various aircraft types employed increasingly from 1941 on the vital air-sea rescue role. These eventually included Supermarine Walrus amphibians, Vickers Wellingtons, and – in the initial stages – virtually any available, adaptable aircraft from 'outside' RAF sources. A prime example of this last category was a Fairchild 91 amphibian, originally in use with Panair do Brasil, which was acquired by the British-American Ambulance Corps and delivered to the ASR Flight in RAF markings, serialled HK832 and carrying the code letter 'M', on 25 November 1941. Given the appropriate identity '*Wings of Mercy*', this amphibian gave sterling service along the North African coastal waters until meeting its fate on 17 May 1943, when it struck a floating object off Benghazi and sank.

CHAPTER EIGHT

Malta Shield

Less than seven hours after the Italian dictator Benito Mussolini declared Italy to be at war with the Allies, on 11 June 1940 air raid sirens moaned their dirge across Grand Harbour, Valetta on the sun-blistered rock island of Malta; the first of more than 3,000 such alerts to be sounded across the island during the next three years. Malta, with its neighbouring island of Gozo, had an area totalling 117 square miles, on which lived a densely-packed population of more than a quarter of a million inhabitants. During the years prior to 1939 the island had been steadily fortified to resist any possible naval or land incursions but – in curious parallel with another island 'fortress', Singapore – its aerial defence had hardly been considered necessary.

In the context of the pre-1940 British Empire, Malta first assumed real importance as a naval refuelling venue from 1869 when the Suez Canal was opened and provided an important trading route to Britain's far eastern colonies and dependencies. The following six decades saw Malta become the HQ for the British Fleet in the Mediterranean, and its defence was based largely on a policy of alliance with France, whereby any threat from nearby Italy could be discounted due to the reprisals from French forces so readily available.

Thus, when France capitulated to Germany in mid-1940, Malta was – in theory – undefendable. A mere 60 miles from the shore of Sicily, and less than 350 miles from the Italian Fleet's harbour at Taranto, the island was, in essence, totally surrounded by Italian-occupied lands – even Tripoli was only some 200 miles to the south. The nearest British naval harbours were Alexandria (820 miles to the east) and Gibraltar (virtually 1,000 miles westwards), while the British forces stationed in Egypt, Palestine, and Iraq would be of little use should Italy invade Malta by sea and air.

Despite its ostensibly undefendable situation, Malta was immediately recognised as a key strategic factor in the burgeoning war in North Africa. The island lay athwart the main sea lanes by which Italy must resupply and reinforce her desert forces, and, like the nodal point of a giant spider-web, Malta *could* be a base for bombers which could attack with almost equal ease targets in Tunisia, Tripolitania, Cyrenaica, Libya, Greece, and Italy itself. All such possibilities hinged on the proviso that Malta remained in Allied hands and, accordingly, within hours of Italy's declaration of war in June 1940, the Allied hierarchy made a decision – Malta *must* fight on. Thus the die was cast for a three years' siege of the island by Axis forces which resulted in a saga of mass and individual courage rarely matched in the turbulent history of mankind.

The full record of those three fateful years has been told in various published accounts over the past 40 years, and it might seem invidious to select any specific facet of that extended siege as being more 'important' than others; without the Royal Navy and merchant marine sacrifices the island might never have been able to sustain its defiance, while the courage of the Maltese civil population under constant aerial bombardment over such a prolonged period outweighs any similar suffering by bombed populations in any other geographical area of the war. Nevertheless, it must be conceded that the most crucial facet of the siege lay with its aerial defences in the face of seemingly impossible odds; a desperate shield which fought off and eventually conquered its assailants and permitted the island to become a jumping-off base for aerial offensive operations which in turn proved significant in finally defeating the Axis in the Mediterranean theatres of war.

The air fighting over Malta, particularly during 1941-42, produced a host of truly outstanding fighter pilots and an intensity of actual combat conditions which led one Malta fighter veteran to describe his period as a Malta fighter pilot as:

One lives here only to destroy the Hun and hold him at bay; everything else, living conditions, sleep, food and all the ordinary standards of life have gone by the board. It all makes the Battle of Britain and fighter sweeps seem child's play by comparison ...

The importance of the fighter pilots' operations was described to one batch of newly-arrived Spitfire men by the AOC, Malta, Hugh Lloyd as:

Malta is like the famous statue of Achilles in Hyde Park, London. Our bombers, torpedo-carrying planes, and submarines are our striking power, like Achilles' sword. Our sword has been blunted but we will sharpen it. Until then Achilles must rely on his shield. The anti-aircraft defences and you pilots flying your Hurricanes and Spitfires are that shield. Malta relies on you.

That shield came to comprise of pilots from virtually every corner of the British Commonwealth and other free countries fighting the Axis powers; English, Scot, Irish, Welsh, Australian, New Zealander, South African, Rhodesian, Canadian, American – all blending readily into a fighting team with a single purpose. Some, like George Beurling, achieved international fame, while others died within days of arriving, killed before they had time to 'get their knees brown' and in relative obscurity. Some were already survivors of the 1939-41 fighting over France, Britain, and the early Middle East campaigns, while many had a violent 'baptism' of operations from the bomb-scarred 'runways' of Luqa, Ta Kali, Safi on Malta; all fought in conditions and against such vastly superior odds that officialdom finally decreed that three months was the longest tour any pilot could expect to endure on Malta.

To describe each man who fought in a fighter's cockpit from Malta would require several thick volumes to do adequate justice to their courage and deeds, but a closer look at the experiences of a few might offer some indication of the types of men who comprised Malta's shield during those crucial years. One such was Wing Commander E.J. Gracie, DFC.

Known to his fellow pilots as 'Jumbo' – partly due to his short-legged, lumbering gait – Edward John Gracie was a Londoner who joined the RAF pre-1939 and at the outbreak of war was serving as a Flying Officer with No 79 (Hurricane) Squadron. At the beginning of July 1940 Gracie, by then promoted to Flight Lieutenant, joined 56 Squadron as a Flight commander, and in the following eight weeks claimed at least eight enemy aircraft destroyed

Hurricanes stowed on the deck of HMS *Furious*, bound for Malta

Hurricane II of 249 Sqn which crashed on arrival at Ta Kali from an aircraft carrier, August 1941. In background a second crashed Hurricane

apart from a share in two others shot down. The last of these, a Dornier, Gracie shot down on 30 August but with his Hurricane badly damaged from enemy fire he crashlanded at base. Next day, though complaining of a 'stiff neck', Gracie was back in action intercepting a raid approaching North Weald, and on landing went to Epping Hospital for treatment to his neck – only to be told he'd broken it in his crash the previous day!

Even this brush with death failed to repress Gracie who was soon back with 56 Squadron on operations again, now wearing the ribbon of a DFC under the pilot's wings on his tunic. By then his reputation as a fighting leader was well established. Brusque in speech, outspoken in criticism, unmerciful to the incompetent, Gracie exuded toughness, but those who flew behind him into battle regarded him with an affection given to few men. He finally left 56 Squadron on 7 January 1941, was promoted to Squadron Leader, and took over command of No 23 Squadron, followed in April 1941 by command of 601 Squadron AAF.

Gracie continued in command of 601 Squadron until 24 December 1941, but was then notified of an imminent posting to No 126 Squadron, a Hurricane unit based at Ta Kali, Malta. Arriving on the island in March 1942 at the head of a batch of reinforcement Spitfires flown off the deck of the aircraft carrier HMS *Eagle*, Gracie was quickly into action and on 2 April claimed a Ju88 as destroyed. Returning to Gibraltar later he next shepherded in Nos 601 and 603 Squadrons from the American carrier USS *Wasp* on 20 April, and within an hour of touching down was airborne again leading 601's Spitfires into a gaggle of incoming bombers and personally destroying two Ju88s, and probably a third. Two days later he shot down a Ju87 and shared in destroying a second.

On 29 April Gracie was promoted to Wing Commander at Ta Kali and continued to lead and inspire the Malta fighters, being by then regarded by his men as the 'soul of Malta' and a man virtually responsible for Malta's fighter defence. Apparently without fear, Gracie not only inspired his pilots in the air but was often seen walking about on the airfield during bombing raids encouraging the indefatigable ground crews as these laboured unceasingly to 'keep 'em flying'.

Finally returning to the UK in 1942 Gracie was rested from

(*Left*) Wg Cdr E.J. 'Jumbo' Gracie, DFC, seen here when OC 601 Sqn AAF in 1941 in England climbing out of a Bell Airacobra fighter

(*Centre*) Pilots of 261 Sqn, Ta Kali, early 1941, including F.N. Robertson, L. Davies, Spiers, and C.S. Bamberger

(*Bottom*) Hurricanes of 261 Sqn at Ta Kali after a Messerschmitt strafe, 1941

operations for a period but in October 1943 he succeeded to the command of No 169 Squadron, a DH Mosquito unit based at Little Snoring, Norfolk, flying *Serrate* sorties in support of Bomber Command's nightly assaults on Germany, but on 15 February 1944 'Jumbo' Gracie, one of Malta's leading defenders, failed to return from a patrol over the Reich.

While Gracie was one of many veteran pilots prior to joining the defence of Malta, no few first fired their guns in anger over the island. Such 'sprogs', providing they survived their first few terrifying sorties, rapidly became old hands in the Malta air struggle, and able to inculcate reinforcement pilots into the tactics – and rules for survival – necessary in an aerial conflict which had no true comparative parallel in any other theatre of war. Two such 'green' pilots were an Australian, Virgil Paul Brennan, and a New Zealander, Raymond Brown Hesselyn. Both arrived on Malta on 7 March 1942, and both left the island a little over four months later having destroyed at least 23 enemy aircraft between them, and collected a DFC and three DFMs as recognition of their prowess.

Brennan had been born on 6 March 1920 at Warwick, Queensland and joined the RAAF early in the war, forsaking his law studies, while Hesselyn had been born just seven days later than Brennan in Invercargill and, after a year in the NZ Army, transferred to the RNZAF in November 1940. Both men received their operational training in England and then joined their first fighter units; Brennan serving with No 64 Squadron while Hesselyn joined No 234 Squadron. By the end of February 1942 both men were embarked aboard the aircraft carrier HMS *Eagle* bound for the Mediterranean and Malta as part of the first batch of Spitfire reinforcements sent to the island.

Landing at the bomb-cratered airfield at Ta Kali on 7 March they joined No 249 Squadron, a unit which had been based on Malta since May 1941 flying Hurricanes and, when Brennan and Hesselyn joined it, was commanded by Squadron Leader S.B. – 'Stan' – Grant, DFC. As newly-arrived Sergeant pilots, the two men spent their first few days 'acclimatising' themselves to the primitive conditions, air raids, and Mediterranean weather before getting their first chance to operate. Then, on 11 March, Brennan flew his first sortie and, despite a failure of his Spitfire's electrical systems, had his first-ever experience of firing his guns at an enemy aircraft when his section tackled some Bf109s. Hesselyn's baptism came in the same week, but it fell to Brennan to score the first kill when, on 17 March, he flew his second sortie and shot down a Bf109 into the sea.

During the following week Ta Kali was heavily bombed and strafed, necessitating 249's Spitfires being moved to Luqa, but on 26 March Brennan scored again, probably destroying a Ju88, though his determined pursuit of the Junkers was flown through intense flak barrage being put up by Malta's anti-aircraft gunners. Meantime Hesselyn had flown half-a-dozen scramble sorties in March without any positive results, but on 1 April he scrambled during he afternoon with three other Spitfires to intercept a Dornier 24 flying boat with a heavy Bf109 escort. Attacking from above and behind, the Spitfires dived in line abreast, each man selecting his own target, and Hesselyn, after overshooting his initial intended victim, fastened on the tail of a second Bf109, gave it a four-seconds' burst, and saw it flip onto its back before plunging straight into the sea. This, his first-ever kill in combat, gave Hesselyn a surge of uncontrolled exultation:

> I was excited as Hell. I told everybody ... that I had shot down my first, screaming over the R/T, 'I've got one! I've got one!' My No 1 called up, 'Shut up, Hess. We all know you've got one'. So elated was I at my success that, foolishly, I began circling round the 109 in the drink, laughing at him. Suddenly Johnny's urgent voice reached me over the R/T. 'For Christ's sake turn, Hess! You've got two on your tail!' he shouted. His words sobered me abruptly. I became aware of two streams of explo-sive cannon-shell passing my port wing. I never worked so hard in all my life as in the next few seconds.*

Hesselyn's inexperience had almost cost him his life, while on his return he realised that he had pressed the wrong firing button, using only his machine guns and not a combined cannon and gun firing. His elation was further dampened when Stan Grant 'tore him off a

---

* *Spitfires over Malta* by P. Brennan/R. Hesselyn; Jarrolds, 1943.

Pilot Officers Virgil Paul Brennan, DFC, DFM, RAAF (left) and Raymond Brown Hesselyn, DFM (Bar), RNZAF

Hurricane P3731 of 261 Sqn at Ta Kali, one of the first to arrive on Malta from HMS *Argus*

strip' for cluttering up the R/T channel with 'unnecessary chatter'. Just 90 minutes later Hesselyn was airborne again, attempting to intercept a large formation of Ju87s heading for the island, accompanied by about 20-30 Messerschmitt Bf109s. Jumped by the 109s the Spitfires became separated but Hesselyn evaded the 109s and fastened on the tail of a Ju87 as it recovered from its bombing dive. At 100 yards' range he slammed a mix of cannon shells and machine gun bullets into the Junkers, and seconds later the bomber burst into flames and fell into the sea vertically.

The first three weeks of April 1942 saw the Luftwaffe greatly intensify its efforts to take out Malta by aerial bombardment and the RAF's airfields came under constant assault, both by night and by day. Inevitably, the pressure on the island's defenders mounted, while the German ploy of attacking Spitfires and Hurricanes as these returned from sorties attempting to land created many problems, apart from occasional casualties, and helped to reduce the number of flyable fighters.

As a result, many pilots found themselves virtually grounded due to lack of aircraft, while a few fighters were henceforth detailed for 'aerodrome defence' i.e. a pair of Spitfires would get airborne some 15 minutes after any operational scramble and then wait out to sea to cover returning Spitfires as these came back to land. Strictly speaking, this 'umbrella pair' had orders to ignore any enemy aircraft in their vicinity while awaiting their returning comrades, but on occasion combat became inevitable.

Hesselyn was detailed for this 'defence' job on 20 April, the day 'Jumbo' Gracie led in a fresh batch of reinforcement Spitfires. At first these were ignored but as the 109s persisted Hesselyn and his No 2 decided they would have to do something, so turned in towards the 109s and began tail-chasing manoeuvres, drifting gradually towards Malta. Two 109s soon climbed away and left the scene but the other two started to dive towards Sicily. Chasing these clear across the island, Hesselyn caught up with his chosen opponent at the coast near St Paul's Bay, gave it a four-seconds' burst, and saw it dive into the sea; while his companion disposed of the second 109 in similar fashion.

Next day the Luftwaffe made a particular effort to destroy the newly-arrived Spitfires on the ground, and during the afternoon

Sqn Ldr A.R. 'Butch' Barton, DFC (Bar), OC 249 Sqn on Malta
Flt Lt Edwin Glazebrook, RCAF who won a DFC for his service with 229 Sqn on Malta in 1942

Sunderland I L5807 of 228 Sqn after being strafed by Bf109s at Kalafrana on 27 April 1941

Spitfire V of 185 Sqn in its pen, Malta, 1942

Belly-landing by Hurricane II, Z2827, 'M' of the Nightfighting Unit at Ta Kali, July 1941

both Hesselyn and Brennan found plentiful action, both men flying the new Spitfire VCs just delivered, each of which carried four 20 mm Hispano cannons instead of the normal two. Hesselyn soon had evidence of the effect of four cannons being fired in 'broadside' when he made a climbing deflection shot at the leader of a bunch of Bf109s. The Messerschmitt literally disintegrated in mid-air, catapulting its pilot into space who fell towards the earth without using his parachute. Evading further Bf109s, the New Zealander climbed higher over Gozo and spotted some Ju87s dive-bombing Ta Kali. Dropping onto the tail of one Ju87 as it came out of its dive, Hesselyn gave it a four-seconds' hosing from dead astern and the Junkers fell burning into the sea off Gozo.

About two hours later Paul Brennan and another Spitfire pilot tackled some 20 Bf109s near Gozo, with Brennan sending one German down into the sea with a full deflection burst. Pulling up to 10,000 feet the Australian heard the fighter controller report Ju88s bombing Ta Kali and promptly dived on one Ju88. Only two of his cannons were actually loaded and one of these jammed shortly after, but Brennan concentrated his remaining cannon's shells on the Ju88's starboard engine and wing root. As his ammunition ran out he saw flames spread along the Junkers which next dived into the sea.

Returning to land, Brennan and his companions were forced to run a gauntlet of marauding Bf109s waiting near the airfield, and the Spitfires spent the next half-hour dodging in and round the nearest valleys amongst a hail of German shells and bullets before finally landing; a nerve-racking ordeal which left each pilot dazed and bathed in sweat.

The following three days brought further intense fighting but on 25 April Brennan added two more scalps to his belt, shattering the wing off a Bf109 and less than a minute later tearing a Ju88 apart in mid-air with his quartet of cannons. Next day Hesselyn led a section of Spitfires – just two aircraft – into some 25-30 Bf109s but eventually destroyed a Ju87 over Ta Kali as it completed its bombing dive. On return he was forced to play hide and seek with the now-usual reception committee of Bf109s over his airfield but finally found his way down safely through the bomb craters on the runway. The previous hour's constant action had left Hesselyn 'shaking like a leaf' and smoking one cigarette after another, 'drawing at them without stopping' (*sic*) and it took him half an hour to regain normality.

From early May Italian aircraft began reappearing over Malta, while the Luftwaffe now began providing fewer bombers in any single formation but increased their fighter escort numbers, often despatching 80 or more fighters to shepherd 30 bombers. In addition pure fighter formations were sent to engage the RAF fighters in the air and strafe them on the ground, and the Spitfire and Hurricane pilots came under close attack even as they attempted to get airborne. Once in the air the overwhelming numerical superiority of the Bf109s meant that Malta's fighter pilots were not uncommonly tackling odds of ten or fifteen to one – yet they returned to the fray undaunted.

On 4 May Paul Brennan was one of four Spitfire pilots from 249 Squadron who were jumped at some 8,000 feet just south of Gozo by a veritable host of Bf109s and each man had to fight desperately to survive. For seemingly endless minutes Brennan was totally absorbed in evading Bf109s which bore in from every conceivable direction, but then one German making a belly attack overshot Brennan, presenting a sitting target. Brennan instinctively fired and the Bf109 fell away pouring glycol.

Five days later Brennan and Hesselyn added further victories. The Luftwaffe sent over a huge formation of Ju87s to bomb the harbour at Valetta, with a horde of Bf109s weaving a protective screen around them, but a combination of anti-aircraft barrage and RAF fighters produced a final tally for the day's actions of 23 enemy aircraft destroyed, 20 more probably destroyed, and about 20 damaged, while RAF losses amounted to two aircraft and one pilot. Of these Brennan had destroyed a Ju87, while Hesselyn had been shot up by a Bf109 which he immediately tore apart with a concentrated burst of cannon shells. By then both men had been notified that each had been awarded a DFM. Over the following three days Hesselyn shot down three more Bf109s while Brennan destroyed a Bf109 north of Gozo on 11 May. On the 12th however Brennan was hit in the arm by cannon shell splinters from a Bf109's head-on attack and was taken into Imtarfa hospital on his return to base, but by the 17th he was back flying and on the 18th shot down

(*Left*) Wg Cdr Anthony J. Lovell, DSO (Bar), DFC (2 Bars) receiving his first DSO from General Wavell on Malta, 25 April 1943. Lovell, who fought in the Battles of Britain and Malta, scored 20 victories before his death later in the war. (*Right*) Sqn Ldr John Dowland who won a George Cross for defusing bombs in the UK, then died in action off Malta

Spitfire Vb, ER220 of 92 Sqn, personal warhorse of Wg Cdr T. Cooper-Slipper, makes a neat 'three-point' landing

an Italian Reggiane 2001 fighter over Zankor Point. That evening he and Hesselyn celebrated the award of a Bar to the New Zealander's DFM.

For the rest of May and most of June enemy air activities perceptibly eased off, though living conditions on Malta also deteriorated as food and other essential stocks diminished. Raids continued but more sporadically until the end of June, then in July the Luftwaffe and Regia Aeronautica returned in strength in their latest attempt to bomb the stubborn island residents into submission. On 7 July both Brennan and Hesselyn, by then both having been commissioned as Pilot Officers, claimed a victory apiece – a pair of Bf109s – but their tours of Malta operations were almost ended, and on 17 July both men climbed aboard a transport aircraft taking them by stages to England, and Paul Brennan added a DFC to his DFM.

Their subsequent careers varied. Hesselyn recommenced fighter operations over Europe and by September 1943 had brought his personal combat tally to 18 confirmed and been awarded a DFC. Then on 3 October 1943, during a bomber escort sortie, he was shot down and taken prisoner. His period as a 'Kriegie'* exemplified his fighting spirit with several attempted escapes from his prisoner of war camps and his assistance in organising others' escaping ventures; efforts which brought him the award of an MBE after the war. He then remained in the RAF as a career officer.

Paul Brennan returned to Australia where he eventually joined the newly-forming No 79 Squadron RAAF to fly Spitfire VCs on operations, but before the unit commenced ops Brennan was killed in an aircraft accident on 13 June 1943.

The experiences of Hesselyn and Brennan were common to most fighter pilots who flew from Malta in 1942; a relatively few weeks of operational intensity which converted green pilots into veterans rapidly – *if* they survived their first two or three scrambles against constantly superior (numerically) enemy formations. In addition to that frantic pace of actual operational fighting they suffered daily and nightly from vicious bombing and strafing attacks on the ground, lived, ate, *existed* in conditions of primitive deprivation that

---

* From *Kriegsgefangener* i.e. Prisoner of war.

might have demoralised less determined men. This combination exhausted men quickly and was exacerbated by the climate and such chronic illnesses as the legendary 'Malta Dog' – a form of advanced dysentery which left its victims debilitated and, on occasion, weak to the point of helplessness. Aircraft, petrol, ammunition, spare parts, food, decent clothing, reasonable accommodation – all were constantly in short supply, leavened on isolated occasions by the heroic efforts of the Royal Navy and Merchant Marine in getting supply ships through the Mediterranean 'battlefield' to the beleaguered island.

By all standards of logic Malta *should* have been a simple plum to pick for the Axis Powers in 1940-42, and had it been occupied by the Axis the eventual outcome of the North African land campaigns might well have been entirely different. Instead Malta became a constant thorn in the side of the German and Italian commanders, a key base for denying the Afrika Korps adequate reinforcement, and much later the springboard for the Allied invasions of Sicily and then Italy.

It should be emphasised that the denial of Malta to the Axis was not solely due to the RAF's fighter pilots based there. The Army, Navy, Merchant Marine, and civilian population of the island all played vital roles in the refusal to surrender Malta. Yet without the prowess, courage, and sacrifices of the fighter pilots all other efforts would surely have been in vain. They were men and virtual boys who hailed from England, Scotland, Wales, Ireland, Australia, New Zealand, Canada, Rhodesia, South Africa, America, and other countries who blended readily into a fighting force with one uncomplicated purpose – to hold Malta at *all* costs. Many died trying – all succeeded.

CHAPTER NINE

George Beurling

George Frederick Beurling holds a unique niche in the annals of Canadian and RAF aerial combat history. In a period of just 16 weeks on Malta in the summer of 1942 he personally destroyed 28 enemy aircraft in individual combat, apart from probably destroying another and severely damaging at least six others. During the last eight weeks of his Malta service he was awarded a DSO, DFC, DFM and Bar, and all these accomplishments were achieved before his 21st birthday. Thus he emerged as Canada's highest-scoring and most decorated fighter pilot from the 1939-45 conflict.

Tall, slim, handsome Beurling was custom-made for the sensation-seeking news media of the period who labelled him variously as the 'Malta Falcon' and 'Malta Knight'. Yet many men in the RAF and RCAF who knew and served alongside Beurling during the war had other less-flattering epithets for this blue-eyed, blonde-haired youth; arrogant, undisciplined, braggart, ill-mannered oaf, even liar. None questioned his dedication to his job as a fighter pilot, or queried his outstanding prowess in actual combat, but relatively few came to regard him as a close 'buddy'. Undeniably, George Beurling did not fit readily into the necessarily disciplined teamwork of an operational RAF fighter squadron. He was the very essence of the legendary lone wolf fighter ace, a complete individual who made only his own rules – with astonishingly successful results.

The complexities of George Beurling's character are not easy to resolve. Born on 6 December 1921 in Verdun, Quebec, he was the first son of five children parented by Frederick and Hetty Beurling. His father was Swedish-born, brought to Canada as a boy, while his mother Hetty (née Gibbs) was Canadian-born of English ancestry. George's father, a commercial illustrator, was a stern parent who abandoned his early Presbyterian beliefs to join the Plymouth Brethren evangelical sect, then veered to the sect's Exclusive Brethren breakaway congregation. Thus, the Beurling household of George's youth was permeated with near-rigid ideals of religious attitude. Such a puritanical background undoubtedly had some part in forming George Beurling's outlook on life, though it should be remarked that on joining the RAF eventually he appeared to have abandoned the Brethren thereafter.

As a youngster George revelled in athletic and other outdoor pursuits, but from the age of seven steadily became obsessed with aviation, making model aircraft and absorbing any literature connected with flying, and forever haunting nearby airfields watching real aeroplanes in action. At the age of nine George Beurling had his first actual flight, a ten-minutes' flip as a passenger in an old biplane, but the experience sealed and focussed all the boy's ambition into a single channel – one day he'd be a pilot; nothing else mattered. By the age of 14 Beurling was flying often with Ted Hogan, a flying instructor at Cartierville airfield who had encouraged the boy's obvious eagerness, and two years later in mid-1938 George Beurling flew his first solo in a Curtiss-Reid Rambler biplane fitted with ski undercarriage.

Still pursuing his sole ambition, Beurling left school and the family home, taking a job in a Montreal radio factory and saving all his spare cash for further flying lessons. In February 1939 he hitch-hiked his way to Toronto to become a co-pilot with a small air-freighting business carrying supplies to the Quebec goldfields at Rouyn, though his co-piloting was mixed with more mundane tasks of loading and unloading equipment *et al*, a routine which soon palled and led him to quit on reading of some American pilots who had volunteered to fight with the Chinese against invading Japanese.

Intending to go to San Francisco to offer his services to these China volunteers, Beurling visited an uncle en route who gave him 500 dollars, with which Beurling promptly went to Vancouver and paid for 50 more hours of flying time in order to build up his log book total before the intended China venture. At the end of June 1939 he once more set out for San Francisco – only to be jailed in Seattle by US immigration officials for illegal entry to the USA, then on 1 September being put aboard a Montreal-bound train with a one-way ticket. On the train Beurling figured out his next step towards his goal. With 120 hours solo in his log, he'd join the RCAF, and within hours of arrival in Montreal Beurling had presented himself at the nearest RCAF recruiting office – only to be rejected!

The next two months saw him taking any job which would help finance further flying time, then he volunteered to fly for the Finnish Air Force in its contemporary fight with Russia. The Finnish Consulate in Montreal tentatively accepted him with the proviso that he obtain his father's written permission – he was still not 21 years old – but Beurling's father refused his consent. A thoroughly dejected young Beurling spent the winter of 1939-40 tackling more odd jobs around Cartierville airport in exchange for more flying time, but in May 1940, having heard that the RAF was in need of experienced pilots, Beurling immediately packed a small bag and got a job as a deckhand aboard a Swedish ship, *Valparaiso*, bound for Britain with a cargo of high explosives.

Arriving in the Clyde, Beurling went to the Glasgow RAF recruiting office where to his delight he was told he'd be accepted – provided he produced his birth certificate. Beurling had forgotten to bring this document, but immediately signed on as a deckhand again with a Canada-bound merchant ship, returned to his home, got the certificate and sailed back to Glasgow in September, when he was at last enlisted as an airman (AC2) in the RAF on 7 September and posted to Hendon to await pilot training.

After some three months of 'peeling potatoes' (*sic*) at Hendon, Beurling finally went to his Initial Training Wing (ITW) in December 1940, then progressed to the FTS at Montrose, Scotland by July 1941 where he first flew Hurricane fighters, and finally was sent to No 57 OTU for operational training as a Sergeant pilot and graduated on Spitfires, under the expert eye of the veteran ace 'Ginger' Lacey.

Throughout his training Beurling had only been truly happy when airborne; on the ground he remained mainly aloof from the other pupils and, as a non-smoking teetotaller, refused to join their off-duty frolicking; while the occasional clash with some book-minded instructional staff members in matters of pure discipline did not enhance his reputation with higher authorities.

Flt Lt George 'Screwball' Beurling, DSO, DFC, DFM

Completing the OTU course Sergeant George Beurling was posted on 16 December 1941 to No 403 Squadron RCAF, a Spitfire unit commanded by Squadron Leader A.G. Douglas (RAF), based at Martlesham Heath but moving base to North Weald on 22 December. From here Beurling flew many sorties over France on bomber escorts etc during the first four months of 1942, but in late April No 403 Squadron was officially 'Canadianised' and Beurling, technically a member of the RAF, was posted to No 41 Squadron based at Merston and commanded by Squadron Leader C.J. 'Nobby' Fee.

The move undoubtedly upset Beurling and he arrived on 41 Squadron with a large chip on his shoulder. The chip quickly increased in size when he was immediately relegated to a greenhorn tail position on his initial sorties with 41. On 1 May, during a sweep over Calais he became separated from the squadron by five Fw190s which riddled his Spitfire, knocking out his guns except for two machine guns in the starboard wing. With these Beurling destroyed one Fw190 which exploded in mid-air, then flew his severely damaged Spitfire back to base – only to be accused by the other pilots of deserting the formation. Beurling's response was brief and pithy!

Two days later Beurling did leave the formation deliberately to destroy another Fw190 over Calais, and on return to base was again accused of desertion by the others. Inviting his critics to ' ... go jump at yourselves', an angry Beurling went to the squadron commander and requested a transfer to another unit. For the following few weeks Beurling became a pariah as far as the rest of the pilots were concerned, ignored in the Mess and seldom being included in the daily battle order for operations.

Then, on 21 May Beurling heard another pilot who had only recently married complaining that he'd been posted overseas, and immediately volunteered to take his place. Next day he was at an Embarkation Depot along with three dozen other pilots and 150 airmen groundcrew. Ten days later, he was aboard a merchant ship leaving England and arriving in Gibraltar. On 7 June along with 31 other fighter pilots he embarked aboard HMS *Eagle*, and the following morning set sail eastwards – destination Malta.

Within 48 hours of leaving Gibraltar Beurling was guiding his

Spitfire Vc down to land at Ta Kali airfield, Malta, and as soon as he finished taxying he (like all other new arrivals) was unceremoniously hauled out of his cockpit as the ground crew Erks swarmed over the aircraft refuelling and re-arming these as fast as possible for resident pilots waiting nearby.

Assigned to No 249 Squadron, Beurling flew his first sortie on 11 June, and next day was one of a four-Spitfire section scrambled to intercept 15 Messerschmitt Bf109Fs approaching the island. In the brief clash which followed Beurling tore the tail section off one Bf109F but since no one witnessed its crash he was only credited with a 'damaged'.

The following three weeks brought only sporadic action for 249 Squadron, a relative lull in the aerial siege of the island, but on 6 July Beurling found plentiful targets as the pace requickened. He flew four sorties that day. The first, early in the morning, was as one of eight Spitfires intercepting three Cant bombers escorted by some 30 fighters heading for Luqa airfield. Ignoring the enemy fighters for the moment, the Spitfires attacked the bombers first, and Beurling riddled one with cannon fire, killing its pilot and leaving its navigator to fly the shattered bomber back to Sicily for an eventual crashlanding. A quick climbing turn brought Beurling onto the tail of a Macchi 202 fighter. Firing a one-second burst into its engine, Beurling saw it erupt in flames and plunge vertically into the sea. Switching his attention to a second Macchi attempting to shoot down a Spitfire, Beurling followed this one down from 20,000 feet to 5,000 and as the Italian began pulling out of his dive hit him at some 300 yards' range with all guns. The Macchi exploded into untold fragments. Beurling returned to Ta Kali for re-arming just 35 minutes after initial take-off.

Two more sorties during the day proved unfruitful, but just before sunset, in company with Daddo-Langlois*, John Williams†, and Norman Lee‡, Beurling scrambled to tackle two Junkers Ju88s escorted by about 20 Bf109s. While Daddo-Langlois and Williams bore in at the Ju88s Beurling and Lee climbed higher to occupy the Messerschmitt escorts. Two Bf109s dropped on Beurling but he

* Wing Commander R. Daddo-Langlois, DFC.
† Sergeant J, Williams ('Willie the Kid'), killed in accident, 1 November 1942.
‡ Flying Officer N. Lee.

twisted onto one's tail and at some 800 yards range gave him a full deflection burst which ruptured the German's glycol tank. Streaming a plume of white smoke the 109 fell towards the sea, then burst into flames prior to diving straight into the sea.

July 7 brought no action for Beurling while his Spitfire was overhauled, but on 8 July he took off with three other 249 pilots to intercept seven Ju88s with a 40 Bf109 escort. The Germans were already over the island, attacking Ta Kali, before the Spitfires reached them and the next few minutes became a maelstrom of twisting aircraft, tracer trails, and overboosted engine cacophony. In the midst of the turmoil Beurling got a fleeting glance of a Bf109's tail in his gunsight, instinctively fired, and saw his target belch black smoke and dive into the sea three miles south of Gozo.

His second scramble of the day was against another batch of Ju88s heavily escorted but this time the Spitfires were already waiting at 25,000 feet as the enemy formation approached the island at some 14,000 feet. Dropping on the Germans in a high speed vertical dive, Beurling selected a Ju88 as his mark and shot its starboard engine into a ball of fire. Seconds later he in turn was the target for five 109s boring in from every angle. Dogfighting all five, Beurling caught one with a burst into its engine and the 109 fell vertically towards Filfola Island, just south of Malta.

Elsewhere in the furious mêlée two of 249's pilots had been killed trying to get at the Ju88s, while Beurling spotted 'Willie the Kid' (John Williams) calmly circling a burning Ju88 he had just shot up and apparently oblivious of three avenging Bf109s about to attack him. Tackling all three Germans head-on, Beurling managed to split them apart, saving Williams.

On 10 July Beurling returned to the fray, destroying a Bf109 on his first sortie, then on the second scramble outfighting an Italian Macchi 202. The latter fought well but made the mistake of trying to loop as an evasive manoeuvre. Beurling's fire hit him at the top of his looping arc, blowing his cockpit apart, and the pilot baled out into the sea. Next day, in company with Sergeant Eric Hetherington, he came upon a pair of Macchi 202s, sneaked in behind them apparently unseen, then gave one a one-second burst. It burst into flames and fell into the sea, but before it reached the waves Beurling had jinked behind its partner, fired briefly, and sent it down to join

Spitfire Vb of 249 Sqn taxies out at Ta Kali, 1942

EXTRACT :- D.R.O's DATED 14.5.42
R.A.F. STATION, TA-KALI, MALTA

A GIBBET HAS BEEN ERECTED
ON THE CORNER OF THE ROAD
LEADING TO THE CAVES. ANY
MAN, WOMAN OR CHILD, CIVILIAN
OR SERVICE PERSONNEL, FOUND
GUILTY OF SABOTAGE, THEFT,
OR IN ANY OTHER WAY IMPEDING
THE WAR EFFORT AND SUB-
SEQUENTLY SHOT, WILL BE
HUNG FROM THIS GIBBET AS
A WARNING TO ALL OTHERS.

An RAF Ta Kali notice dated 14 May 1942

its comrade in the water – two destroyed in merely seven seconds. Added to a third Macchi 202 shot down on an earlier sortie that day – its pilot had taken to his parachute – Beurling had brought his tally to 13 destroyed and others at least damaged.

July 13 proved a quiet day but on the 14th Beurling was about to attack a gaggle of Macchis below him when three Bf109s and two Reggiane 2001s caught him in a scissors' crossfire. Their shells and bullets riddled Beurling's Spitfire, with one bullet nicking his right heel in passing, but he fought them off and limped the shattered aircraft back to base. The following night Wing Commander Gracie* informed Beurling that he had just been awarded a DFM.

There followed two weeks of virtual lull over Malta. Raids still came in and the Spitfires were scrambled, but at less frequent intervals than in the first fortnight of July. This changed in the morning of 23 July when 249 Squadron climbed hard to intercept three Ju88s escorted by some 40 fighters. Beurling hit one Ju88 in its starboard engine in his first attack, then as the enemy fighters came piling down he engaged a particularly aerobatic Reggiane 2001 in a series of tail-chasing rolls and turns before finally getting in a beam attack from below and blowing its port wing off with a full deflection burst.

Beurling's successes over Malta can be attributed to several things. Primarily, there was his single-minded dedication to his role as a fighter pilot. Nothing came before this in Beurling's mind and his whole life at that period was concentrated on the job. When not flying he was always absorbed in calculating deflection angles, testing and improving his superb vision in constant practice at spotting distant objects, thinking over past sorties and analysing his tactics. Alcohol and tobacco did not appeal to him; apart from his Brethren upbringing which forbade such secular pleasures, Beurling considered these might impair his physical state and hence his ability to fight at his best. Another facet of his prowess was his extraordinarily good eyesight; his ice-blue eyes could see an enemy aircraft many seconds before any fellow pilot spotted it, and this gave Beurling an extra edge in preparing for actual battle with any opponent.

* Wing Commander E.J. Gracie, DFC, killed in action 15 February 1944 when commanding No 169 Squadron in the UK.

A third, but equally important 'ingredient' was the boy's incredible, instinctive marksmanship. Fellow pilots have credited Beurling with some God-given natural talent for his accurate shooting but Beurling always denied this, saying it was simply a matter of constant practice, an acquired skill built up by patience, dedication, and wholly concentrated absorption at the moment of firing. If he had any natural talent it was for mental mathematics, a brain which could sift a myriad variables involved in selecting a deflection angle appropriate in every differing circumstance, followed by a lightning decision and co-related action of his body. Between sorties Beurling could often be seen poring over a battered black notebook he maintained as a record of previous combat tactics and dozens of geometrical drawings of deflection calculations and graphs, his 'fighting Bible' (*sic*). Nothing was left to luck or mere chance if Beurling could possibly avoid it.

There can be little doubt that for Beurling Malta was the epitome of all his personal ambitions in life. Not for any glory, decorations, or high rank – to date he had steadfastly refused all offers of an RAF commission, preferring to remain a Sergeant – but because on that battered and beleaguered island he had found his true vocation. On Malta at that desperate period his job was simply to fight. No parades, no routine Service frustrations, even uniforms comprised whatever form of clothing was readily available. Life evolved around a single purpose – to fly and fight; everything else was subordinated to that one aim.

Beurling was in his element, and on 27 July he achieved his greatest day of individual triumph. The day started at 6 am when Beurling and seven other 249 Squadron pilots scrambled to meet a formation of seven Ju88s and 40-odd fighters at 25,000 feet over Ta Kali. Arriving over the enemy bombers as these began releasing their loads, Beurling led the Spitfires down. Spotting four Macchi 202s in line-astern he closed on the rear Italian's tail, shattered its engine, and saw it spin down to crashland on Gozo. Seconds later his fire sent the next Macchi in line down to explode in mid-air. As Beurling began lining up on a third Macchi a pair of Bf109s slid below him and he dived under these, then climbed and sank a burst of shells into one 109's petrol tank, tumbling him down. He next fired at the other Bf109, knocking pieces out of its wings and tail but this one skidded away and left the area quickly.

Landing at Luqa for more petrol and ammunition – his own strip at Ta Kali was bomb-cratered for the moment – Beurling was airborne again as soon as the sweating groundcrews had given him the OK to go. Climbing to 17,000 feet above some 20 Messerschmitts, Beurling and his companions dived hard. Picking out one Bf109, he split-assed around with the German for several minutes until the German went into a dive. Following him down Beurling put a one-second squirt into its glycol tank. The 109 flicked over in a snap-roll, then dived a thousand feet headlong into the sea. Beurling next tackled another 109 but only managed a fleeting burst at its tail, causing the Messerschmitt to trail black, greasy smoke as it fled hell-bent towards its Sicilian base.

His exploits on 27 July led directly to the award of a Bar to his DFM, though official notification of this only came through a month later. On 29 July Beurling engaged a Bf109 which jumped him out of the sun's glare and shot away the Spitfire's cockpit canopy. As the 109 flashed past him Beurling whipped around onto its tail, fired a one-second burst which riddled the German from nose to tail, and watched it plunge in flames into the sea just off Valetta. Next day Beurling was informed that, like it or not, he was now a Pilot Officer.

Within 48 hours George Beurling was effectively rendered *hors de combat* by becoming the latest victim of the 'Malta Dog' – a debilitating form of violent dysentery brought on by poor rations and lack of an adequate diet; an affliction suffered by most men serving on Malta at that time. Weakened by combat tensions and inadequate food, Beurling had already lost some 35 pounds in weight since arriving on the island, and the bout of 'Dog' put him prostrate on his bed for the first week of August.

On 8 August, though still weak, Beurling joined a scramble to engage 15-20 Bf109s reported coming in and shot one down into the sea. His Spitfire then juddered under the impact of another 109's cannon-fire, taking a burst in its engine. Nursing the Spitfire back to Malta, Beurling glided in over the cliffs at a bare 200 feet with a seized engine, dipped his port wing to take the impact first, then bellied in for a crashlanding ploughing through one of the tiny stone walls which proliferated on the island.

Recurring bouts of the 'Dog' racked Beurling for several days but he was airborne again on 13 August and shared the destruction of a solitary Ju88 with two other pilots. For the following five weeks this became the pattern for Beurling – bouts of chronic dysentery interspersed with an occasional sortie when strength permitted. Meantime he lost a further 25 pounds in weight and now looked gaunt and drawn when he appeared at dispersal.

By late September Beurling had almost recovered from his illness and was back in action more frequently, particularly on 25 September when in the course of a single sortie he destroyed two Bf109s and despatched a third on its way to Sicily spewing black smoke. Days later came the news that he had been awarded a DFC, but yet another lull occurred in the day operations in the first week of October; a sure sign to the Malta veterans that 'Jerry' was preparing for the next big assault.

Enemy fighters continued to appear over the island in the interim, two of which Beurling destroyed on 9 October while carrying out an air test on his recently serviced Spitfire, but the next real blitz began shortly after and on 13 October Beurling's share of one sortie's destruction amounted to two Bf109s and a Ju88 shot down and a second Ju88 set afire but unwitnessed and therefore only credited officially as 'Damaged'.

Next day, 14 October, Beurling flew just one sortie, fated to be his ultimate from Malta. Shortly after noon 249 Squadron scrambled at full strength to meet an incoming raid of eight Ju88s protected by some 50 fighters. The fight which followed split the opposing fighters all over the Malta sky, with individual dogfights happening at all altitudes. Beurling nailed a Ju88 in flames, then destroyed a Bf109 but also had his port wing sieved and a couple of cannon shells punch holes in his perspex canopy.

An R/T call for help with '20 Mes' over Kalafrana Bay took Beurling down in a fast dive to tackle Bf109s trying to kill 'Willie the Kid' Williams, and he blasted the left wing off one Messerschmitt. In doing so he was in turn attacked from behind. A Bf109 sank an accurate burst into Beurling's Spitfire's belly, shattering the controls and wounding Beurling in his left heel, elbow, ribs, and left leg. The throttle control was jammed open and the Spitfire fell in a full-power spin. Jettisoning his cockpit hood, Beurling tried to bale out without success, then as the engine erupted in flames at about 3,000 feet he tried again and managed to step onto the port wing root.

At 1,000 feet he finally separated from his aircraft, his 'chute opened at 500 feet, and he fell into the sea. Inflating his dinghy, Beurling clambered into it with blood pouring from his heel and other wounds, but was retrieved by a rescue launch about 20 minutes later and taken to hospital for surgery.

For the next two weeks Beurling remained in hospital; by now his skeletal frame had been reduced to 125 pounds weight and, unknowingly, he had reached the limits of his capability to fly and fight due to combat fatigue. His wounds merely completed the knockout punch. On 25 October Beurling received a surprise visit from the AOC Malta, Air Vice-Marshal Keith Park, who told the Canadian that he had been awarded a DSO, and that as soon as he could travel he would be sent home to Canada at the request of the Canadian government. Accordingly, on 1 November Beurling was put into a Liberator bomber on Luqa airfield.

Also being repatriated with him were 25 other Malta veterans, including A.H. Donaldson,* and Beurling's particular fighting partners, Pilot Officer, 'Hether' Hetherington and 'Willie the Kid' Williams. At 3 am the Liberator took off from Malta heading for Gibraltar as the first stage of its flight to England, but on the approach to Gibraltar's runway, in foul weather, it stalled at 40 feet and plunged into the sea. Beurling and Donaldson were among the few passengers who managed to escape from the crash – 'Hether' and 'Willie' were killed, an ironic death for men who had survived the hell of Malta.

It was a desperately tired and frail Beurling who eventually arrived at Montreal's Dorval Airport on 10 November 1942, where he was reunited with his family, then whisked to Ottawa for a formal hero's welcome by the Canadian Prime Minister and the media. A further blaze of national publicity followed and, after a spell in hospital to restore his gaunt, undernourished physical state to normal health, Beurling spent many weeks in early 1943 on bond-selling tours and other public chores.

* Later, Group Captain A.H. Donaldson, DSO, DFC, AFC.

George Beurling discussing tactics with Captain Roy Brown, DSC, the Canadian WW1 fighter 'ace' officially credited with shooting down Rittmeister Manfred von Richthofen in April 1918

Beurling shows his medals to Miss Jean Johnson, USA Red Cross Service, after his Buckingham Palace investiture

Another Canadian Malta veteran, Sqn Ldr 'Wally' McLeod, DFC, RCAF

He then formally requested a transfer from the RAF to the RCAF which was eventually granted with effect from 1 September 1943, but meanwhile Beurling returned to RAF duty in Britain in May 1943, being posted to a gunnery school as a fighting instructor. Here he survived three crashes in various accidents but began to agitate for a return to combat duties, and his pre-Malta arrogance and lack of discipline in day to day matters now became evident again.

On official transfer to the RCAF on 1 September, Beurling got his wish for more combat when he was posted to No 403 Squadron RCAF. Here his constant and flagrant disobedience in remaining with a unit formation – often breaking away to hunt alone – combined with outright insubordination to his superiors on occasion led his CO, Wing Commander Hugh Godefroy, to place Beurling under open arrest pending a court martial.

RCAF HQ was horrified at the thought of a national hero being court-martialled, however well-deserved, and hushed up the furore, at the same time having Beurling posted on 7 November 1943 to No 412 Squadron at Biggin Hill where, as a Flight Lieutenant, he was given command of the squadron's 'A' Flight. With 412 Squadron he was to add two more victories to his tally in December 1943,* a pair of Fw190s, but by then his outright flouting of discipline and ill-considered social behaviour had earned Beurling many critics at higher level.

In the event he was sent home to Canada at the end of April 1944, where he was employed as a mundane ferry pilot; duties which frustrated Beurling so much that in June 1944 he tendered his resignation as an RCAF officer. His resignation was promptly accepted by RCAF Headquarters and on 16 October 1944 George Beurling was formally retired from the Service into civilian life.

As a civilian in wartime Beurling was a fish out of water. He made various attempts to join or rejoin the USAAF, RAF, and RCAF, only to be politely rejected in each case; nobody wanted a problem child pilot. The early peace years too were troubled ones, including a failed marriage and occasional clashes with authorities, but in early 1948, with the imminent partition of Palestine and creation of Israel

* He had also destroyed a Fw190 on 24 September with 403 Squadron.

due in May, Beurling was recruited to fly with the Israelis by an ex-RCAF Beaufighter pilot, Syd Shulemson, DFO, DFC.

On 1 May 1948 he flew out from Montreal to New York, and four days later was in Rome. Here he spent his working hours at Urbe airfield, just north of the Eternal City, where intending Israeli crews and aircraft were being checked out, then ferried to Israel. On 20 May 1948 Beurling was detailed to air test a Norseman freight aircraft. As co-pilot he had with him Len Cohen, an ex-RAF pilot who had achieved slight fame when, flying a Swordfish from Malta, he had forcelanded on Italian-occupied Lampedusa where, to his astonishment, he received the surrender of the entire Italian garrison of the island.

At 11.10 am (local time) Beurling took the Norseman off Urbe's runway, made two steady circuits of the field, then began an approach for a practice landing. At 300 feet a thin streak of blue flame suddenly trailed from under the Norseman's fuselage, then increased in volume, and as the aircraft's wheels touched down engulfed the cockpit. The bystanders heard its engine roar in a surge of power, the aircraft veered hard left towards the nearby river Tiber, then exploded in a giant orange-tinged fireball.

The Italians buried Beurling in Rome's Verano Cemetery in a funeral of opulent ceremony – at least, he was *officially* interred then, though in fact his casket was stored in a warehouse for claiming by relatives. The casket was later buried privately by his legal widow in Rome's Protestant cemetery, then on 9 November 1950 the caskets containing the mortal remains of George Beurling and Leonard Cohen were flown in to Haifa airport in Israel where hours later they were finally laid to rest in the Zahal military cemetery at the foot of Mount Carmel. The marker stone on Beurling's grave was engraved 'Fell in action' – George Beurling, the 'Knight of Malta', would have appreciated that tribute ...

CHAPTER TEN

Adrian Warburton

The Desert Air Force, along with its predecessors and successors, tended to produce a host of highly individual, even totally unorthodox air crew men; loners who might never have been acceptable to the selection boards of the rigidly disciplined – and often blinkered – pre-1939 mode of RAF life. Yet in the Mediterranean air war such men seemed to find a vocation in the wholly unbureaucratic atmosphere of any operational unit, where the book had little relevance and life evolved around the rock-basis of fighting – and, of course, survival.

In particular, the besieged island of Malta, constantly assaulted by the Axis air arms, witnessed herculean efforts by its RAF air and ground crews, and from its lengthy ordeal emerged several such singular personalities for whom Malta appeared to epitomise their innermost ambitions; a place and a moment in history which gave full rein to their peculiar talents. The name of George Beurling comes immediately to mind as perhaps a prime example of such 'lone wolves' who scorned Service formalities, yet he achieved lasting fame for his prowess and made his own rules.

Another pilot to regard Malta as his spiritual home was a tall, slim, blond-haired individual who also broke all the rules and became a legend in his own short life. Men who knew and/or flew alongside him have described him variously as tireless, mercurial, cynical, aloof, arrogant; an iconoclast who also came to be called 'King of the Mediterranean', 'Malta's Lawrence', and by the AOC-in-C, Middle East, Air Chief Marshal Tedder, as 'the most valuable pilot in the whole RAF'. His name was Adrian Warburton.

Warburton's connections with Malta began when he was christened aboard an RN submarine there in 1918 – his father, Geoffrey, being an RN submariner* – but his education came in

* Later, Commander G. Warburton, DSO, OBE, RN.

England, after which young Adrian became a bank clerk and, in 1937, joined the Territorial Army in the ranks of the Royal Tank Corps. In late 1938, however, he applied for a Short Service Commission in the RAF, was accepted on 14 January 1939, and trained as a pilot. Graduating in late 1939, Warburton was considered merely an 'average' pilot by his instructors – indeed, his assessments as a pilot were either 'below average' or at best, 'average' throughout his RAF career – and his first posting was to No 22 Squadron to fly Bristol Beauforts from Thorney Island and, from 8 April 1940, North Coates in Coastal Command. With this unit his flying remained unremarkable, while his off-duty activities soon brought him into bad odour with his COs, Wing Commanders H.M. Mellor and, from June 1940, F.J. St G. Braithwaite (later, AVM, killed in flying accident, December 1956).

Meanwhile in Malta the island's meagre air strength had been slightly strengthened in August 1940 with the arrival of three Martin Maryland twin-engined bombers for general fighter-bomber duties. The AOC, Malta, Air Vice Marshal Maynard, decided to use this trio to form a new unit, No 431 Flight, and requested three more Marylands to be sent out from the UK for 'spares cannibalisation', and 22 Squadron undertook the latter request, having in the same month converted a few air crews to Marylands on evaluation flights at North Coates.

Accordingly, Flight Lieutenant E.A. Whiteley (later, Group Captain, CBE, DFC) and two other pilots undertook the long, direct delivery flights to Malta, with Adrian Warburton being included in one crew as a navigator. Crossing enemy-occupied France, the three aircraft avoided landing at Gibraltar* and reached Malta in early September. On 8 September 1940, the Flight made its first operational sortie when Pilot Officer Terry Foxton, with Warburton as his navigator, flew a photo-recce of Tripoli, obtaining a set of perfect pictures.

For the first few weeks on Malta Warburton flew only as a navigator, and was appointed as 431 Flight's Photographic Officer, but being short of pilots Whiteley decided to train Warburton as a unit pilot, though Warburton's initial practice flights in a Maryland

* Indeed, they were *forbidden* to land at Gibraltar, contrary to past published accounts.

were hardly encouraging; his first solo attempt ended in a shaky landing with half the boundary fencing wrapped around the aircraft's tail wheel! His next few attempts to master a Maryland led to a variety of weird and hairy take-offs and, especially, landings, yet his usual crew of Sergeants Paddy Moren* and Frank Bastard† (W/Op AG and navigator respectively) remained loyal to 'Warby'; Moren eventually completing more than 100 sorties and Bastard about 50 sorties with Warburton at the helm.

During October and November 1940 the prime task for 431 Flight was photo-reconnaissance of Italian naval anchorages and harbours, during which Warburton showed early signs of his total disregard for personal danger and an aggressive determination not only to complete any given duty but to hit back at all enemy opposition. On several of his early sorties enemy fighters attempted to intercept his Maryland but were driven off by Warburton's gunners; nothing would prevent him getting through to his objective or from bringing back his vital photographic evidence.

Priority targets for Warburton's cameras were the Italian ports at Taranto, Brindisi and other possible refuges for the Italian navy, these being usually well protected by ground gunners and Italian fighters, but Warburton simply ignored such hazards – as Paddy Moren was to describe him later: 'Warby was a man who knew no fear'. Although, like every PR pilot, Warburton regarded his 'evidence in camera' as the top priority, to be brought back to base at all costs, he invariably mixed that prime consideration with purely offensive action whenever an opportunity presented itself; as on 30 October 1940 when, during a recce of Taranto and Brindisi, an Italian Cant seaplane tried to interfere and was promptly shot down for a forced landing on the sea, then coolly photographed by Warburton before he continued his reconnaissance.

Three days later he was attacked by three Fiat CR42 fighters and a flying boat, but fought these off leaving one Fiat to limp away trailing smoke. On 7 November four Macchi 202s engaged his Maryland, but again Warburton's gunner sent one fighter home with severe damage, and the recce was completed without further incident.

* Later, Fight Lieutenant, DFM, then Lt, DFM, RN.
† Later, Squadron Leader, DFM.

Wing Commander Adrian Warburton, DSO, DFC

The many recces flown by 431 Flight's crews over Taranto during October-November 1940 culminated in specific sorties on 10 and 11 November as preliminaries to a planned Fleet Air Arm torpedo-bomber attack on elements of the Italian navy harboured there. Warburton and his CO, Whiteley, each carried out close photographic surveys of the harbour on 10 November, thus providing the Fleet Air Arm with detailed evidence of each Italian ship's location, while on 11 November Warburton again visited Taranto and, though his camera evidence this time proved abortive, he nevertheless provided detailed visual information on the Italian ships' actual disposition. The outcome was the famed attack by FAA Swordfish on the night of 11/12 November which crippled virtually half the Italian Fleet and drastically re-balanced sea-power in the Mediterranean Sea at that time.

Though the Taranto affair received world-wide acclaim, to No 431 Flight it was merely 'one more job', albeit one in which its part had been so crucial for the ultimate success of the FAA strike. Photo-recce sorties continued apace, with Warburton well to the fore in accumulating a rapidly escalating total of successful sorties. On 13 November, this time crewed with Sergeant Gingell and LAC Levy, Warburton photographed Cagliari, Monserrato, Oristana, and Alghero, despite being persistently harried by four Italian fighters; while on 15 December, when flying near Syracuse, he spotted a surfaced Italian submarine and calmly dived and strafed this. On Christmas Eve he carried out a recce over Naples, meeting a Savoia-Marchetti SM79 bomber en route and shooting it down in flames; while two days later he was back over Taranto running a gauntlet of seven Fiat CR42s, then having to evade a pair of Macchi 200s on his return to Malta.

By then No 431 Flight possessed a total of five operational Marylands* and on 10 January 1941 the Flight was retitled as No 69 Squadron, with Squadron Leader Whiteley as its initial commander, and Adrian Warburton a Flight Lieutenant, and remained based at Luqa. In the same month Warburton received his first DFC, the first of an eventual six gallantry awards. The unit's new label made little, if any, difference to its tasks and Warburton's increasingly daring PR

---

* Theoretically, 69 Squadron's full 'paper' establishment from 10 January 1941 amounted to twelve marylands and ten Bristol Beauforts.

sorties continued to produce excellent intelligence. The value of 69 Squadron's activities was by now fully appreciated by the Italians, and the unit's crews found themselves increasingly opposed by enemy aircraft. On 7 March, for merely one example, Warburton set out to cover Taranto yet again and had four Macchis pursue him well out to sea before he could outrun them, then was attacked by two more fighters as he returned over Malta.

In May 1941 a new AOC arrived on Malta, AVM (later, ACM) Hugh Lloyd, whose philosophy for his new command could be summed up in one word – 'offensive'. His constant policy for the air units based on Malta was to attack the Axis however and when-ever possible, and from the outset Lloyd recognised the immense value of the photo-reconnaissance crews, and in particular men like Adrian Warburton. Certainly, Lloyd recognised in Warburton all the qualities he required from his pilots – skill, courage, perse-verance, perfectionism – and he was perceptive enough to realise that loners like Warburton could only produce their finest efforts if they were permitted to do things in their own peculiar ways.

His view was perhaps more than fortunate for Warburton specific-ally, whose deliberate flouting of normal standards of dress and behaviour expected of RAF officers by more Service-minded senior officers might well have robbed the Middle East RAF of possibly its most outstanding recce pilot. Warburton's daily uniform could vary from thigh-length, privately made sheepskin waders topped by a scruffy Army battle dress jacket and battered, grease-stained peaked hat, to pyjamas, carpet slippers, and a lengthy brightly patterned woollen scarf. Indeed, he seemed to delight in being nonconformist in all such minor matters, and could often be found mucking in with the ground crews servicing his aircraft out on dis-persal, or when off duty living *en famille* in Valetta with a particularly attractive cabaret artiste and going to work daily in a second-hand car.

Yet Hugh Lloyd would brook no criticism of Warburton and gave him complete freedom from any routine disciplines – to Lloyd the photo intelligence gathered by Warburton was the *raison d'être*, and in return Warburton came to regard his AOC almost as a father-figure, for whom no effort was too great to attain. It was as if by some unfathomable stroke of fate that Lloyd, Warburton, and Malta had been brought together at the only moment in history that such a combination would benefit from such an unlikely trio of men and venue. Even so, it should be remembered that Warburton's reputation was already well founded before Lloyd's arrival on Malta – under Air Vice Marshal Maynard's command he had already totted up some 80 operational sorties – but it remains a simple fact that under Lloyd's fatherly protection Warburton blossomed into the legendary figure ever associated with his name.

Warburton's various encounters with enemy aircraft, though not in the main of his own choosing in these early sorties, were nevertheless frowned upon by his CO, Ernest Whiteley, to whom the prime objective of obtaining photographs *and* bringing them back was of far greater value and importance than the destruction of a few enemy aircraft. His priority for his PR crews was to avoid trouble at all costs; PR crews and aircraft were too few and too valuable to 'waste' in aerial combat.

A case in point was the occasion when Warburton during a running fight with Italian fighters had a bullet smash through the Maryland's nose, miss the navigator's head by inches, then plough through Warburton's instrument board and penetrate his chest. Landing shakily back on Luqa, Warburton was fortunate to be alive, the bullet having spent most of its force before wounding him, and he was back on operations the following day.

Though always conscious of the paramount need to return with his photographic evidence, Warburton continued to take the offensive against enemy aircraft when an opportunity arose in the course of any sortie; as on 20 June when, during a reconnaissance around Italian air bases in Tripoli, he flew across Misurata airfield and strafed a gaggle of Savoia-Marchetti SM79 bombers on the ground, setting at least three on fire and riddling others. Four days later he was flying alone, piloting a Hurricane (V7101) for the first time and flew a recce over Catania, but on the 25th was back at the controls of his Maryland during a bombing sortie against an enemy merchant convoy, hitting one ship amidships with one 500 lb bomb. By the end of June 69 Squadron had said farewell to Ernest Whiteley (recalled to the UK for engineering specialist duties) and a new CO had taken over command, Squadron Leader John Dowland, GC*,

* Dowland had won his George Cross (awarded 7 January 1941) for defusing enemy bombs during the 1940 Luftwaffe blitz on the UK. He was killed in action off Malta on 13 January 1942.

an ex-Cranwell Cadet who was serving on Malta in mid-1941 as an armament staff officer at Air HQ.

For Dowland his appointment gave him his first opportunity to fly operationally, and he quickly established a reputation as a press-on type, constantly in the air on PR sorties. Meanwhile Warburton continued his one-man war, attacking a Cant Z506 east of Syracuse on 22 July and setting it on fire after it forcelanded on the sea; then bombing San Giovanni on 9 August. A few days later came the award of a Bar to his DFC. On 7 September he was reconnoitring the Tunisian coastal areas when he spotted seven enemy bombers and calmly attacked these, even though a pair of SM79s reinforced the opposition. Making five passes, he claimed several as 'damaged' only, but on the 24th, while patrolling over the Ionian Islands, he jumped two Italian aircraft escorting a merchant convoy and sent one, a Cant Z506, down onto the sea and then strafed it to destruction.

On 29 September he engaged in his last aerial clash of his first tour of operations, being attacked by a Macchi 200 which his gunner, Paddy Moren, shot into the sea, then on 1 October 1941 Adrian Warburton was posted for a 'rest' to non-operational staff duties, followed in December with a further posting to No 2 PRU at Heliopolis, Egypt where he was asked to evaluate the Martin Baltimore design for possible PR use. His verdict on the Baltimore was succinct – 'No bloody good' – but while at Heliopolis he borrowed a standard Beaufighter, had all its guns and armour plate protection stripped out, and fitted vertical cameras in its fuselage, then tested it locally.

With promotion to Squadron Leader, Warburton returned to 69 Squadron on 11 August 1942, ferrying in a Spitfire (BP911) and taking over command of the unit's 'B' Flight*. Next day he flew his Spitfire to Taranto, photographing a host of enemy shipping in the harbour from 21,000 feet, and continued to use a Spitfire for the rest of 1942, with occasional sorties in a Baltimore when necessity demanded a crew to accompany him. On many of his sorties he was attacked by enemy fighters but usually managed to outmanoeuvre and outrun these, though on 15 November, over Bizerta, his Spitfire

* 69 Squadron by then had Baltimores ('A' Flt), Spitfires ('B' Flt) and Wellingtons ('C' Flt).

(BR646) was badly damaged by Bf109s and, with a smashed compass and oil leaking steadily, he was forced to land at Bone.

While still at Bone he was promoted to Wing Commander on 20 November, and next day left Bone to deliver a new Spitfire (ER674) to Malta. En route, near Zamba, he ran across a pair of Ju88s at 1,000 feet, attacked and destroyed one, then started chewing pieces off the other when his cannons jammed and the Ju88 escaped in cloud. By early 1943 Adrian Warburton had become widely acknowledged as the supreme master of his craft, flying constantly to objectives all around the Mediterranean with consummate ease and skill, utterly disdainful of opposition and danger, yet always the epitome of individualism. In October 1942 he had received a second Bar to his DFC, and in February 1943 he was appointed as the first commander of a new unit, No 683 Squadron, a Spitfire IV unit formed on 8 February at Luqa by expanding and separating 69 Squadron's 'B' Flight.

The squadron's initial role was high altitude photography of Italian harbours and coastal towns and cities, and in April 1943 it began receiving Spitfire IXs; Warburton flying EN391 over Sicily on 26 April. For the following four months Warburton changed from high to ultra low-level sorties as the Allies prepared for their invasion of Sicily and, later, Italy itself. Such sorties inevitably incurred savage flak opposition but Warburton seemed to bear a charmed life, often returning with damaged aircraft but always with the vital films. In July, as the Sicilian invasion commenced, Warburton was flying daily, and on one sortie was badly shot up by trigger-happy American gunners. Returning to Luqa with holed wings, shattered ailerons, and a rear fuselage resembling a pepperpot, his Spitfire limped to dispersal where, on leaving his cockpit, Warburton's sole laconic comment to his ground crew was; 'My R/T is u/s' ...

His ultimate sortie with 683 Squadron was flown on 6 September and on 1 October 1943 he was posted to La Marsa to take command of No 336 PR Wing, comprised of four PR units, Nos 680, 682, 683, and 60 SAAF Squadrons, equipped with Spitfires and Mosquitos. By then he had added a DSO to his awards, and his co-operation with the USAAF's 3rd and 5th Photo Groups later led to the award of an American DFC. To the American PR airmen Warburton was

Warburton (centre) with (L-R) Lts German, Spencer, Sculpone, Webb, and Bury of the USAAF's North African PR Wing detachment to Malta, on 2 April 1943

Warburton (far rt) talking with ACM Sir Charles Portal, CAS on the latter's visit to Malta, 1943

something of an heroic cavalier, totally unlike any other relatively senior RAF officer they had met, and he often borrowed an American Lockheed P-38 for operations.

On one P-38 take-off he experienced engine trouble, returned, crashlanded, then coolly extricated himself from the burning wreck and climbed into another Lightning and was away again – all within 20 minutes. However, after only a few weeks in command of the PR Wing Warburton was seriously injured in a motoring accident in Tunis and was invalided home to the UK before the year was out.

By then he had completed more than 300 operational sorties by his own admission*, and a Bar to his DSO was promulgated in 1943 with a citation quoting his 'great courage and devotion to duty'. Officially 'unfit for flying', Warburton displayed his usual contempt for officialdom by leaving the UK on 24 October 1943 to ferry a PR Spitfire to the Middle East, via Gibraltar.

Warburton remained in the UK until early 1944, but on 12 April 1944 borrowed a P-38 Lightning from an American unit at Mount Farm and set out to cross the Alps and visit his old Wing, now based at San Severo, Italy. His aircraft was reported sighted over Lake Constance by a USAAF pilot – then he vanished without trace. The manner and location of his death remains a mystery. Perhaps, like the legend of the World War One French fighter ace Georges Guynemer, Warburton had 'flown higher and higher until he could never return to earth', but whatever his final moments his disappearance at the height of his fame in such mystifying circumstances was in a way fitting. Supreme individual, inspiring leader, yet averse to all forms of rigid bureaucracy and authority, Adrian Warburton, 'King of the Mediterranean' could never have slotted readily into any humdrum peacetime existence.

* Anthony Spooner, in his book *In Full Flight* (Macdonald, 1965) saw Warburton's log books and quoted a figure of '... 500 or more operational sorties ...'

CHAPTER ELEVEN

Billy Drake

By mid-1941 a number of Uk-based fighter pilots who had fought
through the battles of France and/or Britain in 1940 re-entered the
operational scene on posting to the Mediterranean war theatre,
where many such 'veterans' were to embellish their fighting prowess
and gain high success, honours, and senior rank. One such was Billy
Drake* whose operational experiences included fighting over
France, North Africa, Sicily, Italy, and northern Europe throughout
the 1939-45 conflict.

Born in London on 20 December 1917, Drake was accepted for
pilot training in the RAF on 7 September 1936, trained at No 6 FTS,
Netheravon from 19 September that year, and on completion of his
course was posted to No 1 Squadron on 22 May 1937. Commanded
at that time by Squadron Leader F.R.D. – 'Ferdie' – Swain, AFC† and
based at Tangmere, No 1 Squadron was flying sleek biplane Hawker
Fury I fighters when Drake joined the unit, but in February 1939 the
squadron exchanged these for Hawker Hurricanes and two months
later received a new CO, Squadron Leader P.J.H. 'Bull' Halahan‡,
who still commanded the unit when, on 7 September 1939, the
squadron commenced its move to France as part of the British
Expeditionary Force's Air Component.

No 1 Squadron, in common with most RAF units in France, saw
virtually little action through the winter of 1939-40, and only
claimed its first combat victory on 29 March 1940 when a Bf109
from III/JG53 was shot down and its pilot wounded. Drake's first
blooding came on 20 April when four 'A' Flight Hurricanes tackled
nine Bf109s. Three of the Messerschmitts gave their undivided

* Drake's Christian name Billy is *not* a diminution of William, as stated in some
previously published books.
† Later, Air Commodore, CB, CBE, AFC.
‡ Later, Wing Commander, DFC.

attentions to Drake, but he fastened on the tail of one Bf109 which dived away to ground level, chasing it at tree-top height until the German made the mistake of turning to port suddenly and presenting Drake with a full deflection shot. His bullets ripped into the 109's engine, black smoke spumed, and the Messerschmitt bore straight into a hill and exploded in a gout of flames.

On 10 May 1940 the so-termed 'Sitzkrieg' terminated savagely as German forces poured across the borders of France and the Low Countries, and No 1 Squadron began its first full day of combat at 5 am. Shortly after noon, while flying to a new airfield, Drake was in a 'B' Flight formation which met a mixed batch of German bombers and in the fight which followed Drake destroyed a Heinkel He111.

Three days later 'B' Flight was scrambled to intercept a reported raid approaching Rheims shortly after dawn. At altitude Drake's oxygen system failed and he began to return to Berry-au-Bac, but en route he spotted four Dorniers. Pouncing on these he quickly destroyed one, probably destroyed a second, but was then attacked from behind by a Bf110 whose cannon shells riddled Drake's Hurricane and wounded him in his legs and back. Baling out, Drake was retrieved by nearby Allied troops and taken to a hospital at Rethel.

Evacuated to England shortly after, Drake was initially posted to Sutton Bridge as a Flight Lieutenant, but in October 1940 joined No 91 Squadron and on 7 December shared in the destruction of a Dornier bomber. Awarded a DFC and further promoted to Squadron Leader, Drake joined No 53 OTU, Llandow as a fighting instructor in early 1941, but returned to operations in September 1941 as commander of No 128 Squadron. Though ostensibly an operational unit, 128 Squadron had been formed at Hastings, Sierra Leone for defence of vital ports and bases in that part of West Africa, and its Hurricanes saw no combat until August 1942. Drake remained in command of 128 until April 1942 but was then posted to North Africa where, on 25 May 1942, he joined No 112 Squadron as its latest commander. On that date 112 Squadron was based at Gambut Main airfield, flying Curtiss Kittyhawk 1a fighters, and had become renowned throughout the North African campaigns for the shark's mouth insignia painted around the engine cowlings of its aircraft as well as its fighting record.

Wg Cdr Billy Drake, DSO, DFC after his award of an American DFC

By May 1942, however, the 'Sharks' were flying both pure fighter and fighter-bomber roles as required, and on the day after his arrival at Gambut Drake was one of six pilots who strafed and bombed Tmimi airfield. That same night General Rommel launched his latest offensive by attacking around Bir Hakeim towards El Adem, and from 27 May the 'Sharks' were fully engaged in daily bombing and strafing sorties over the battle areas.

Such operations meant accepting the inevitable hazards of all ground-level sorties – intense ground opposition, with the ever-present possibility of being bounced by roving Messerschmitts – but throughout June 112 Squadron wrought great havoc among enemy transports and troop concentrations, though six pilots were either killed or made prisoner, while several other Kittyhawks were shot down and their pilots 'walked back' to resume operations within days.

Drake flew daily during his squadron's intense operations, bombing a gathering of enemy troops apparently being addressed by some senior officer on 4 June, and two days later probably destroying a Bf109 near Bir Hakeim. The Axis advance forced the squadron to move to El Daba (LG106) on the night of 26 June, but operations continued without pause and by the start of July the Kittyhawks were being used as bomber escorts. On 2 July, flying Kittyhawk ET510, Drake sent one Bf109 down with glycol pouring from its engine; while on 8 July he led ten Kittyhawks from 112 Squadron in a strafe of LG21 and claimed a Bf109F of JG27 as destroyed in a brief combat over the target area. On 16 July Drake received notification that he had been awarded a Bar to his DFC, and celebrated the honour three days later by destroying a Junkers Ju88 on the ground during a multi-squadron strafe of the enemy air strips at LG21. On the 24th he led 112 as part of a 239 Wing attack on LGs 20 and 104, and shot down a Bf109F from JG27 in the process. By then the retreating Eighth Army had dug in along the El Alamein lines and Rommel's advance had slowed to a temporary standstill due to the length of his resupply lines and heavy losses in tanks and other land transports. Thus, throughout August 1942 the land fighting became fairly static as each army hastily built up strength, and 112 Squadron took advantage of this 'simmering' period by taking unit mass leave from 3 August until the 10th, and did not resume operations until 21 August when an 'armed reconnaissance' was flown over the central El Alamein front. Four days later the squadron moved to LG175 at Amriya – mainly because LG175 was less dusty – but continued its attacks on German troop convoys the same day, followed by similar strafes in the following days. On the last day of August Rommel began another offensive in the southern area of the El Alamein line, but the Allied air forces now held virtually total air superiority and the German thrust was heavily bombed and strafed from the outset.

For 112 Squadron, September 1942 commenced with two bomber-escort operations before mid-day, and after 'tiffin' (lunchtime) 239 Wing's fighters were scrambled to intercept reported Luftwaffe intrusions, but later met a force of 50-plus Ju87s, escorted by more than 30 German fighters. In the ensuing mêlée Drake destroyed two Ju87s, while other 112 pilots accounted for three others without damage or loss to the squadron. After the initial fierce clashes of the first week of the battle, the tempo of aerial fighting eased off for a few days, but on the 13th Drake led the Wing (Nos 3 RAAF, 112, 250 and 450 RAAF Squadrons) in a scramble over the fighting zone to tackle some Bf109s reported as bombing El Alamein. These were, in fact, Bf109s from JGs 27 and 53 escorting Ju87s, but Drake only found a batch of 109s and immediately tangled with these, personally sending Uffz König of I *Gruppe* down to forceland near El Daba. The remainder of the month brought 112 Squadron relatively little trade and much time was spent on inculcating newly-arrived pilots replacing casualties, and some American pilots of the USAAF's 64th Squadron, in desert tactics.

Action resumed sharply on 1 October, however. At 5.30 pm the squadron took off as top cover for No 250 Squadron and were vectored on to a force of 18 Ju87s from III/St G 3, escorted by 34 Bf109s from II and III *Gruppe* and III/JG53, attacking Allied positions at El Taqa. As the Kittyhawks dived at the Ju87s these promptly jettisoned their bombs and tried to flee, but Drake, flying EV168, shared the destruction of one Ju87 with Flight Lieutenant G.W. Garton, DFC*, and then probably destroyed a second Ju87; while the other 112 pilots claimed one destroyed, three probables,

* Later, Wing Commander, DSO, DFC, who retired from the RAF on 13 February 1962.

and two damaged – all without loss to themselves.

The next three weeks brought a series of bombing sorties, armed recces, and bomber-escort duties, interlaced with occasional clashes with German fighters; the only real break in flying coming on 16-18 October when blistering sand and dust storms obviated any possibility of operations.

October 22 saw 112 Squadron combine with No 145 Squadron and the USAAF's 66th Squadron for a fighter sweep over the El Daba area, led by Drake; a so-termed 'de-lousing' operation in support of a coincidental RAF bombing operation against LG104. On the return flight Drake spotted four Bf109s below and promptly attacked, probably destroying one, while the other three became one destroyed and two damaged by his fellow 112 pilots. Next day the battle of El Alamein commenced, and 112 Squadron flew 30 individual sorties that day, bombing LG104, and at 10 pm Allied infantry moved forward – the beginning of an advance which would ultimately drive the Afrika Korps out of North Africa and suffer final defeat and surrender in Tunisia in the following year.

Aerial opposition from the Luftwaffe proved scanty during the battle's opening phase, though Drake destroyed a Bf109F on 26 October as a sideshow during the squadron's intensive attacks on various German landing grounds. Next day Drake led 12 Kittyhawks as close escort for an RAF bombing formation attacking Fuka. Over the target the RAF formation was bounced by three Italian Macchi 202s but all three were swiftly despatched, with Drake accounting for one as destroyed.

On the last day of October 112 Squadron had something of a field day of combat. At 7.20 am the squadron sent off eleven Kittyhawks, led by Drake, to bomb an enemy tented camp, protected above by 250 Squadron, and after bombing were vectored on to a gaggle of Ju87s heavily escorted by Bf109s from JGs27 and 77, later reinforced by some Macchi 202, intent on dive-bombing the forward positions of the 9th Australian Division. The Kittyhawks arrived on the scene just as the Ju87s commenced their bombing and tore into them, with Drake destroying one Ju87, and the others eventually claiming a Ju87 destroyed, three Bf109s and a Macchi probably destroyed.

A second sortie just before noon encountered another Ju87

(*Above*) Sharkmouth – the near-legendary nose art of No. 112 Squadron's Tomahawks seen here circa September 1941

(*Right*) Wg Cdr F.E. Rosier (later ACM Sir Frederick) who saw distinguished service on fighters in the desert war

formation with fighter escorts and 112's pilots claimed five destroyed, one probable, and two damaged, while the only loss was the Kittyhawk (FR281) piloted by Pilot Officer D.A. Bruce* which ditched in the sea, though Bruce returned to his unit next day.

By the close of October 1942 a measure of the Allied air forces' superiority in sheer quantity over the Luftwaffe in the north African struggle was the strength of No 112 Squadron, which had a total of 36 pilots; 22 of these being senior NCOs. In mid-month too the squadron had begun exchanging their Mk 1 Kittyhawks for Mk IIIs with a consequent improvement in performance and weight-carrying capacity, though in clinical terms the Mk III Kittyhawk still fell short of the Bf109F in all-round combat agility.

The squadron opened November with a day of 46 individual sorties throughout the first six hours of daylight, bombing enemy troop camps and accounting for six Ju87s destroyed, a seventh probably destroyed, and at least three others severely damaged; all at a cost of one pilot wounded who nevertheless returned to base safely. On 5 November Drake in FR293 led eleven Kittyhawks off at 9.25 am to the area west of Fuka, patrolling at 18,000 feet. Spotting six Bf109s some 6,000 feet below he led his men down to attack, destroying one Messerschmitt and damaging a second, while three other Bf109s fell to the other pilots' guns.

On return to base, Drake led the whole squadron off again to move forward to a fresh base at LG102, then on the following day moved further forward to LG106 and, en route, carried out a bombing and strafing attack on 'Charing Cross' and the Sidi Barrani road. The general forward movement continued for several days, with 112 arriving at LG76 (Sidi Haneish) on 11 November and the same day despatching twelve Kittyhawks on a long-range scouring sweep of the El Adem-Tobruk-Gambut areas; an operation which gave the squadron two combat victims (Ju52s over Gambut) and several damaged enemy aircraft on the ground including a Bf109 thoroughly sieved by Billy Drake.

Two days later 112 Squadron had leapfrogged forward yet again, this time to Gambut Satellite 1, but within 24 hours had moved on to and by the 15th was occupying Gazala No 2 LG. This same day a

* Bruce was eventually reported missing on 10 March 1943 in Kittyhawk FR295 some 40 miles north-west of Fuma/Tatauin during combat with Bf109s of JG77.

Worthy opponents. Messerschmitt Bf109E-4/Bs of JG27 over typical North African desert panorama

Billy Drake, when OC 128 Sqn in West Africa

sweep was carried out along the road west of Cirene, strafing various enemy vehicles with visible success, while Drake quickly shot down a Heinkel He111 which strayed across the path of the marauding Kittyhawks.

The next few days continued the squadron's 'roving gipsies' mode of living with some of the unit moving to Martuba and others still operating from Gazala 2, and it was from the latter that Drake took off on his second sortie of the morning on 19 November, returning within 30 minutes with claims for a Bf110 destroyed and another damaged.

Five days later the squadron became based at Martuba No 3, where it joined the USAAF's 57th Fighter Group for future cohesive operations, though it had already flown several operations alongside the Americans in previous weeks.

Towards the end of November and in early December operations became partially restricted by a series of torrential rainstorms which turned the bald desert landing grounds into murky lakes, but 'opportunity' ground-strafing sorties continued between these downpours when ground conditions permitted, maintaining constant pressure on the retreating German armies. On 27 November official notification reached 112 Squadron of the award of a DSO to Billy Drake, an event duly celebrated that evening in traditional manner, but by 1 December the 'Sharks' were once more on the move, to Belandah 2 LG; a move delayed until the 6th eventually due to continuing rainstorms.

Flying Kittyhawk FR293, Drake led eleven aircraft as escort for a USAAF 66th Squadron attack on enemy tented camps and vehicles on 11 December. On the return flight the formation was attacked by six Bf109Fs which were soon joined by several other Messerschmitts and some Italian Macchi 202s. Drake fastened on the tail of one 109 and shot it down in enemy territory, then chased a Macchi 202 out to sea where it 'voluntarily' (*sic*) spun into the sea and disintegrated on impact. As he turned to rejoin his formation Drake was jumped by seven Bf109s and, being bereft of ammunition by then, had no alternative but to run for the Allied lines as fast as possible, eventually bellylanding near an 11th Hussar troop, and returning to his squadron later in the day in a 'borrowed' Hurricane.

Rain and low cloud precluded operations on the 12th, but the following day Drake, in FR338, led twelve Kittyhawks on a bombing strafe, but en route was informed of some Ju87s south of El Agheila. Jettisoning their bombs, the 'Sharks' intercepted these Ju87s, which were being escorted by ten or more Bf109s. In the dogfight which followed four enemy aircraft were shot down and two others damaged; Drake's contribution being a half-share with Sergeant A. Shaw in the destruction of one Bf109F.

. The rest of the month brought few operations and little contact with the Luftwaffe and this relative inactivity continued during the first week of the new year, 1943. On 9 January, however, 112 Squadron continued its travels by moving base to Hamraiet, commencing operations from there two days later as top cover for some Tac-R (Tactical Reconnaissance) aircraft in the Buerat-Gedabia area. Further operations as bomber escorts and Tac-R protection occupied the next few days, but Billy Drake was then notified that he was being taken off operations, and accordingly handed over the reins of command of 112 Squadron to Squadron Leader G. W. Garton on 15 January, and three days later left the 'Sharks' to report to Air HQ in Cairo.

Shortly after he was awarded an American DFC by the USAAF authorities for his invaluable work alongside various USAAF units over the previous months. To date Billy Drake had been officially credited with an overall total of 15 enemy aircraft destroyed, five probably destroyed, half-shares in the destruction of three others, and three more damaged in aerial fights apart from uncounted aircraft shot up while on the ground.

Promoted to Wing Commander, Drake spent the first six months of his rest from operations as an instructor in Egypt, but in June 1943 he returned to operations on appointment as commander of a Spitfire Wing on Malta, one of three such Wings moved to that island in preparation for an eventual invasion of Sicily and, later, Italy. He remained with his Wing until November 1943, during which period he added at least six more combat victories to his tally, but then returned to England, where he was appointed to No 20 Wing, flying Hawker Typhoons over western Europe.

In mid-1944 Drake finally left the operational sharp end when he was sent to the USA in an advisory appointment, returning in 1945 with a posting to Biggin Hill. Granted a permanent commission in the postwar RAF, Billy Drake ultimately retired from service as a Group Captain on 1 July 1963.

CHAPTER TWELVE

Clive Caldwell

In April 1942 the AOC-in-C, RAF Middle East, Air Chief Marshal Sir Arthur Tedder, took the near-unique step of sending for a fighter pilot's flying log book and entering a personal assessment, 'A fine commander, an excellent leader, and a first class shot'. The log book's owner was an Australian, Clive Robertson Caldwell, who was about to be repatriated to his native country and who was destined to emerge as Australia's highest-scoring fighter ace of the 1939-45 war. Yet almost exactly four years later Caldwell was to end his RAAF career with a court-martial and consequent demotion and resignation from the service. During the desert air war his icy determination, restless aggression, and constant outspokenness had earned him the soubriquet 'Killer' – and his combat record justified such a chill nickname.

Born in Sydney on 28 July 1911, Caldwell was an enthusiastic competitive sportsman from his earliest schooldays, representing his grammar school in swimming and athletics and later becoming the New South Wales champion over the quarter-mile and 120 yards hurdles, apart from rowing representative in the Great Public Schools competition. On finishing his academic education he was employed variously as bank clerk, jackaroo in Queensland, garage owner, and insurance broker, and in 1938 he began taking flying lessons with the New South Wales Royal Aero Club, going solo after less than four hours of dual instruction. The outbreak of war in Europe on 3 September 1939 prompted Caldwell to enlist in the RAAF within 24 hours with the prime intention of becoming a fighter pilot, and he commenced training in February 1940 as a potential officer pilot. To his dismay he discovered that he and his fellow students were already earmarked as future flying instructors, and his reaction was to get himself released from the course, and on 27 May he re-enlisted in the RAAF as an Aircraftman 2nd Class

(AC2), U/t Pilot. Eventually gaining his wings on 14 November 1940, Caldwell was commissioned as a Pilot Officer on 12 January 1941, and by the close of that month was en route to the Middle East for operational service.

Kicking his heels for several weeks in an aircrew pool, Caldwell was then posted to No 250 Squadron on 7 May. Formed at Aqir, Palestine on 1 April 1941, No 250 Squadron was equipped with Curtiss Tomahawk IIbs and by May had brought together its various detached Flights to assemble as a complete squadron at Mariut, commanded initially by Squadron Leader J.E. Scoular, DFC. In June 1941 the squadron became based at Sidi Haneish South, from where it flew a series of convoy escort patrols, then undertook low-level strafing operations along the North African coastal area, in support of *Operation Battleaxe*, beginning on 14 June. Two days later the squadron made its first combat claims for two Bf109s damaged over Bardia, but on 18 June, while strafing the Capuzzo-Tobruk-El Adem sections of the coast road, four Tomahawks were lost in clashes with Bf109s.

By 26 June Caldwell had flown some 30 operational sorties and on that date was one of ten Tomahawk pilots of 250 Squadron escorting bombers to raid Gazala when his formation was attacked by about 30 Italian and German fighters. Caldwell fired inconclusively at several enemy aircraft before getting on the tail of a Bf109 which he shot down west of Capuzzo – his first combat victory. On 30 June Nos 73 and 250 Squadrons joined up to escort a Tobruk convoy and were soon embroiled with an Axis formation of 20 Ju87s and about 30 fighters. Caldwell quickly destroyed two Ju87s, then shared with Sergeant Whittle* in the destruction of a Bf110 of III/ZG26.

A week later, on 7 July, 250 Squadron joined several other units for a large-scale scouring sweep of the Bardia area but met no opposition. Caldwell, however, became separated from his Flight and just before 7 pm met two Fiat G50s some 25 miles west of El Adem. Attacking these immediately, he shot one down, then completed his sortie by using up the rest of his ammunition against various ground targets on his way back to the unit base. Two days

---

* Later, Squadron Leader R.J.C. Whittle, DFM.

later he added a Bf109 destroyed to his score. The next few weeks saw the squadron primarily employed on coastal convoys' protection, involving constant clashes with enemy aircraft, intermingled with straightforward fighter offensive sweeps and ground-strafing of opportunity targets, and by late August 1941 it had shifted its base to LG07.

On 29 August, in the late afternoon, 250 Squadron was escorting shipping to Tobruk when Bf109s from I/JG27 intercepted and bounced the Tomahawks. What followed is described by Caldwell in his after-combat report:

> ... whilst acting as 'weaver' I was attacked by two Me109s, one coming from astern and the other from the port side, neither of which I saw personally. Bullets from astern damaged tail, tail trimming gear, fuselage and starboard main plane, while the aileron on that side was destroyed and a sizeable hole made in the trailing edge and flap ... evidently by cannon shells, a quantity of splinters from which pierced the cowling and side of the cockpit, some entering my right side and legs. Fire from the port side damaged the fuselage a number of bullets entering my left shoulder and hip, small pieces of glass embedding in my face, my helmet and goggles being pulled askew across my nose and eyes – no doubt by a near miss.
>
> As a result of the hits on the mainplane and probable excessive avoiding action the aircraft spun out of control. Checking the spin I blacked out when pulling out of the ensuing dive, recovering to find flames in the cockpit. Pulling the pin from the safety harness I started to climb out to abandon the aircraft, when the fire, evidently caused by burning oil and not petrol as I thought, died out, so I decided to remain and attempt a landing.
>
> Looking behind me as I crossed the road at about 500 feet some six miles east of Sidi Barrani I saw a number of planes manoeuvring in a manner suggesting an engagement. As my plane seemed to answer the controls fairly well, apart from turns, I made a gradual turn and climbed back towards said aircraft, finally carrying out an attack on what I believed to be a Me109. Having previously lost the pin to my harness I was holding the straps in my left hand for security which, together with damage

Group Captain Clive Caldwell, DSO, DFC, RAAF

sustained to aircraft, (made it) inadvisable to attempt much in the way of quick change of altitude, so I carried straight on to very low level and continued to base arriving at 2010 hours. Using half flap only (because of damage) I landed to find the starboard tyre flat as the result of a bullet hole ...*

In fact, Caldwell shot down a Bf109 during the engagement when he was wounded and flying a crippled aircraft. The German pilot responsible primarily for shooting him up was Leutnant Werner Schroer of JG27 (who flew back to base and claimed a victory), a pilot destined to claim 114 victories during the war, 61 of these in North Africa. Caldwell's report of this sortie, laconic in tone and totally honest about how the Bf109s had surprised him on their initial scissors attack, exemplified his mental attitude to his role; never giving up a fight, no matter what the circumstances, and ever determined to maintain the offensive.

Within 48 hours Caldwell was back in action, narrowly avoiding being shot down by an aggressive Bf109 pilot on 1 September, and on 12 September he was promoted to Flight Lieutenant as a Flight commander. Four days later the 4th *Staffel* of I/JG27 returned from Germany equipped with 13 Messerschmitt Bf109Fs, the first examples of this much-improved Bf109 which would soon give the Luftwaffe in North Africa at least technical fighter superiority. On 27 September, ten Tomahawks from 250 Squadron joined No 3 Squadron RAAF to escort nine Maryland bombers of No 21 Squadron SAAF to Bardia, but 15 miles south of Buq Buq they were attacked by Bf109s. Caldwell destroyed one Bf109 in the general dogfight which followed, and next day claimed another Bf109 as probably destroyed, being unable to see his victim's ultimate fate.

In the same month 250 Squadron received a new commander, Squadron Leader E.J. Morris, who led the unit almost daily over the following weeks of escalating aerial activity as the Allies prepared to launch *Operation Crusader*, an offensive which finally got under way in the morning of 18 November 1941. By then both Allied and Axis air forces had been greatly increased in strength, but the Allied push on 18 November caught Rommel by surprise and Axis aerial

* *Air War against Germany and Italy, 1939-43* by J. Herington; AWM, 1954.

opposition took several days to become serious in quantity.

By the 22nd, however, German and Italian aircraft were making their greatest challenge to the RAF's desert air arm and combat became fiercely high in intensity and casualties on both sides. 250 Squadron was well to the fore in this offensive and, on 23 November ten of its Tomahawks, with eleven Hurricanes from the Royal Navy's Fighter Squadron, patrolling over South African infantry advancing on Sidi Rezegh, met six Ju88s with an escort of 24 German and Italian fighters. The outcome was the loss of one Tomahawk and one Hurricane, but claims were made for five enemy fighters destroyed, three probables, and five more damaged, with Caldwell claiming one Bf109 destroyed and a second damaged from this toll.

The same day saw *Crusader* begin to crumble as Rommel inflicted heavy casualties upon the Allied tanks, followed next day by a rapid dash towards Egypt by his own armoured columns. By the end of the month, after savage fighting, Sidi Rezegh was in Axis hands and the Tobruk garrison was isolated again.

December 5 proved to be Caldwell's most destructive single day's combat. Twelve Tomahawks from 250 Squadron, led by Caldwell, with seven more from 112 'Shark' Squadron as top cover, met a force of 40 Ju87s with more than 30 fighter escorts some 15 miles south of El Adem and virtually massacred the enemy formation, claiming no less than 17 destroyed, four probables, and four damaged for the losses of four Allied fighters (the pilots of two of these returning to their units).

Caldwell led his men straight for the Ju87s and his first victim exploded, setting fire to a second nearby. He then switched his sights to other Ju87s and destroyed three more in rapid succession; five confirmed victories in the course of less than ten minutes' action. Seven days later, during an offensive sweep, Caldwell destroyed a Bf109 during a clash with another escorted Ju87 formation. His fighting record had been well noted by higher authority and on 26 December Clive Caldwell was awarded both a DFC and Bar – a rare honour.

A few days later he was promoted to Squadron Leader, and on 13 January 1942 arrived at Antelat to take up his appointment as commander of No 112 'Shark' Squadron. Wasting no time with formalities he was in the air next day leading seven other aircraft on

One of several Polish pilots who served under Caldwell's command in 112 Sqn, taxying out for a sortie with an 'Erk' on the wing to smooth out the 'bumps' of the desert landing ground

Italian-marked Junkers Ju87 down in Allied lines

a sweep of the forward fighting areas. 112 Squadron had only just exchanged its Tomahawks for the better Kittyhawk versions of the Curtiss P-40F, though the new fighters were still inferior in many respects to the German Bf109Fs when it came to pure dogfighting action.

By the end of January 1942 Allied forces were once more in retreat eastwards, creating a series of quick moves of base for 112 Squadron, though fighter sweeps continued to be flown whenever possible, and by mid-February the squadron had become firmly (at least for the moment ...) at Gambut. From here, on 21 February, Caldwell led eleven Kittyhawks on a sweep near Gazala just before noon and near Acroma spotted six Bf109s from I/JG27 at higher altitude, obviously preparing to attack. One Bf109, piloted by Leutnant Hans-Arnold Stahlschmidt, lagged behind his companions and Caldwell, carefully waiting for the exact moment, suddenly whipped up the nose of his Kittyhawk to near-vertical attitude and fired. Stahlschmidt's Messerschmitt received Caldwell's burst in its engine and nose, rolled onto its back, then spun down with flames licking back. Finally regaining control the German – with his leader, Hauptmann Gerhard Homuth's angry voice ringing in his ear 'Which idiot let himself be shot down?' – crashlanded in the 'No-Man's Land' area between the opposing armies' forward positions and was soon after picked up by an Axis patrol and returned to his unit at Martuba by early evening. Stahlschmidt was eventually to claim 59 *Luftsiege* in the North African campaigns, but his escape from death that day had been razor-thin; Caldwell's accurate shooting being described by the German pilots involved as 'fabulous'.

A combination of bad weather and lessening aerial activity followed over the next two weeks, but on 10 March Caldwell took off in a Kittyhawk loaded with an unfused 250lb GP bomb strapped under its fuselage for the first experiment in possible use of the aircraft as a fighter-bomber. The trial was successful and next day he took a live bomb to the enemy airfield at Martuba, though the bomb fell wide of his target.

Three days later 112 Squadron flew its last operations of their contemporary tour. In the afternoon Caldwell led twelve Kittyhawks on a diversion sweep to Gambut to intercept any enemy fighters attempting to interfere with a bombing operation by Bostons against Martuba. Near Bir Hakeim Caldwell saw two Kittyhawks being chased by four Italian Macchi 202s and a pair of Bf109s, and immediately turned his formation in pursuit of the pursuers. The Bf109s swung to attack Caldwell's men, shooting two down, but Caldwell and his No 2, Sergeant Urbanczyk, followed the Messerschmitts down in their dive and shared in destroying one of these. Climbing back into the mêlée above him, Caldwell attacked the Macchis, one of which jerked up its nose violently. Seconds later a fawn-coloured parachute swayed downwards and the empty aircraft fell towards the desert to certain destruction.

Next day 112 Squadron set off for Sidi Haneish for several weeks of rest and refurbishment of equipment, and well-earned leave in the fleshpots of Cairo and Alexandria, being officially declared non-operational with effect from 1 April.

On 27 April Caldwell left 112 Squadron, being posted back to Australia, via the USA, to take up a further operational post with the RAAF defending his native land against the Japanese. By then he had been officially credited with at least 20 enemy aircraft destroyed, apart from shares in others and a number of damaged.

Throughout his operational career, especially when in command of a Flight, squadron, or (later) Wing, Caldwell had always laid great stress on the prime importance of accurate shooting, something he constantly practised. In his own words; 'A pilot who can't shoot straight might as well remain on the ground because he's useless in a fighter squadron'. A man of alert brain, lightning reactions in any tight situation, fast-talking (usually with abrupt honesty of opinion and judgment), Caldwell was supremely self-assured, having faith in his own abilities and exuding that self-confidence to a degree which bolstered the confidence of his subordinates. In combat he was totally aggressive, channelling his abundant energies into explosive bouts of action; while on the ground he was a natural leader, mixing easily with the men under his command from Flight commander to the lowliest Erk ground crew.

Arriving in Australia in late September 1942, Caldwell was promoted to Wing Commander and assigned as the Wing Leader to the newly-forming No 1 Wing RAAF, comprised of Nos 54 RAF, 452 RAAF and 457 RAAF Squadrons, equipped with Spitfires. After

Caldwell after his return to Australia

working up at Richmond, the Wing moved to Australia's North-Western Area for the defence of Darwin and its adjacent area. Here the Wing drew its first blood on 6 February 1943, while Caldwell, flying Spitfire Vc, BS234, bearing his initials-code letters CR-C, opened his account on 2 March by destroying a Japanese Type O and a Type 97 during a Japanese attack on Coomalie.

In the following five months Caldwell was to add six more Japanese destroyed to his tally, his final victim being a *Dinah* shot down on 20 August 1943. Two months later came the award of a DSO, and Caldwell became OC and CFI at No 2 OTU, Mildura in South Australia. By April 1944, however, he had returned to Darwin as a Group Captain to form and command No 80 Wing of the Australian 1st Tactical Air Force (TAF), flying the superb Spitfire VIIIs, a variant of R.J. Mitchell's brainchild which was superior to any contemporary Japanese opponent.

With the gradual retreat of Japanese forces during 1944-45, Caldwell's Wing was moved forward to keep in contact with the enemy but was to be almost exclusively employed on ground-strafing operations; sorties that Caldwell personally termed 'futile and wasteful, flying maximum sorties against a well-armed but captive enemy ... being the square of stupidity, and losing aircraft and pilots'.

By February 1945 Caldwell's disgust with this lack of 'proper' fighter operations was voiced to several senior RAAF officers, emphasising the wastefulness of such sorties and their lowering of morale amongst his men who deeply resented what amounted to near-inactivity in their proper role.

Matters finally came to a head by April 1945 when Caldwell along with seven battle-experienced unit leaders tendered identical applications to resign their RAAF commissions. The internal furore dragged on throughout the remainder of the year, culminating for Caldwell personally in January 1946 when he faced a court-martial on a somewhat trumped up charge of 'trafficking in liquor using RAAF aircraft'; a reference to Caldwell's unofficial activities during 1945 when he helped initiate a barter system of Australian beer and spirits for American troops in exchange for much-needed spares for his Wing's aircraft. With characteristic candour, he did not deny his 'trading', though made it perfectly plain that no personal financial gain had accrued. He was, however, found guilty and received a modest 'punishment' – reduction in rank and loss of pay – but on 5 March 1946 Clive Caldwell resigned from the RAAF and returned to civilian life to organise an import-export business which quickly prospered.

CHAPTER THIRTEEN

Neville Duke

The name of Neville Frederick Duke is primarily associated in many aviation buffs' minds with his many years as a test pilot for the products of the Hawker aircraft firm in the 1948-60 period and later; pioneering flying of the Hawker Hunter and other jets, intermingled with various world records in the air. Yet before Duke became a test pilot he had completed three tours of operations as a fighter pilot, flying a total of 486 operational sorties in Europe and the Middle East, earning four gallantry awards and being credited with 28 enemy aircraft destroyed and at least 16 others probably destroyed or at least damaged.

Duke's enthusiasm for and love of flying began even as a small boy, crystallised on an Easter holiday at the age of ten when he paid the sum of five shillings for a flip in an Avro 504K biplane at Pickhill, Kent; a ten minutes' baptism of the sky which sealed his ambitions for his future.

Born at Tonbridge on 11 January 1922, Duke's schooldays passed wholly immersed in a world of aircraft models and aviation literature, with a near-equal interest in boats and the sea, but on leaving school in the summer of 1939 he was employed as a clerk in an estate agent's office while marking time until his 18th birthday, on which date he planned to apply for an RAF Short Service Commission as a pilot.

The outbreak of war months later nullified that ambition but Duke immediately volunteered to join the RAF, only to be rejected because he was too young. Dismayed but still determined, he applied again on his 18th birthday and eventually donned RAF uniform in June 1940 as an AC2 (U/t Pilot). After the initial bull of ITW, he was posted to No 13 FTS at White Waltham where he made his first Service flight on 20 August 1940 in a DH Tiger Moth (N6790), and eventually progressed to No 5 FTS, Sealand and Tern

Hill, completing his instruction at No 58 OTU, Grangemouth, earmarked for training as a fighter pilot and a commission.

In April 1941 Neville Duke joined his first operational unit, No 92 Squadron, based at Biggin Hill, commanded by Squadron Leader 'Jamie' Rankin*, as one of the first two wartime-trained pilots to join this squadron. Engaged mainly on day offensive sweeps and bomber escorts over France, Duke's first combat claim came in the same month, a Bf109 damaged, but on 23 June he became separated from his formation over Le Touquet and was jumped by five Bf109Fs. Hitting one Messerschmitt which attacked him head-on, Duke saw it disappear from the fight trailing black and white smoke, then fought off the others in a fast, jinking flight back across the Channel.

He merely claimed the Bf109 as damaged, but next day was part of a Wing escort for Blenheims attacking St Omer which was bounced by several Bf109s, one of which Duke shot down to crash just inland of Dunkirk. Cracked ear drums resulting from an ultra-fast dive in combat a few days later put Duke in hospital for two weeks, but on his return to 92 Squadron he was given the signal honour of becoming the No 2 to the Wing Leader, Wing Commander A.G. – 'Sailor' – Malan, DSO, DFC, whenever Malan flew on operations, an experience which was to prove invaluable to Duke later. August 1941 brought Duke claims for one Bf109 destroyed and another damaged, but at the end of October he was notified of an imminent posting to Egypt and left England in a Sunderland flying boat on 3 November, having been told by officialdom that his stay in the Middle East would only be for 'six weeks, old boy' – it was to be three years before Duke saw the green fields of England again ...

On arrival at Air HQ Middle East Duke was detailed to join No 112 Squadron based at Sidi Haneish, flying Curtiss P-40 Tomahawks, and he arrived on the unit on 12 November. His first flight in a Tomahawk next morning produced an expensive crashlanding due to Duke's unfamiliarity with the aircraft, but 112 was already in the process of moving base to LG110, Sidi Barrani and commenced operations from there on the 14th, but five days

---

* Later, Air Commodore J.E. Rankin, DSO, DFC.

Neville Duke

later had moved further forward to LG122, Fort Maddalena to keep up with the Allied forward infantry positions. On 21 November, flying Tomahawk AK402, Duke was one of three pilots who forced a Fiat CR42 down to crashland, whereupon Duke concentrated on destroying this aircraft while his two companions calmly strafed the escaping Italian pilot and killed him; an act which shocked Duke.

Next day he was flying one of nine Tomahawks of 112 Squadron which combined with twelve fighters from No 3 RAAF Squadron for a fighter sweep over enemy lines. South-east of El Adem they were bounced by about 20 Bf109Fs from I and II/JG27 and Fiat G50s and a lengthy combat ensued, during which Duke gave one Bf109 a burst from 100 yards using only his fixed ring and bead sight – his gunsight was unserviceable – and saw the German's cockpit canopy and chunks of fuselage fly off. Its pilot, Offizier Waskott, took to his parachute and was closely circled by Duke until reaching the earth where he became a prisoner of war.

On 24 November Rommel's panzers began their eastward push to Egypt, followed by several columns of Afrika Korps infantry, one of these columns being seen to swing south-east and thereby creating a fair amount of 'panic' among the various Allied air units directly in this column's projected path. Accordingly LGs 123, 124, 132, 134, and 136 were rapidly evacuated and all aircraft flown in to Fort Maddalena; a conglomeration of some 170-180 RAF aircraft all on one relatively small landing ground, and thus a tempting target. In the event the German column missed Fort Maddalena by some ten miles in its headlong advance towards Egypt, blissfully unaware that it *might* have effectively captured or wiped out the bulk of the Desert Air Force's frontline fighter strength in one blow …

With Rommel's forces still moving towards Egypt, 112 Squadron spent the next few days on intense ground-strafing sorties against the German troops and transports, but also had several fierce clashes with enemy aircraft supporting the German advance, as on 25 November when a combined force of 23 Tomahawks from 112 and 3 RAAF Squadrons met nearly 60 German and Italian fighters and bombers attacking forward New Zealand infantry positions. By the end of the resulting maelstrom of dogfighting ten enemy aircraft had been claimed as destroyed, three more probably destroyed, and eight others damaged, while 112 Squadron lost one pilot, Sergeant

Glasgow in AK461 who was shot down by Oberfeldwebel Espenlaub of I/JG27.

November finished on a dramatic note for Duke who, on the 30th, was flying AK402 with a formation of 24 Tomahawks which intercepted nearly 40 enemy aircraft intent on bombing Tobruk. Diving into the enemy formation Duke suddenly found a Fiat G50 in front of him which dived fast to ground level then fled. Following the Fiat Duke riddled it and saw it crashland. He was then attacked by some Bf109Fs and Italian fighters, managed to hit one 109 which spurted glycol, then dived to deck-level and ran for home.

One Bf109F persisted in pursuit of Duke and soon put some bullets through the Tomahawk's wings and rear fuselage. Turning violently to avoid this punishment, Duke presented the German, Oberfeldwebel Otto Schulz from II/JG27, with a full deflection shot, and his cannon shells blew a hole in the Tomahawk's port wing, then caused Duke to roll over onto his back in an involuntary complete circle at some 500 feet above the ground. The Tomahawk completed its wild barrel roll, hit the sand on its belly, bounced into the air again, then crashlanded. Scrambling out of his cockpit Duke sought frail cover behind a nearby scrub bush as Schulz turned to strafe the grounded Tomahawk, his shells causing the Curtiss to erupt in flames, then flying back to his own lines. Picked up by some nearby infantry, Duke hailed a passing Westland Lysander which flew him back to his squadron.

Duke extracted a modicum of revenge for his defeat of 30 November when, on 4 December, flying Tomahawk AN337, he was one of 22 Tomahawk pilots from 112 and 250 Squadrons who attacked some 15 Ju87s and 15-plus Bf109s, Fiat G50s, and Macchi 200s over El Adem-Sidi Rezegh. Duke attacked one gaggle of five Ju87s, destroying one and damaging a second which dived out of the mêlée pouring smoke, then found himself dogfighting an Italian Macchi 200. As the fight progressed Duke's guns and cannons jammed up one after the other leaving him ostensibly unarmed, but he continued chasing the Macchi and delivering dummy attacks. Skimming at zero height along the sea shore the Macchi headed over Tobruk but as Duke made yet another dummy attack the Italian pilot steep-turned, stalled, flicked violently, then dived into the ground and exploded in flames.

Duke landed at Tobruk, shared the customary bully beef and hard tack biscuit 'lunch' with the Australian soldiers defending Tobruk, then flew back to his unit. He was to return to Tobruk next day in rather different circumstances! December 5 brought 112 Squadron one of its greatest combat successes since its heroic part in the ill-fated Greek campaign. Seven Tomahawks from 112, including Neville Duke flying AN337, joined with 250 Squadron in tackling a force of 40 Ju87s, escorted higher up by some 35-40 German and Italian fighters in two layers.

While 250 Squadron attacked the Ju87s, 112's pilots took on the top cover fighters. Within seconds the sky became a milling mix of bombers and fighters, and Duke, whose aircraft radio was defunct and had its windscreen plastered with sand on take-off, failed to see a Bf109 which blew a hole in the right side of his cockpit, wounding him in the right leg and filling his cockpit with blinding smoke.

From 10,000 feet Duke's Tomahawk spun down, its right elevator shot away, an aileron shot through, and its starboard wing badly torn at the root. As he prepared to bale out of the uncontrollably spinning fighter, Duke felt it straighten out of its dive at 2000 feet and flew the machine down for a 150 mph bumpy landing at Tobruk. Having his wounded leg attended to in the Tobruk emergency hospital while a German bombing *blitz* was under way, Duke was airlifted back to his squadron in a Blenheim; the unit's only 'loss' from a fight in which 112's pilots had claimed ten destroyed and 250 Squadron had destroyed a further twelve enemy aircraft.

After a few days' recuperation leave in Cairo, Duke rejoined 112 Squadron which had again begun moving forward with the Eighth Army's advance, and claimed his next victims on 22 December. Flying Tomahawk AK354, he was one of six pilots who made a surprise attack on Magrun airfield, base for the German JG27 fighter *Jagdstaffeln*, among other Luftwaffe units. With his No 2, Sergeant Carson, Duke strafed a circling Ju87, then attacked a Bf109F which was climbing to attack the 'intruders'.* Shortly after Duke ran into a formation of Ju52 tri-motor transport aircraft heading for Benina and promptly shot up a Ju52 straggling behind

* Though claimed by Duke as destroyed, this Bf109, piloted by Leutnant Sinner, is not recorded as lost in German records.

112 Sqn pilots at Fort Maddalena (LG122) on 30 November 1941. L-R: Leu; Duke; Soden; Humphreys; Sqn Ldr Morello (OC); Ambrose; Dickenson; Burney; Westenra; Sabourin; Bowker; Bartle; Carson

112 Sqn Kittyhawk 1a, AK772, GA-Y, carrying a surface-impact fused 250lb GP bomb, Gambut Main, March 1942. This aircraft was shot down on 30 May 1942 and its pilot, Plt Off H.G. Burney reported 'Missing'

'Aces' from 112 Squadron. L-R: Flt Lt D.F. Westenra, DFC; Flt Lt N. Duke, DFC; Flt Lt P.J. Humphreys, DFC. All have the top tunic-button undone, the unofficial mark of the fighter pilot then

Spitfire JF476, QJ-D, of 92 Squadron

its companions. As the bulky Junkers started to fall away, Duke found himself the target for some Bf110s which came out of cloud above him and, being very low on ammunition, Duke evaded these and flew back to Mechili.

The next few days brought little air activity, though several ground-strafing sorties were flown, while on 29 December the squadron received its first seven Curtiss P-40E Kittyhawks, and next day handed its battle-weary Tomahawks over to No 250 Squadron, while 14 pilots flew to Kasfareet on the Suez Canal to collect and ferry back further Kittyhawks to 112 Squadron. From then until 9 January, 1942 the squadron flew only practice flights with the new Kittyhawks, on that date flying the first Kittyhawk operations with a Blenheim escort mission north of El Agheila.

Four days later a new commander arrived for the unit, Squadron Leader Clive Caldwell, DFC, who had recently served in its brother unit, 250 Squadron.

On 14 January the squadron completed a move to Antelat LG – the rear party arriving while a pitched dogfight was in progress over the airfield with four Bf109s – but exactly a week later Rommel's forces commenced an offensive which was destined to push the Eighth Army back to the Egyptian border again. No 112 Squadron hastily evacuated Antelat, moving base 40 miles back to Msus, followed three days later by a further retreat to Mechili, some 85 miles to the north-east. These moves were interlaced with offensive sweeps by available Kittyhawks daily, strafing and bombing the advancing Afrika Korps vehicle and troop convoys, but on the 28th Benghazi was captured by the Germans and that afternoon the squadron began yet another shift of airfield, moving back to Gazala, some 65 miles further east.

At the close of January 112 Squadron had a total of 24 pilots, 17 of these non-commissioned SNCOs, and on 2 February 'A' Flight flew to El Adem, while 'B' Flight followed next day and flew on to Gambut, the latter LG being attacked by enemy aircraft based in Crete on the 5th. By 7 February the whole squadron was together at Gambut and next day escorted Blenheims bombing Derna, during which operation 112's pilots claimed three Bf109s shot down. Further enemy attacks on Gambut followed over the following days but 112 fought back, scoring a particularly heartening success on 14

February. On that day Duke in AK578 was part of a ten-Kittyhawks' formation from 112 which joined eight from 3 RAAF Squadron in scrambling to intercept an incoming batch of Italian and German bombers and fighters reported over Acroma. The ensuing 'Valentine's Day Massacre' resulted in 112 Squadron alone claiming 12 destroyed, two probables, and three damaged, of which tally Duke accounted for two Macchi 200s, both destroyed. On 12 March he was informed by 'Killer' Caldwell that he had been awarded a DFC, but his time with 112 Squadron was almost ended, and on 22 April Duke was posted as an instructor to the Fighter School at El Ballah near the Suez Canal. By then his log book showed that he had flown totals of 161 operational sorties to date, involving 220 ops hours of flying time.

While instructing at El Ballah Duke heard that his old unit in England, 92 Squadron, had arrived for operations in North Africa, and immediately agitated for a posting to the squadron, only to be told that he must complete his six months' rest period before returning to 'ops'. 92 Squadron had left England on 13 February 1942 and finally assembled as a complete unit again at Heliopolis in late April, and on 2 June its commander and 12 of his pilots were attached to 80 Squadron at Amriya for operational experience in Middle East conditions, flying their first sorties two days later.

Over the next ten weeks 92 Squadron accumulated much operational flying time, scoring several combat victories in the process, and by 12 August was declared fully operational with a total of 22 Spitfires (mainly Mk Vbs), and by 18 November – on which date Neville Duke finally 'escaped' from his instructional rest with a posting to 92 – the squadron was based at Gambut, moving shortly after to Msus, commanded by Squadron Leader J.H. Wedgewood, DFC,* who was succeeded as CO on 2 December by Squadron Leader J.M. Morgan, DFC, who in turn handed over command on 20 January 1943 to Squadron Leader W. Harper. It was a period of constant changes of landing grounds too as the Eighth Army followed up its successful offensive from El Alamein with its air support keeping pace with the ever-changing front lines.

---

* Wedgewood, returning to England, was killed in a Halifax crash on take-off from Malta shortly after.

On 8 January 1943 ten Spitfires of 92 Squadron, flying from the forward LG at Hamraiet, scrambled to meet a force of Ju87s heavily escorted by fighters. Tackling the high cover of Macchi 202s at some 13,000 feet, Duke and his wingman, Flight Sergeant Sails, dived out of the sun and Duke followed one Macchi to ground level where, after several accurate bursts, his fire sent the Italian down to crash in flames and disintegrate in a shower of hurtling metal debris.

Three days later was Duke's 21st birthday and he marked the anniversary well. Flying two sorties in the morning and early afternoon without results, Duke led 92 Squadron off for a third sortie to intercept an enemy bombing formation approaching Tamet. A total of 40 Italian aircraft from 13°, 18°, and 23° *Gruppi* were involved in the raid, but Duke spotted a group of five Macchi 202s first and promptly dived on these. On seeing the Spitfires piling down four of the Macchis quickly dived away but the fifth climbed, and Duke fastened onto the latter, his cannon shells striking its fuselage just behind the cockpit. The Macchi rolled onto its back and its pilot parachuted to earth to become a prisoner of war. He was Maggiore (Major) Gustavo Garretto who had only just taken command of the 18° *Gruppo*, and in postwar years rose to become a General in the Italian air force.

Continuing his hunt for opponents Duke, and his No 2, Pilot Officer McMahon, found another Macchi flying very low over the desert. With the sun's glare behind them both Spitfires dived on this Italian, making several attacks before the Macchi pilot lowered his aircraft's flaps, crashlanded and evacuated his cockpit at high speed, to be taken prisoner a little later.

Moving further westwards to keep pace with the Allied advance, 92 Squadron was based at Wadi Surri by 21 January on which date twelve Spitfires spotted some Italian Ju87s near Castel Benito (now Idris). Diving from 18,000 feet to the Ju87s' altitude of 1,000 feet, Duke's Spitfire was leading the rest when he lined his gunsight on one Ju87 and splashed it with bullets and shells with no visible effect. Tackling a second Ju87 his cannon shells ruptured the bomber's starboard wing root and it burst into flames, spiralling down crazily until it exploded into the ground.

On return to Wadi Surri the Wing Leader, Johnny Darwen, told Duke that he was now promoted to Flight Lieutenant as a Flight commander in 92 Squadron, while a few days later came an award of a Bar to his DFC. The squadron moved to Castel Benito on 7 February but by the end of the month had moved to Ben Gardene, from where Duke claimed seven more victories in the first week of March 1943. On 1 March he shot down two Macchi 202s, both pilots baling out from shattered aircraft, then two days later attacked a lone Bf109F which fell vertically, breaking up as it fell and trailing thick smoke.

Next day while patrolling the Mareth Line at 8,000 feet eight Spitfires from 92 Squadron met two Bf109s escorting three or four bomb-carrying 109s attacking Hasbub airfield. Duke attacked the escorts, forcing one pilot to bale out, then chasing the second Messerschmitt through flak bursts until his shooting caused the German to crash and explode.

On 7 March Duke rounded out a most successful week by destroying a Bf109F over Medenine during an early patrol, and then, with only two other Spitfires, tackling a formation of 20 Bf109s near Neffatia in the early afternoon and shooting one down, its pilot taking to his parachute.

On 13 March the squadron received its first four Spitfire Mk IXs as the start of re-equipment from its battle-worn Mk Vs, and on 23 March Duke attacked a Junkers Ju88 which proved particularly tough in opposition, its rear gunner putting several bullets through his Spitfire's wings, propeller, and a wheel tyre. In the event it escaped, although certainly damaged.

Four days after his brush with the pugilistic Ju88 Duke was telephoned by Air Vice-Marshal Harry Broadhurst, 'boss' of the Desert Air Force, to congratulate him on an immediate award of a DSO; an event duly honoured on 29 March when Duke was leading seven Spitfires over an area north of Gabes and destroyed a Bf109G from six which bounced the Spitfires out of the sun. Duke's victim exploded into the ground close to a German Red Cross hospital – his 20th officially credited victory. With the Eighth Army on the verge of driving Rommel's Afrika Korps out of the desert into Tunisia 92 Squadron continued moving bases to keep up with the advance, operating from Fauconnerie and Goubrine, flying mainly escort sorties covering Kittyhawk 'bombers', Hurricane IIC 'tank-busters', Baltimore, Mitchell, and Boston bombers in pursuit of the retreating Germans.

On 16 April ten Spitfires of No 145 Squadron took off, led by Wing Commander Ian – 'Widge' – Gleed, DSO, DFC, the 244 Wing Leader, for a sweep of the Cap Bon area, with Duke leading three Spitfire IXs from 92 Squadron at 20,000 feet as high cover. Duke spotted some 18 Savoia-Marchetti SM82 tri-motored Italian transport aircraft below – some of the Axis aircraft now being used for hasty evacuation of troops from Tunisia to Sicily – and reported these to Gleed.

Ian Gleed, unable yet to see the SM82s from his lower altitude, told Duke to 'lead the way' and Duke dived to attack, overshooting his first selected target but quickly shooting two SM82s into the sea shortly after. As he lined his sights on a third SM82 he was attacked by a Focke Wulf Fw190, veered out of immediate danger, and found himself virtually surrounded by a host of enemy fighters, including the élite German JG77. In the shambles of desperate fighting which ensued 'Widge' Gleed and his No 2 wingman were lost, but the Spitfires claimed correctly seven SM82s shot down along with four enemy fighters.

Two days later, on Palm Sunday, 18 April, Duke was to be virtually a spectator to an aerial clash thereafter known as the 'Palm Sunday Massacre'. At 5 pm a total of 46 Curtiss P-40Fs from all three squadrons of the USAAF's 57th Fighter Group and the 314th, and eleven Spitfires from 92 Squadron as top cover, set off to hunt for Axis transport aircraft in the Cap Bon area.

An hour later a mass formation of Junkers Ju52s, escorted by German and Italian fighters, was sighted some six miles off Cap Bon, leaving Tunisia en route to Sicily. With 92 Squadron and the USAAF 64th Fighter Squadron remaining 'upstairs' to ward off fighters, the rest of the Allied fighters dived in to shatter this prime target, creating great slaughter among the troop-filled Ju52s.

Apart from chasing away a Bf109 Duke remained aloft, witness to an amazing scene, where eventually 24 Ju52s, nine Bf109s and one Bf110 were lost in the sea, and 35 other Ju52s force-landed or crashed on the nearby coastline. These *actual* Axis losses were far less than the optimistic American claims for almost 150 enemy aircraft destroyed made initially, though this figure was later officially watered down to less than 80 destroyed. German records show that the initial formation comprised 65 Ju52s, escorted by 16 Bf109s and

Macchi 202s, and five Bf110s. Duke's own epilogue to this astonishing fight was: 'As dusk fell we looked down to see burning aircraft glowing over an area of many square miles. It was a blood-chilling sight ...'.*

Apart from several escort sorties in the next few weeks, Duke was virtually tour-expired and flew the last sortie of his second operational tour on 11 May. Expecting a posting back to England, he was told by RAF HQ in Cairo that he was to become a Squadron Leader on a staff job; a prospect which totally dismayed him. In mid-June, however, he took up the post of Chief Flying Instructor as Squadron Leader at No 73 OTU, Abu Sueir, near Ismailia, a job which involved plentiful flying and compensated to some degree his disappointment in having to remain in Egypt. Once reconciled to staying in the Middle East for the foreseeable future, Duke quietly looked around for a chance to return to operations, and a chance meeting in Cairo with Brian Kingcome, a friend from his initial spell with 92 Squadron in the UK and by now Group Captain commanding No 244 Wing in Italy, led eventually to Duke being posted to Kingcome's Wing in early March 1944 where, on 13 March, he took over command of No 145 Squadron, a unit flying Spitfire VIIIs and based at Marcianise, near Caserta.

By May the squadron was based at Venafro, and on 13 May Duke re-opened his tally by damaging one Bf109 and destroying a second, while next day over the Cassino area he shot down another Bf109 engaged in bombing Allied positions. A few days later, while flying to a rendezvous to escort some American Baltimore bombers, Duke and his men met 18 Fw190s. Wheeling into the leading section of Focke Wulfs, Duke hit one at short range which burst into flames, then splashed cannon shells all over a second Fw190. Its hood flew off and the German pilot baled out.

On 3 June 1944 Duke was awarded a second Bar to his DFC, but four days later while engaged in strafing some trucks in the Rieti area he had a close brush with death. On passing over the line of burning vehicles his Spitfire was hit in the engine radiator, the engine vibrated alarmingly, then began spewing flames. Climbing for height quickly, Duke's cockpit filled with dense smoke and the

* *Test pilot* by N. Duke and A.W. Mitchell: Wingate, 1953.

engine fire intensified. Sliding his canopy back, he turned the Spitfire on its back to bale out, but remained jammed in the cockpit by his parachute pack being caught up. Kicking hard he eventually fell out, then on pulling the ripcord handle had one shoulder strap break, nearly spilling him out of his 'chute harness.

Falling into a lake, his troubles were not over yet because one leg strap kept him tied to his billowing parachute canopy which, blown by the wind, began dragging him across the water, part-submerged and almost drowning him. In the event he was rescued by some local peasant farmers and within days was back with his unit.

The following three months saw diminished Luftwaffe opposition and 145 Squadron undertook a variety of fighter-bomber and general escort operations, its chief enemy now being the deadly accurate 88mm predicted flak encountered on every low-level sortie. On 3 September, however, Duke and his No 2 flew a pre-dawn patrol of the Pesaro-Rimini battle zone and north of Rimini found three Bf109s flying in line-abreast formation. Chasing these hard, Duke riddled one whose pilot baled out, then caught a second in a climb and set it on fire, its pilot also escaping by parachute.

Three weeks later Duke was told he was to come off operations and hand over command of 145 Squadron to Squadron Leader S.W.F. Daniel, DFC. By then Neville Duke had accumulated an overall total of 486 operational sorties (712 flying hours) in his three operational tours, and had been officially credited with $28\frac{1}{2}$ enemy aircraft destroyed, three probables, and at least five more damaged. On the last day of October 1944 Duke flew out of Italy en route to England, almost exactly three years from the start of his 'six weeks' posting to the Middle East ...

Back home, though offered a Wing Commander, Assistant Air Attaché's posting at Chunking, Duke voluntarily dropped a rank to Flight Lieutenant in order to become a test pilot with Hawker Aircraft from 1 January 1945, and in June 1946 became a member of the RAF's High Speed Flight at Tangmere. Deciding that his future lay in test-piloting Duke left the RAF in June 1948 and commenced a full career with the Hawker Company, eventually becoming its Chief Test Pilot and a pioneer of the early supersonic world of flight.

CHAPTER FOURTEEN

Bombers' Tales

In the overall context of the air war in North Africa it is perhaps inevitable that the deeds and exploits of fighter pilots take a lion's share of publicity; not least because fighter squadrons predominated in numerical strength in the desert air arm during the years 1940-43. Nevertheless, the efforts of the bomber units contributed in no small measure to the offensive against Axis forces from the first hours of the North African campaigns and provided the long arm of Allied aerial strategy until the ultimate victory.

As with the UK-based RAF during the early years, bombers were classified as light or medium, being twin-engined and of modest weight-carrying and long-range performance, exemplified by the Blenheim of pre-war design which equipped nine RAF squadrons under Middle East Command control – a total of 102 aircraft – on 10 June 1940; the day Italy formally declared war against the Allies. The only other bomber units in the Command then were Nos 14, 47, and 223 Squadrons, all flying Vickers Wellesleys, and Nos 70 and 216 Squadrons, classified technically as bomber-transports flying Valentias and Bombays respectively. Of this relatively meagre force, 26 Blenheims, drawn from three squadrons struck the first blow against the Italians in the early dawn of 11 June by attacking the Italian airfield at El Adem, thereby initiating a policy of constant offensive which was to become the *raison d'être* of succeeding bomber crews over the desert.

Reinforcements for the bombers were relatively slow to arrive in Egypt; the needs of the East African campaign absorbing a number of squadrons exclusively for several months. One unit to join the Middle East war in May 1941 was No 24 Squadron SAAF, only recently formed in South Africa and equipped with Martin Marylands. This unit commenced actual operations on 14 May, and on 20 October the squadron received its first example of the

American-designed Douglas Boston bombers which were to replace the Marylands for future sorties which commenced by November. The initial Boston sorties by the South Africans were often made by single aircraft, unescorted, and consequently suffered casualties to roving Luftwaffe fighters.

An example was 7 December 1941 when a single Boston was sent off to recce the El Adem-Acroma-Gazala area at dawn. Near Gazala it was attacked by Oberfeldwebel Schulz of II/JG27 whose fire set one of the bomber's engines on fire and its wing spread the flames. Its pilot, Lieutenant A.M. Kingon, ordered his crew to bale out which the Observer did promptly. As Kingon began to undo his own safety harness prior to evacuating his seat he heard on the intercom that his two air gunners, Sergeants C. Lucas and W. Hendrick, were too badly wounded to obey his order. Buckling himself in again, Kingon set the burning Boston down on the desert in a crashlanding, then carried each gunner to a place of safety 100 yards away. Then, ignoring the flames and detonating bullets, Kingon plunged back into the Boston to extricate the emergency water supply and the first aid kit. Kingon and his Observer were captured and sent to Italy, but, ironically, the two wounded gunners, initially taken to Derna hospital for treatment, were later 'liberated' by advancing Allied army personnel. Later that same day a second Boston was despatched on a similar recce, only to be shot down near El Adem by Leutnant Remmer of I/JG27, with just one crew member, an RAF air gunner, escaping by parachute.

Three days later, on 10 December, came the blackest day in the squadron's history – the 'Boston Tea Party', as it came to be titled in the unit history. Six Bostons were detailed for an attack against retreating enemy troop columns west of Laib Esem, to be led by Major E.N. Donnelly who had succeeded to command of a Flight of 24 Squadron SAAF only five days before, and for whom this was to be his first operational sortie. At almost the same time as the Bostons took off, Messerschmitt Bf109s of I/JG27 left their airstrip to escort a formation of Ju87s on a bombing raid against forward Eighth Army troop positions. As the two forces neared Laib Esem, the Bf109 leader spotted the six unescorted Bostons below him through a break in the clouds and promptly ordered twelve of his men to attack these. What followed was a near-massacre of the unprotected bombers.

Boston III of No. 24 Squadron SAAF on air test

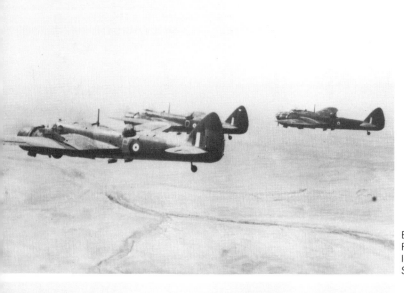

Blenheim IVs of No. 14 Sqn RAF over Iraq bound for a leaflet-drop on Iran, September 1941

View from the nose of Blenheim IV, Z5867, of 113 Sqn RAF during a strafe of a Italian road convoy on the coastal main road of Libya, south of Benghazi, 26 October 1941, piloted by Vic Cashmore

The Bostons were flying in the two Vics-of-three formation and the No 3 of the rear Vic, piloted by Lieutenant Jim Williams was the first victim. Attacking him from above and abeam came Leutnant Willi Kothmann whose shells severely wounded both air gunners, Lieutenant R.A. Joiner and Sergeant D. Newall, shattered Williams' instrument panel, damaged both engines, and set the Boston on fire. Williams gave the order to abandon aircraft but only seconds later Kothmann swept in from the beam again and further riddled the bomber, damaging its tail heavily. Jim Williams felt the aircraft dropping its nose and had to pull his control column fully back to prevent a vertical dive. Repeating his order for the crew to bale out, he was about to jump himself when he realised one of the wounded gunners was still aboard. Dropping back into his seat, Williams continued the struggle to keep the Boston's nose up until the gunner finally left, then at 1,500 feet finally evacuated his burning aircraft.

The two gunners landed one and a half miles apart, one of them unconscious, and were picked up by an Indian Supply Unit, but the Boston's Observer, Lieutenant Bernard Alexander, was not seen to leave the aircraft and was presumed dead. Unbeknown to the crew their victor, Kothmann, had himself been badly wounded by the crossfire of the Boston gunners and only just managed to land safely at Tmimi.

The next Boston to suffer was that piloted by Lieutenant Gerry Genis, flying No 2 to the formation leader. He was attacked by Feldwebel Franz Elles and wounded, and his aircraft set on fire. Seeking cover in nearby cloud, the wounded Genis managed to maintain flying attitude and offer his crew reasonable time in which to take to their 'chutes. The Observer, Lieutenant D. McPherson, managed to bale out but Genis and his two air gunners, Sergeants Roger Bowerman and David Ross, both RAF men, were too badly wounded to leave, and all three died as the Boston spun down and exploded into the ground. Captain Frank Goch, leading the second Vic, then came under attack from Hauptmann Erich Gerlitz and fell away burning fiercely. Goch and his Observer, Lieutenant H. Raw, managed to take to their parachutes though Goch's head injuries and bullet wounds led to his death two hours later. Both gunners, Sergeants Bertie Delaney and Mildmay Clulee, failed to bale out.

The remaining member of the rear Vic, piloted by Lieutenant B.

Blenheim I, L6823, come to grief

Wellington – 'Wimpy' – believed of No. 38 Sqn RAF

Wellington JN-A (R1016?), 150 Sqn, May 1943. The cartoon figure was of 'Captai Reilly-Ffoul' of the *Daily Mirr* strip cartoon 'Just Jake'

Middleton-Stewart, also erupted in flames as it was attacked by Oberfeldwebel Hermann Fôrster. With his intercomm useless, the pilot baled out, but his crew, Flying Officer Edwin Harding, RAAF, and Sergeants Jack Handley, RAF, and Johannes van Dyk, perished when the Boston exploded in mid-air.

Leutnant Friedrich Körner then attacked the third Boston of the lead-Vic, setting one engine and a wing on fire. Its pilot, Lieutenant D.R. Haupt, and his two gunners, Sergeants Vincent Black and L.E. Venter, baled out just before the aircraft shed its damaged wing, though Venter was wounded and Haupt hit the tailplane. Vincent Black fell straight through the continuing hail of fire from Körner's guns and his body was riddled with bullets when it touched earth, while the Observer, Lieutenant Leslie Bensimon, was not seen again and was presumed to have died still in the doomed Boston. Only the leading Boston, piloted by Donnelly, escaped. Though severely damaged, it jettisoned its bombs and eventually managed a forced landing near LG76. Of the 24 men who had set out originally, twelve had been killed. It was the last time Bostons were sent on operations without fighter escort, while Jim Williams later received a DFC for his selfless actions that disastrous day.

Not all casualties among the bomber crews were directly a result of enemy action; accidents were inevitable in the makeshift conditions on desert airfields commonly bereft of such niceties as air traffic control, radar, and all the amenities for safety normally installed on any peacetime aerodrome. On 4 December 1941 Nos 45 Squadron RAF and the Free French 'Lorraine' Squadron, both flying Blenheim IVs, were based at opposite ends of LG75 airfield. The 'Lorraine' squadron had only arrived in Egypt on 5 November from Iraq, though it had seen previous operations in Libya, and recommenced sorties in North Africa on 21 November. On 4 December a Lysander crew reported sighting an enemy convoy of cars, trailers, and self-propelled artillery crawling along the coastal road, and the Blenheims were quickly briefed for an attack on this inviting target.

A total of 39 aircraft were detailed for the operation and, unbeknown to each other, the first Vics of three Blenheims of both 45 and the Free French squadrons commenced take-off in close formation from opposite ends of Gambut, neither able to see the other due to a wide hump in the centre of the airfield. Despite frantic waving and other attempts by personnel on the ground at the side of the LG, both squadrons' leading Vics of three Blenheims reached airborne speed as they came from opposite directions over the field's hump, heading nose-on at each other.

Time was not available for conscious thought, only instinctive reaction as each pilot suddenly realised the situation. The leading French pilot, Charbonneaux, slid only inches beneath the 45 Squadron leading Blenheim, losing his aerial as this was chopped off. The No 2s clipped wing-tips and staggered on but the French aircraft exploded into the ground 200 yards further on, scattering metal and human remains over a wide area. The third pair of Blenheims met head-on when only six feet off the ground. The French pilot, Sergeant Fifre, was crushed and died two hours later, his Observer, de Maismont, received severe injuries leaving him in a coma for two days but eventually recovering. The wireless operator/AG, Soulat, was trapped in a fuselage resembling a semi-closed concertina and ground crews had to axe him out of his near-coffin. After only a few days' convalescence in Alexandria, however, Soulat was declared fit enough to return to his unit. A young pilot, Arnaud, was sent to fetch him in a Bloch light 'hack' aircraft, but on the return trip they passed over a Free French Army camp and, in a burst of patriotic zeal, young Arnaud decided to salute his compatriots with a deck-level beat-up. As the Bloch swept across the waving infantry Arnaud's judgment of height proved at fault, his slipstream collapsed a large tent, a wing grazed a lorry, and the aircraft ploughed a long furrow in the sand, virtually demolishing itself in the process. Both men were able to walk away from the crash, but Arnaud then found himself having to explain why he had blown down General Koenig's private accommodation! Wisely, perhaps, Soulat decided to complete his journey by road ...

De Maismont took some eight months to recover fully from his injuries but rejoined the 'Lorraine' squadron in 1944, by which time the unit was based in England as part of No 2 Group, RAF, only to be killed shortly after D-Day when flying back to his beloved France.

By virtue of the longer range of operations flown by the bomber crews, any mishap _ whether due to enemy action or sheer technical troubles – meant landing deep inside enemy-held territories, and, *if*

(*Right*) Free Frenchman. Insigne (Cross of Lorraine) on the original Free French 'Lorraine Squadron' Blenheim IV aircraft

(*Centre*) Blenheim IV, N3622 of the 'Lorraine Squadron' about to take off

(*Bottom*) Free French pilot and his wrecked 'steed'

the crew survived the landing, a seemingly impossible task of regaining the Allied lines. By October 1942 Rommel's armies had reoccupied virtually the whole of North Africa and were facing the Allies inside the Egyptian border, leaving any crashed air crews many hundreds of miles of desert between themselves and 'friendly' land. On 8 October 1942 Wellington DV504, 'G' of No 40 Squadron RAF left its base at Kabrit, alongside the Suez Canal, bound for Tobruk on a bombing sortie. At the controls was Flight Sergeant 'Bob' Spence RCAF whose crew included an Australian and several Britishers, and he arrived over the target shortly before 3 am. As Spence made his bombing run fierce flak began straddling his Wimpy and seconds after releasing his bombs one engine was hit, erupting in flames, followed by its propeller wrenching itself away into space. As the Wellington fell, the flames spreading rapidly across its fabric-skinned wings, Spence gave his crew the order to abandon, and all six men apparently escaped by parachute; apparently, because Spence met only three others near the wreckage of his aircraft shortly after and never knew the fates of the other two.

At dawn the four men took stock of their situation. Apart from a sprained ankle sustained by the rear AG, Sergeant A.W. Butteriss, Spence, his Wireless Operator, Sergeant J.K. Wood, RAAF, and another air gunner, Sergeant E.A. Linforth, were all uninjured, though two had very slight leg strain from their parachute landings. As far as they could calculate, the nearest Allied line was at least 300 miles to the east but if they were to avoid capture they would need to detour southwards first, adding probably a further 50-odd miles onto the trek. Gathering all possible sustenance from the aircraft wreckage they counted three full water-bottles, six tins of bully beef, 16 small packets of biscuits, some milk tablets, chocolate, chewing gum, a little packet of toffee, some benzedrine tablets, matches, and four tiny compasses. Figuring that it would take 20 days to reach the Allied lines, they set out at dawn that morning and kept walking until 4 pm, finding a rain-filled cairn en route and an abandoned two-gallon can which they filled with the rainwater, then each dined on two milk tablets and slept.

On the second day they walked south-east and made camp at 6 pm beside a water-hole, where they met six Hindus who had escaped from Tobruk, were well-provisioned with food and water, and intended walking south, so Spence gave them one of the compasses. By the fourth day both air gunners were suffering from strained ankles and feet, having only their flying boots, and on the sixth day (having walked all through the previous night) Sergeant Butteris could not carry on, being very weak from his exertions trying to keep up with the others with a greatly swollen ankle. By then the party was near the coastline, so Spence arranged to leave Butteriss where he was, giving him two bottles of water and some chocolate, then the remaining trio set off again south-eastwards walking through the cool of night.*

By the evening of the eighth day the other gunner, Linforth, could not go any further, having almost crippled his feet walking so long on loose rock in his clumsy flying boots. Spence and Wood gave Linforth water, chocolate, milk tablets and some chewing gum, figuring he was about a day or so from the coast where he could be picked up and tended to, and then took stock of their remaining rations – four tins of bully, three tins of chocolate, about 16 biscuits and 20 milk tablets, three full waterbottles and a can of about $1\frac{1}{2}$ gallons of the precious liquid. Still calculating 20 days to complete the overall journey, with eight days already gone, they agreed to stretch one tin of bully to last the pair of them three days with sparing use of water.

Forty-eight hours later they had to seek shelter in an old tomb as a fierce sandstorm raged around them, while on the twelfth day they met two nomadic Arabs driving a herd of camels to the Siwa Oasis, and bought three pints of water and two handful of dates from these men with the only money in their pockets, 45 piastres (*45p in modern English currency*).

By the 14th day both men's RAF issue shoes were in a dilapidated condition, and soles had to be secured to the uppers with twisted wire, which soon cut into the hikers' feet, and next day, on reaching the cliff-edge of the Qattara Depression, they ruined their footwear in scrambling down the cliff-face to the hot, salt marsh land in the valley. The next three days passed in a scorching heat and the agony of walking along the undulating salt crags, and by the eighteenth day sheer exhaustion, lack of food, and dwindling water rations had

---

* Both Butteriss and Linforth were captured shortly after.

begun to make sleep impossible for both men, but towards dusk that day they met three Bedouins driving camels, and the Arabs made them two rounds of a local bread called 'grassa' which, though giving Spence and Wood agonising indigestion, they swallowed 'to the last morsel' (*sic*).

Setting out again that night they found themselves walking on soft salt, making very heavy going and only permitting them to cover at most 15 miles per night, apart from the added physical strain on their weary legs. Despite the strict rationing schedule they had set themselves, their meagre food supply finally ran out on the twentieth day, and water was now reduced to two full waterbottles, but that evening they were given a handful of dates and some salty water by five Bedouins driving a herd of 70 camels. With the daytime temperature now easing a little, they decided to walk a few miles by day as well as night, and on the twenty-first day of their walk encountered two Bedouins grazing camels who fed the travellers with rice and water-diluted camel's milk. Next day they came across an Arab encampment where they were treated to a 'meal' of dates, rice, oil, and salty water, but their physical condition was by then very weak.

Finally, on 2 November, the twenty-fourth day, Spence and Wood heard the sound of an engine, a motor lorry, which eventually appeared over the brow of a nearby hill. It belonged to an advance Allied armoured division and picked up the two airmen a few miles north of El Maghra. Wood was later commissioned, while Spence was awarded a DFM. Both men epitomised the motto of the Late Arrivals Club – 'It's never too late to come back' – and joined that Club's membership which, by the close of 1942, already numbered 345 hikers who had refused to surrender to man or nature.

That the desert could be an implacable killer was borne out only too tragically in May 1942. No 15 Squadron SAAF, a Blenheim IVF unit based at Amriya, sent three of its aircraft on detachment to the Kufra Oasis, some 550 miles south of Gazala, just prior to the Gazala battle as a 'precautionary' measure to deny Kufra as a likely base of operations against Egypt by the Afrika Korps. Three Blenheim IVFs, specially modified to carry a forward-firing, fixed 20 mm Hispano cannon in the starboard nose section, were flown into Kufra on 28 April 1942 by the detachment commander Major J.L.V.

de Wet and Second-Lieutenant L.T.H. Wessels and J.H. Pienaar. Their nearest supply base was Wadi Halfa, some 650 land miles away, and de Wet had been advised to restrict flying to one operational sortie per day, if possible, to conserve fuel and maintenance.

On 3 May he briefed his three crews (each of four men) for a 'practice flight' locally of 281 miles round-trip. Next day all three Blenheims took off, led by de Wet in Blenheim Z7513, with four days' rations and water aboard, but de Wet had already set a pattern for the ensuing tragedy, when he refused a weather balloon test for calculating wind strength and direction, and shortly after the trio left Kufra the only available forecast, on which the air crews were relying, proved false when the wind strength increased and its direction was 65 degrees different to that forecast. Though two ground posts at Rebiama and Bzema – 83 and 134 miles away – had been warned to expect sight of the Blenheims, and therefore not to fire at them*, neither ground station saw or heard the Blenheims, despite excellent visibility conditions in their areas.

Major de Wet soon became hopelessly lost, due to adhering to the false forecast of the wind and hence incorrect course, and told his wireless operator to contact the direction-finding station for a fix and course to steer. The DF station sent back a snap bearing '120-3=0527' – meaning 'Steer 120 degrees (zero wind), 3rd Class Fix, time 0527 hrs GMT', but de Wet's operator only recorded the figures 3, 0, and 5 – and de Wet promptly altered his course to 305 degrees! After an unrecorded spell of time he then turned and flew a reciprocal course of 125 degrees, but at about 9 am one Blenheim's engine started cutting so de Wet ordered all three aircraft to be landed in the open desert. On crosschecking it was found that none of the navigators had made any record of the flight as yet. Two exploratory flights by De Wet and Wessels proved fruitless and both rejoined the others. Fuel was transferred from the engine-defect Blenheim to the other two aircraft and a third flight undertaken of only 43 miles, again to no avail in spotting any form of landmark though its radio operator managed to send out calls on the D/F frequency.

* Aircraft recognition training was virtually non-existent then, and in any case Blenheims resembled Junkers Ju88s to the untutored eye.

Meantime Major de Wet failed to give any orders for conserving the water stock and the crews used most of this merely to keep cool in the blistering heat, while no attempt was made to lay out air recognition strips or to make a petrol/sand fire to attract attention. Back at Kufra a request was sent to No 203 Group HQ for search aircraft to find the now over-due Blenheims at 1 pm. Group HQ agreed, detailing a Blenheim and a Bristol Bombay transport for the task, to be flown up next morning – but neither reached Kufra due to unserviceability of the Blenheim, and a breakdown in communications regarding the Bombay which, unaware it was needed, left Wadi Halfa on a previously scheduled flight to Khartoum instead.

On the morning of 5 May de Wet had all remaining petrol put in Blenheim Z75513 and Second-Lieutenant Pienaar set off for another attempt to find Kufra – but never returned. That night de Wet's men with the two useless Blenheims fired Very Lights and fired bursts from the gun turrets, and next morning (6 May) the last of the water was issued, one bottle per man. By then all were tormented by thirst and when the water had been drunk, turned to drinking oil from some tins of sardines and the sweet syrup-juice from some tinned fruit. By now HQ Middle East had ordered three Bombays of No 216 Squadron RAF at Khanka to fly to Kufra, and sent a senior officer from Khartoum to meet these at Wadi Halfa and organise the projected search. The latter's aircraft force-landed en route and he completed the journey by goods train, arriving at Wadi Halfa too late to meet the Bombays, one of which had in any case returned to its own base with engine troubles. In the interim a ground search party set out from Kufra to a point 60-odd miles away, based on a faint and brief signal received on 4 May (which may or may not have been from the stranded Blenheims), but by night this patrol had failed to sight anything.

Even as these measures were proceeding de Wet and his party were in a parlous state, and the crews began playing aircraft fire extinguishers' fluid on their bodies to cool off – only to have their flesh break out in blisters which soon became open running sores. Attempted first aid with gentian-violet, then morphia, did little to relieve their agony as the ultra-hot sun bore down. In a torment of thirst the men began drinking alcohol from the aircraft instruments,

(*t*) Wing Commander Hugh
olm, OC 18 Sqn who was killed on
cember 1942 leading an
corted low-level raid, and was
umously awarded a Victoria Cross

(*w*) Blenheim V, BA727, of 114 Sqn
nrobert, December 1942

compass and bombsight fluid, and were soon showing signs of temporary madness as a result, even trying to shoot each other. One man in fact shot himself, while two others then died in their extremis.

A violent sandstorm adding to the stranded crews' problems also created chaos elsewhere, blanking out Kufra and causing the two search Bombay aircraft to overfly the oasis and make a forced landing 40 miles away, where they too became stranded; while the ground search party struggled manfully across broken desert to within five miles of the 'fix' position they had set out to reach originally but could get no further. Next morning (7 May) the Kufra garrison commander sent out a second ground search party, despite the sandstorm having reduced visibility to barely 100 yards. That day Major de Wet recorded in a daily-kept diary: 'We expect to be all gone today. Death will be welcome – we went through Hell'. The stranded Bombays could not take off all that day, and indeed next day, being too low on fuel for any protracted air-search, flew back to Wadi Halfa for batteries' recharging. As the Bombays made their way back to base on 8 May, Major de Wet wrote his final lucid diary note: 'It is the fifth day, second without water, and fifth in a temperature well over 100, but "Thy Will be done, O Lord" ....'

Meanwhile the ground parties had come within two miles of the de Wet party and three miles from Pienaar's Blenheim, though they were still unaware of this. Wellingtons of No 162 Squadron at Bilbeis had been detailed to join the search, but had been delayed for two days with engine problems, and even when they finally set out for Kufra the first could not locate the oasis, having been given an incorrect call-sign for Kufra's D/F station ...

Finally on 9 May, after a 5½ hours' search, Squadron Leader D.G. Warren found the Blenheim last flown by Pienaar. Its crew were all dead, lying in the shade of its wings, the aircraft fuel tanks were dry, and examination of the instruments *et al* showed that its engines had been overboosted. A doctor's examination concluded all had died from thirst the previous day. On board were no navigator's logs, only a map and a hand sketch, and on 11 May Warren returned to Pienaar's Blenheim's location, then set course from the map and sketch, and only 24 miles away spotted the other two Blenheims, nose to nose in the shade of a small hill, with a parachute draped over a nearby hummock. As he flew over these a lone figure was seen struggling to lay out a ground strip – Air Mechanic N. Juul, the sole survivor.

The subsequent Court of Inquiry laid most blame on the inexperience of the crews in desert flying conditions, poor air crew efficiency, and above all the crews' overt ignorance of desert survival techniques. The final irony of this tragic 'incident' was Major de Wet's nickname, *'Jannie sonder koers'* ('Off-course Johnnie') – given him since the occasion when as a Captain serving with No 11 Squadron SAAF during August 1940 he had led four Fairey Battles on a bombing sortie, had his aircraft instruments smashed by an attacking Fiat CR42 and Italian flak, and had led his men off-course deep into Abyssinia and Italian territory before realising his error and leading them back to Lokitaung, crashing his own Battle on landing.

For the first two years of the desert air war the Allied bomber force relied exclusively on twin-engined stalwarts such as the Blenheim, Maryland, Boston, and, especially the Wellington, but by the spring of 1942 the need for heavier, longer-range bombers had become paramount, and a request for heavy bombers sent to Winston Churchill was agreed by late June, and two squadrons of Halifaxes, Nos 10 and 76 RAF, were ordered to fly to Aqir, Palestine under a strict cloak of secrecy. These began arriving almost individually in early July and were to form No 249 Wing of No 205 Group, and commenced operations on 11/12 July when a single Halifax of 10 Squadron attacked Tobruk.

Two nights later four Halifaxes of 10 Squadron set out for the same target but Pilot Officer Drake's W1171 was badly damaged by flak over the target and crashlanded at Almaza, near Cairo on return, his aircraft being burnt out and several Egyptian firemen being killed when a bomb exploded in the wreckage. No 76 Squadron suffered its first loss on operations shortly after when W7762, 'D' was hit by flak and eventually crashed near LG09, though without any crew casualties. The first few months of Halifax operations, mainly against Tobruk and similar priority objectives, produced a long list of purely technical problems for the ground maintenance crews, particularly with engines overheating, hydraulic oil leaking, and insufficient (as yet) stocks of spares to replace

Heavy stuff. Liberator II,
AL566 of 108 Sqn at Fayid,
Egypt in March 1942

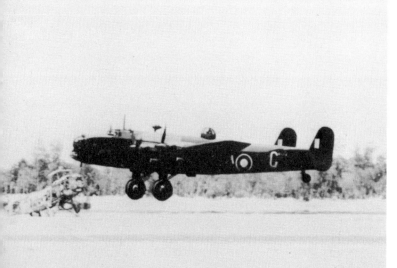

Halifax W1174, ZA-G, of
No. 10 Sqn RAF

Halifaxes of 462 Sqn RAAF at
Messina, August 1943

recalcitrant items. Nevertheless, operations continued sporadically with occasional losses to flak damage or engine failures resulting in aircraft being ditched in the Mediterranean.

On 5 September 1942 No 249 Wing was ordered to mount a raid on Heraklion aerodrome, Crete, a Luftwaffe base used heavily by transport aircraft supplying Rommel's forces in North Africa, and Nos 10 and 76 Squadrons were initially required to despatch six Halifaxes each. The continuing saga of technical problems caused three of the projected twelve-aircraft formation to abort the operation before or shortly after take-off, while a fourth jettisoned its bomb load and returned to base with engine failure trouble before the formation reached its target. The remaining eight crews, flying in three sections, approached Heraklion and commenced a straight and level bombing run across the crowded airfield. The leading section of three aircraft from 76 Squadron saw their bombs burst among the many dispersed German aircraft, crater the runways, and cause several fires in the airfield zone.

Following in at 9,000 feet, the second section, comprised of two Halifaxes (one each from 10 and 76 Squadrons), ran head-on into a fierce flak storm from the now-alert ground defences and Flight Lieutenant J. Bryan's aircraft (W1114,'Q') became an immediate victim, spiralling down in flames, with only two of its crew managing to take to parachutes. His companion, Wing Commander Seymore-Price, OC 10 Squadron, flying W1174,'G', released his bomb load on target but was immediately attacked by two Bf109s from the Crete *Schwarm* of III/JG27.

Their first attack sliced open the Halifax's wing between its starboard engines and punctured the airframe in a dozen places, while the continuing flak slashed both the tail wheel and starboard main wheel, ripped chunks out of the fuselage, and ruptured the main hydraulics leaving the pilot without flaps or control of the gaping bomb bay doors. Successfully evading two more attacks by the Bf109s, Seymore-Price nursed his Halifax back for a safe landing at Fayid, Egypt.

As the third section of three Halifaxes made their bomb-run, the leading aircraft, W7679,'C' of 10 Squadron, piloted by the veteran Squadron Leader Hacking, was attacked by the Bf109 of Feldwebel Liebhold of III/JG27 whose cannon shells set its starboard outer engine on fire as the Halifax finished its bombing run. The bomber banked, fire spread along its wing, and it eventually crashed south-east of Castelli Padiada, though several parachutes were seen in its wake. Both the remaining Halifaxes sustained flak damage and hits from the defending Messerschmitts but eventually returned to base safely.

Though nominally titled Nos 10 and 76 Squadrons, both Halifax units were in fact only detachments from those units whose main formations were still UK-based, and on 6 September 1942 orders were received from 205 Group HQ for these two detachments to be amalgamated and thereby form a fresh unit, No 462 Squadron RAAF, with Wing Commander D.O. Young, DSO, DFC, AFC as its appointed commander, but still based at Fayid, alongside the Suez Canal in Egypt. The decision to title 462 as a unit of the Royal Australian Air Force seemed to those on the squadron puzzling, to say the least; all its ground crews and all but one of its air crew personnel at that time were *non*-Australian!* For the following eight months No 462 plodded on as the sole Halifax squadron operating regularly from Egypt and points west as the Allies advanced from El Alamein.

On 10 October the Halifax crews returned to one of their early targets, Crete, and on that day Squadron Leader P. Warner's aircraft (W1183,'M') was hit by flak over the objective; a 'near-miss' which put both outboard engines out of action as the burst shattered the aircraft's nose, severing all electrical services in the forward fuselage. The navigator, Flight Lieutenant F. Collins, was seriously wounded by shell splinters but remained at his post and received first aid treatment *in situ*. The Halifax lost altitude immediately and continued down to 1,100 feet before the bombs in the belly bay were finally hand-released, while Warner contrived to put some life back into the port outer engine. The crew then began throwing overboard every piece of unwanted equipment not bolted down to help lighten ship as Warner struggled to keep the aircraft airborne despite the dead weight of the still-loaded wing bomb racks. Height continued to be lost, though only shallowly, and Warner finally succeeded in making a safe forced landing some twelve miles from

* Paradoxically, when 462 Squadron was retitled as No 614 Squadron RAF on 3 March 1944, its complement of Australian personnel was at its highest quantity ever ...

Dikirnes without further crew injuries. For his courage and devotion to duty the navigator, Collins, received an immediate DSO award.

In the prelude to Montgomery's Alamein offensive 462's crews amassed a total of 183 sorties against Tobruk alone between 6 September and 24 October, and thereafter concentrated on direct tactical support for the Eighth Army with night raids against enemy transport concentrations and airfields. On these latter sorties the Halifax crews became virtual ground-strafers, bombing from as low as 1,200 feet eventually until mid-December 1942. Then, after a non-operational 'pause' to replace the tour-expired air crews – almost 90 per cent of its aircrew strength – 462 resumed operations, this time concentrating heavily on targets in Sicily from 29 January 1943. The ever-present problems of engine failures continued to plague the maintenance crews until, in April, two-thirds of the unit's aircraft were returned to No 61 Repair & Salvage Unit (RSU) to await new motors. At that time, in an attempt to ease the strain on Halifax engines, nose and mid-upper gun turrets were generally removed.

In late May a second Halifax unit appeared alongside 462 when No 178 Squadron, based at Hosc Raui, began exchanging its B-24 Liberators for Halifaxes, and despatched its first Halifax sorties – two aircraft – on the night of 31 May 1943, alongside six of its Liberators. No 462 Squadron moved to the same base by the end of May but by then the North African campaign had ceased in Tunisia, and the squadron spent the remaining war years heavily engaged in the conquering of Italy, having changed its unit number to 614 Squadron and shortly thereafter becoming No 205 Group's 'target marking force' – or 'Path Finders', and flying its ultimate Halifax war sortie on 3 March 1945.

CHAPTER FIFTEEN

Beau Men

In May 1941 the Middle East RAF received its first Bristol Beaufighter units, Nos 252 and 272 Squadrons, which initially staged via Gibraltar to Malta. By early June Beaufighters of 272 Squadron had begun a few offensive operations from Egypt, being based at Edku, some 25 miles east of Alexandria. Thus the 'mighty Beau' entered the lists in North Africa. From then until the end of the Mediterranean war Beaufighter crews were to wreak great havoc and destruction among the land, sea, and air forces of the Axis 'partners', both by day and by night. With its four 20 mm Hispano cannon in the belly and up to six 0.303-inch calibre Browning machine guns in the wings, the Beau was the RAF's heaviest-armed fighter of the 1939-45 war; while its ability to carry additional under-wing 3-inch rocket projectiles (RP), bombs, torpedoes, or long-range fuel drop-tanks, gave the Beau a versatility in operational roles denied to virtually all its contemporaries.

Moreover, the design's rugged construction could absorb astonishing amounts of damage and still deliver a live crew from any potentially disastrous crashlanding; an asset which gave the Beau crews utter confidence in their warhorse in almost every circumstance. Admittedly Beaufighters were heavy, requiring no small amount of physical strength to execute violent manoeuvres in any emergency, but once familiar with the Beau's idiosyncrasies most pilots swore by the aircraft.

Though the Beau's particular *forte* in the Middle East was low – *very* low – strikes against land and shipping targets, its performance in the air against the Luftwaffe and/or Regia Aeronautica proved equally doughty, and no few Beaufighter pilots accumulated impressive aerial combat kill tallies over the desert and Mediterranean Sea. Probably the most successful, certainly one of the greatest Beaufighter pilots in this context was Wing Commander

John Kenneth Buchanan. A native of Southsea, 'Buck' Buchanan joined the RAF with a Short Service Commission on 3 May 1937, and after training at No 8 FTS, Montrose was posted to No 101 Squadron at Bicester on 27 November 1937 to pilot lumbering Boulton Paul Overstrand bombers, though in June 1938 the unit replaced these with Blenheim Is. Buchanan was to remain a bomber pilot during the following four years, being posted to the Middle East and gaining a DFC in July 1940.

By November 1941 he had become commander of No 14 Squadron, succeeding Wing Commander Deryck Stapleton (later, AVM, CB, CBE, DFC, AFC), flying Blenheim IVs from LG75 and Gambut. By then he had already gained a considerable reputation in Middle East RAF bomber circles as an adventurous, even cavalier pilot, yet never foolhardy. His constant interest in and obvious love of flying were exemplified by his mounting total of operational sorties flown, apart from seizing every opportunity to be airborne between sorties on training flights, testing flips, or simply 'to keep my hand in' (*sic*).

His appearance, in view of his high reputation, was highly misleading to newcomers. Of slender build – to quote one pilot's description, 'a figure like a girl's ...' – 'Buck' was always immaculately turned out, no matter what form of dress or uniform, with carefully combed hair and a neat Ronald Colman moustache. To his ever-neat appearance he added a coolly 'English' Oxford accent and almost affected gestures when discussing any subject, yet beneath this studied, near-effeminate pose Buchanan's natural authority and leadership qualities soon emerged when the occasion demanded. His quiet self-confidence and instinctive charm obviously captivated Morley Lister, the female American war correspondent from *Life* magazine, when she visited Gambut on 13 January 1942. During the next ten days she accompanied Buchanan on at least two bombing sorties, before a shocked Cairo-based superior *ordered* her to return from her unauthorised flights over enemy territory.

In May 1942, with a total of some 230 operational sorties already recorded in his log books, Buchanan was posted to an HQ staff job and shortly after was awarded a Bar to his DFC, its citation mentioning his keenness for operational work as 'outstanding, no task being too arduous or too hazardous. Throughout he has displayed courage, initiative and tremendous enthusiasm'. Buchanan accepted his enforced rest with great reluctance and spent the six months he was to endure in a chairborne capacity constantly harassing his superiors for an active post.

His wish was finally granted in November 1942 when he was sent to Malta to take up an appointment as commander of No 272 Squadron at Ta Kali airfield. His arrival on the squadron typified Buchanan's quiet, unflurried approach to all situations. Attaching himself to the next unit operation, Buchanan told his crews, 'I have only flown a Beaufighter once in my life but I shall do my best to learn quickly'.

How quickly he learned soon became evident when, on 21 November during a sweep over Sfax and Gabes, he attacked a Heinkel He115 floatplane near Linosa Island. Firing just one crisp burst of 20mm cannon he sent the He115 down in flames into the sea. Next day Buchanan and one of his pilots discovered a lone Cant Z506b en route to Tunisia. Buchanan ordered his No 2 to attack while he deliberately flew to one side of the Cant to attract the Italians' attention away from the second Beaufighter. His No 2 made one pass, then Buchanan closed on its tail and shot it straight into the waves. Shortly after the two Beaufighters met a four-engined Junkers Ju90 transport and in turn attacked the unwieldy aircraft, knocking pieces of metal off it. Buchanan's voice then came over the R/T, cool and drawling, 'My guns have jammed … very thoughtless of them' …

Three days later, on 24 November, Buchanan led four of 272's Beaufighters off shortly before 8 am to scour the Gulf of Tripoli for Axis aircraft attempting to supply Rommel's Afrika Korps. Two hours later a Junkers Ju52 was spotted some 40 miles from Linosa and Buchanan carried out an astern attack, his shells causing the Ju's starboard engine to erupt in flames before the tri-motored transport curved down to crash. As Buchanan swept low over the wreckage he saw about ten surviving passengers swimming in the sea.

On 26 November Buchanan was again airborne early, leading three pairs of Beaus off minutes before 8 am to patrol the Gulf of Tripoli. Just east of Pantellaria two hours later a Ju52 flew overhead,

14 Sqn crew (Blenheim) at Gambut, January 1942. Centre is Wg Cdr J.K. Buchanan,
DSO, DFC

'Buck' Buchanan (rt) talking to a *Daily Mail* war correspondent on return from a
Beaufighter sortie, 30 January 1943

obviously heading for that island, and Buchanan immediately climbed in pursuit. Closing on its tail as it neared the coast he fired one sustained burst, shattering the Ju's starboard engine and sending it down to explode on impact with the sea. Next morning Buchanan and his wingman were sweeping the Zarzis-Cap Bon area and spotted a pair of Messerschmitt Bf110s about 20 miles south-east of Zarzis flying low at 1000 feet. Attacking one of these from below and astern, Buchanan saw pieces flying off its starboard wing before it dived to sea level and fled southwards. One Bf110 then attacked Buchanan in a series of frontal quarter onslaughts lasting some 15 minutes before breaking away with Buchanan in pursuit and eventually being shot down.

On his second sortie of the same day Buchanan attacked a Ju88 near Cap Bon. His first stern attack produced no visible result but the Ju's rear gunner's fire hit the Beaufighter's port engine. Closing to 75 yards' range Buchanan poured a long burst into the Junkers' starboard wing and engine, watched it spin down into the sea in flames, then nursed his crippled Beaufighter back for a safe landing at Ta Kali.

Buchanan's daily scoring continued on 28 November. During a morning sortie he spotted a Savoia-Marchetti SM79 flying low over the sea and dived to carry out his customary astern attack, his fire causing the Italian's starboard engine to burst into flames before it fell into the sea and quickly sank. Climbing away Buchanan saw a large formation comprised of some 60 Ju52s with Bf109 escorts and decided discretion was the better part of valour for a lone Beaufighter in the circumstances, but shortly after he came across an SM81 off Cap Bon and immediately bore in for a kill, only to be driven off by a determined Macchi 202 fighter. Later that day 272 Squadron switched to ground-strafing attacks on airfields and vehicles in the Tripolitanian zone and a particularly successful strike against the enemy seaplane base at Bon Chemmakh despite fierce flak opposition from the base defences. This latter base was again the Beaus' target early next morning with Buchanan destroying one of four moored Cant Z506bs which sank and riddled the other three.

December 1942 began with a determined German offensive in the Tebourba area, causing the Allied First Army to withdraw. RAF activities concentrated on opposing this 'push' despite appalling weather conditions of heavy rain which reduced most Allied airstrips to bogged mud, while the Malta-based units maintained their scouring patrols of the Mediterranean seeking Axis resupply aircraft. On 9 December Buchanan was leading four Beaufighters at low-level in the Lampedusa area when at least 30 Ju52 transports, escorted by two Bf110s and a pair of Ju88s, were seen. Buchanan led his men in a head-on attack, his cannons knocking chunks of metal off one Ju52 before a Bf110 fastened on his tail and damaged his Beaufighter. Shaking off the Bf110 Buchanan again attacked a Ju52 from astern, chewing pieces out of its wings and fuselage, only to be jumped again, this time by the two Ju88s. This pair chased him for some ten minutes, their fire causing yet more damage to Buchanan's aircraft before he was able to outrun them and return to base.

Within 48 hours of that narrow escape from destruction, Buchanan extracted 'revenge' when, in the early morning of 11 December, he led six Beaufighters, accompanied by eight Spitfires from 249 Squadron, to sweep Pantellaria-Lampion-Kirkenna and eventually encountered 32 Ju52s with at least five escorts near Lampion. While the Spitfires tackled the enemy escorts, Buchanan led his Beaus into the gaggle of Ju52s, personally shooting one into the sea and creating severe damage to two others. The other Beaus and the Spitfires soon claimed a further eleven destroyed, one probable, and three damaged, but lost one Beaufighter.

On 14 December Buchanan again co-operated alongside 249 Squadron, flying his lone Beaufighter at the head of five Spitfires over the Lampedusa area in the mid-morning and attacking a Ju88 of II/KG30 which was finally destroyed by the Spitfires, due to Buchanan's cannons jamming. Three hours later he left Malta again, with four of 249's Spitfires, and shared in shooting down a second Ju88 from II/KG30 west of Lampedusa which flamed and spun to a watery grave. This daily routine of patrols off Tunisia and North Africa continued apace, with the Malta squadrons flying two, sometimes three sorties per man each day, with increasingly fruitful results. December 19 saw Buchanan take off with one other Beau crew* and four 249 Squadron Spitfires for an offensive patrol at 0840 hours, and just after 11 am a Dornier Do24 flying boat and a

---

* Crewed by Sergeants H.F.M. Pien and R.W. Lane (Nav).

Ju88 were engaged near Delimara; the flying boat being quickly shot down by a Spitfire. Seconds later Buchanan saw his companion Beaufighter explode into the sea and joined with two Spitfires in destroying its victor, the Ju88 from III/KG76.

Sunday, 27 December, brought a VIP flight for Buchanan when he took off from Malta to escort a second Beau from 272 Squadron which had on board Air Vice Marshal K.R. Palmer for a flight to Egypt. En route their flight path was crossed by two Focke Wulf Fw200 four-engined aircraft and Buchanan instantly swung into attack on these. Making four attacks on one Fw200 Buchanan's aircraft was damaged by return fire, though he had at least damaged its port outer engine before being forced to break off. The second Beau also attacked, only to be similarly damaged by Fw200 gunners, and both Beaufighters returned to Malta. Two days later Buchanan, at the head of four Beaus and four Spitfires, trapped a Ju88 of II/KG54 near Pantellaria and shot it down, three of its crew taking to parachutes.

His aggressive leadership of 272 Squadron brought Buchanan the award of a DSO in January 1943, and within the next four months he added four more enemy aircraft destroyed or damaged to his tally before, in June, handing over his command to Wing Commander W.A. Wild. Never content with staff paperwork, Buchanan soon returned to the operational scene when, in October 1943, he was appointed CO of No 227 Squadron, another Beaufighter unit, based then at Nicosia, Cyprus and later Berka 3 airfield. 227's prime roles were anti-shipping strikes and convoy protection in the Aegean theatre of war, and it was while returning from one such sortie several weeks later that Buchanan had to ditch his flak-damaged Beaufighter in the sea. He and his navigator were seen to get aboard their dinghy safely but subsequent air searches failed to relocate them until days later, by which time 'Buck' Buchanan had died of exposure and thirst.

The report of his death in such tragic circumstances deeply affected many of the men who had flown with him over previous years. As one contemporary said of him:

Buck, had he lived in another era, would have been a buccaneer by natural inclination and character. His dandyish outward

hter pilots on Malta,
luding Wg Cdr J.K.
:hanan (centre) and M.M.
:phens, DSO, DFC (in white
:rall). Behind is the personal
itfire of Wg Cdr P.P.
osser' Hanks, DFC and
:hanan's usual Beaufighter

o of Beaufighters about to
ave on a strafing search

:au men of 600 Sqn. From
Des Hughes; Reg Gillies;
:wton

appearance belied his courage and dash, because he had the guts of a lion when the chips were down. He was one of very few men whom I've always felt highly privileged to have known.

'Buck' Buchanan's operational record was outstanding by any standards in the context of Beaufighters but he was not alone in establishing a high reputation while flying a 'Bristol Brute'. A contemporary with 272 Squadron, Squadron Leader Anthony Watson, eventually achieved near-equal fame for his exploits in Beaus. An ex-farmer from Surrey, Tony Watson was a Blenheim pilot with No 203 Squadron in May 1941 involved with the Rashid Ali uprising in Iraq which was threatening the RAF station at Habbaniyah. During a bomb attack on Fort Rutbah he saw a fellow Blenheim shot down and, despite nearby rebel armoured cars and troops, coolly landed in open country and retrieved the Blenheim pilot; a feat which brought him a DFC award two months later.

On 8 August 1942, as a Flight Lieutenant, Watson joined 272 Squadron as a Flight commander and quickly demonstrated his skill as a fighting pilot by shooting down an SM81 and then strafing a Fiat CR42 on the ground during an attack on an Italian airfield. On 25 October Watson led eight Beaufighters into an attack on a force of 35 Ju52s with six escorting Bf110s north of Tobruk and personally destroyed two Ju52s, while five days later he was one of five Beau pilots attacking El Adem airfield, destroying two Ju52s on the ground, then shooting down a third Ju52 as it came in to land. While escorting some Beaufort torpedo-bombers on 2 November Watson, by then promoted to Squadron Leader, intercepted and shot down a Ju88 which attempted to interfere.

On 10 November 1942, just 48 hours after the Anglo-American invasion of Oran, Algeria – *Operation Torch* – reconnaissance photos had revealed a force of more than 100 Axis aircraft gathered at El Aouina airfield, just north of Tunis. Nine Beaufighters from Malta-based 272 Squadron took off shortly after 4 pm and swept in at deck-level across El Aouina, creating havoc among the tightly parked aircraft and destroying at least ten apart from damaging a further 16 for certain; Watson's share of the carnage being the total destruction in flames of a Messerschmitt Me323 *'Gigant'* transport of KG.zb.V.323, and damage to two Ju52s. Next day, while patrolling the Cap Bon area Watson joined four other pilots in destroying a Heinkel He115 floatplane over the sea; while on 12 November he was prominent in a mini-massacre of some Italian transport aircraft. On that Thursday he and six other 272 Beaufighters were sweeping the sea between Tunis and Sicily when they spotted six enemy twin-engined aircraft flying northwards near Pantellaria. The engagement was brief, with all six Italian SM75s being shot down; Watson destroying two and sharing a third with a Belgian pilot, Charles Delcour.

Two days later Watson returned to El Aouina at the head of seven Beaufighters of 272 Squadron, only to be greeted by a fierce flak barrage from well-alerted ground defences. Strafing a Ju52 on the ground, Watson's Beaufighter was hit in its starboard engine and he had to force-land on a beach six miles away. Setting fire to his wrecked Beau, Watson and his navigator then set out to walk to the Allied lines and eventually returned safely, becoming the latest members of the 'Late Arrivals Club'. Shortly after Watson was awarded a DSO, its eventual citation quoting him as credited with eleven enemy aircraft destroyed in the air, apart from 'many' more damaged on the ground, and also credited with the sinking of an enemy 'schooner'. On 29 December Watson left 272 Squadron to take over command of No 227 (Beaufighter) Squadron, but his command was destined to be brief, being reported missing after a sortie to Tunis.

Buchanan and Watson were two leading personalities from a host of Beaufighter pilots whose depredations of the Axis forces throughout the Mediterranean struggle played a significant part in the ultimate Allied triumphs. Men like George Tuckwell, a Sergeant pilot with 272 Squadron who accumulated a victory tally of eight destroyed, two probables, and many damaged; or H.H.K. Gunnis, DFC, of 252 Squadron who claimed at least five confirmed combat kills over the desert. In a sense aerial combat victories for the Beaufighter crews who flew day sorties were a bonus in many cases; in that their prime function was tactical and semi-strategic support of the Allied armies by acting as long-range 'artillery'; strafing and bombing enemy road and sea transports, troops, airfields, installations. Naturally, their function overlapped into pure air fighting, as witness the scale of destruction of Axis transport aircraft

(*Left*) Wg Cdr George Stainforth, AFC, OC 89 (Beaufighter) Sqn who died in Beaufighter X7700 on the night of 27/28 September 1942 (*Right*) Sqn Ldr R.M. McKenzie, DSO, DFC, AFC who served with Nos 89, 46, and 227 Squadrons

(*Left*) Wg Cdr C.P. Green, DSO, DFC, OC 600 Sqn AAF watches his navigator Fg Off Reg Gillies, DFC painting up the latest victim tally. (*Right*) Sqn Ldr (later, AVM) F.D. Hughes, DFC of 600 Sqn AAF

plying the routes from Sicily and Italy to Libya, Tripoli, and Tunis, engagements which on occasion amounted to near-massacres of the unwieldy multi-engined Axis machines, their crews, and (often) troop passengers. Such forays added significantly to the deprivation of supplies and reinforcements for Rommel's Afrika Korps and the Luftwaffe and Regia Aeronautica units in North Africa. One sphere of Beaufighter operations was, however, pure air combat – night fighting. From the start of 1942 until the very end of the Mediterranean war nightfighter Beau squadrons established fighting reputations and victory tallies comparable with many day fighter units.

The first radar-equipped nightfighter Beau unit earmarked for Middle East operations was No 89 Squadron, formed at Colerne from 25 September 1941 for that specific purpose, and commanded by Squadron Leader George Stainforth, AFC*. The move to Egypt by air and ground crews was spread over the next three months until all aircraft and crews were finally assembled at Abu Sueir in December. Operations commenced on the night of 3 January 1942 – the squadron's role was defence of the Egyptian Delta area – and the unit's first victory claims were made on the night of 2/3 March when Squadron Leader D.S. Pain and Flying Officer R.C. Fumerton, a Canadian, each claimed a Heinkel He111 destroyed over Alexandria. In February a detachment of 89's Beaus was based at Edku, while at the end of March a second detachment became based on Malta where the squadron's 'score' soon began to escalate. Robert Carl Fumerton – known to all as 'Moose' – was to become 89's highest-scoring nightfighter pilot in the Middle East theatre and, incidentally, the top-scoring Canadian nightfighter pilot of World War Two in the context of enemy aircraft destroyed in aerial combat.

Born in 1913 at Fort Coulonge, Canada, Fumerton joined the RCAF in November 1939. By June 1941 he had joined No 406 Squadron RCAF flying Beaufighter IIs and on the night of 1/2 September 1941, in R2336, scored his, and his squadron's, first night kill, a Ju88 shot down over Bedlington. A week later he

---

* Stainforth, a former RAF High Speed Flight member of Schneider Trophy fame, was killed in action in Beaufighter X7700 on the night of 27/28 September 1942.

claimed an He111 as damaged, but in October joined 89 Squadron as it prepared to move overseas. Re-opening his score on 2/3 March 1942, Fumerton's next victims came on the night of 7/8 April when he shot down two He111s from II/KG26 over the Delta area. Awarded a DFC, he was sent to join the unit's Malta detachment in June and on the 24th destroyed a Ju87 and a Ju88, while five nights later he claimed two more Ju88s destroyed.

On 1 July he added yet another Ju88 to his tally, and within two weeks had claimed two further Ju88s before rejoining 89 Squadron's main party again in Egypt. Here he destroyed a Ju88 over Port Said on 22 July, then returned to Malta in August for 'more action'. He found rather more 'action' than he bargained for, being shot down into the sea on 10 August, but after a safe retrieval he returned the compliment by destroying a Cant Z1007 four nights later. On 27 August he indulged himself with an intrusion sortie over Sicily, destroying a Ju88 on the ground in the process, and in October came off operations temporarily with promotion to Squadron Leader.

By mid-1943 he returned to England, where as a Wing Commander he was appointed OC his old unit, 406 Squadron RCAF on 25 August, and added just one more kill to his score on 14 May 1944. Two months later Fumerton returned to his native Canada.

During 1942-43 several more Beaufighter squadrons joined 89 in nightfighting roles over North Africa, Malta, Sicily, and later Italy and the Aegean zones. One of the most successful of these to operate in the Mediterranean was No 600 Squadron, AAF ('City of London'), arriving initially at Blida, Algeria on 18 November 1942. As one of the UK-based pioneering units for operating AI-equipped Beaufighters, the 'Gallant 600' (its usual soubriquet) had a number of well-experienced crews and opened its North African account on 29 November when Flying Officer Hilken shot down a Cant Z506b during an afternoon recce of Cagliari harbour in Sardinia.

On 7 December the squadron moved base to Maison Blanche where on 26 December it received a new CO, Wing Commander C.P. – 'Paddy' – Green, DFC with his regular navigator Pilot Officer Reg Gillies. Another nightfighter veteran from the UK also joined 600 that month when Squadron Leader Desmond Hughes, DFC arrived on the 19th and took over command of 'B' Flight. Hughes, with his normal navigator Pilot Officer Laurie Dixon, wasted little time in enlarging the squadron's 'game bag'. In the evening of 23 January 1943 they contacted a Ju88 shortly after take-off, closed to 200 yards range, sank a burst into its port wing and engine, and saw it burn down into the sea. Continuing their patrol they found another Ju88 less than 30 minutes later. Closing to short range, Hughes fired one long burst and the Junkers exploded, its debris falling into the sea about a mile off Philippeville's shoreline.

The lethal destructive power of a Beaufighter's 20 mm cannon battery was exemplified in the early hours of 1 May 1943, when a 600 Squadron crew, Flight Sergeant A.B. Downing and his radar operator, Sergeant J. Lyons, shot down five Ju52s in a mere ten minutes of action some 30 miles south of Cagliari; a feat which brought DFM awards for both men shortly after.

By the beginning of June 1943 the squadron had claimed nearly 50 victories since its arrival in North Africa, and on 24 June moved to Luqa, Malta from where it quickly began boosting the unit's bag. On the night of 12/13 July its crews claimed six enemy aircraft shot down, one of these falling to the Green/Gillies duo who repeated their success the following night, then less than 24 hours later returned from a patrol in which they had disposed of four 'bogies' and damaged a fifth. That same night other crews claimed a further four Ju88s destroyed. Double and triple kills were by no means uncommon, as on 11/12 August when Desmond Hughes claimed three victories, Flight Lieutenant Turnbull bagged two, and Paddy Green and Flying Officer Mellersh destroyed one apiece. Hughes received a second Bar to his DFC shortly afterwards while his regular navigator Laurie Dixon added a Bar to his DFC. By then 600 Squadron had moved into Cassabile, Sicily – a move made on 21 July – and continued to find plentiful 'trade' in the night skies, and soon registered its 100th victory when the Downing/Lyons*/team shot down a pair of Ju88s.

After Sicily had been secured by the Allies, invasion of the Italian mainland followed quickly, with 600 Squadron's Beaufighters ever alongside the spearhead invasion forces, often based on the battled

---

* Later, Flying Officer A.B. Downing, DFC, DFM and Pilot Officer J. Lyons, DFC, DFM. Lyons died after baling out into the sea on 1 February 1944.

beachlines. Continuing its progress northwards with the advancing Allied armies throughout 1944 the 'Gallant 600' ended its war at Campoformido in May 1945. Its war tally by then amounted to 165 enemy aircraft destroyed, 13 'probables', and 34 damaged, apart from at least 77 trains, trucks and barges destroyed or badly damaged. Throughout its lengthy period of operating Beaufighters, 600 Squadron had produced a host of outstanding pilots, men like Paddy Green, Desmond Hughes, Alwyn ('Ace') Downing, Angus Horne, Johnny Turnbull, Owen, Jim Bailey, to name simply a few; each of whom had been splendidly teamed with superb navigators and radar operators like Reg Gillies, John Lyons, Laurie Dixon, S.V. McAllister and others who deserved an equal credit for the successes of their 'drivers'. The unit's long list of gallantry awards befitted the nickname 'The Gong Squadron' for the 'Gallant 600'.

The limited space available in any single book such as this precludes adequate mention of the many other equally courageous men who flew Beaufighters by day and/or by night in the Mediterranean skies during the 1940-45 years of conflict. Thus, those mentioned already should be regarded as representatives of that silent majority of Beau men whose contribution to the final Allied victory was both prodigious and significant.

Victim. Junkers Ju52, adapted for degaussing sea mines, about to die

CHAPTER SIXTEEN

Vignettes

Unlike those air crews whose operational flying was (mainly) confined to northern Europe from bases in Britain, where they were ready subjects for media exploitation, the men of the desert air forces were far removed from the limelight of publicity, fighting and – too often – dying in relative obscurity. Their deeds made no immediate impact on the consciousness of the British lay public, for whom the importance of achieving mastery in such foreign countries as Libya, Cyrenaica, Egypt, or Greece was not so overtly evident as the need to ward off Luftwaffe depredations of homes and families on the spot in the United Kingdom. Thus, as far as UK newspapers and other media outlets were concerned, coverage of Fighter and Bomber Commands of the RAF outshone the exploits of crews in the Middle East (and even more so those serving in the Far East) as far as headlines were concerned.

Yet such bias was truly ironic because many desert airmen achieved fighting records and reputations equal to and, often, even greater than many UK-based equivalents. Such reputations were, in no few cases, confined to local campaigns, whereby they rose from virtual initiate to fighting leader solely in the course of the desert air war, and in some instances died tragically at the peak of their esoteric fame. Perhaps the most obvious example of such unknown greats was the South African, Marmaduke St John Pattle, DFC, whose record as a fighter pilot at the moment of his death in action over Greece in 1941 placed him at the head of RAF fighter aces for the entire 1939-45 war.

Another outstanding figure of the desert aerial conflict, who became almost a legend for his courage and 'dash', was Group Captain John – 'Jackie' – Darwen, DSO, DFC. He had joined the RAF in December 1933 as a Cranwell Cadet, and on graduation from the college on 14 December 1935 had been posted first to No 25

Squadron to fly Hawker Fury I fighters. By early 1939 Darwen was serving with No 27 Squadron on the North-West Frontier Province of India (now, Pakistan) piloting Westland Wapitis on the RAF's thankless task of 'air control' duties, and in June that year was promoted to Flight Lieutenant. Returning to England, he was further promoted to Squadron Leader and, in June 1941, became commander of No 152 Squadron, flying Spitfires on (mainly) bomber escort sorties interspersed with assistance to Coastal Command operations around the Western Approaches.

Such routine operations were not to Darwen's personal liking; on the night of 8 March 1941 his wife had been killed in a Luftwaffe bombing raid which destroyed the Café de Paris, London, and Darwen nurtured a deep, uncompromising hatred for all things German thereafter, a private vendetta exemplified in his constant urge to get to grips with the enemy at every opportunity. In pursuit of that singular aim Darwen henceforth showed total disdain for death or hazard on operations, setting a standard of courage hard for his subordinates to follow – as one pilot put it; 'Jackie was never one to hang about when there were Huns to be attacked, and set his own pace leaving the rest of us straining to keep up with him.'

In mid-1942, as a Wing Commander, Darwen arrived in the Middle East Command to become Wing Leader of No 244 Wing and immediately set a fierce pace indeed, constantly spearheading fighter sweeps against German and Italian aircraft and airfields. One such sweep – later to be dubbed 'The Daba Prang' – took place on 9 October 1942 when Darwen led the combined Hurricane strength of Nos 33, 213, 238, and 1 SAAF Squadrons in an attack on the Axis airfield at El Daba. Coming into their target from the nearby sea, the Hurricanes flew south towards the Qattara Depression before turning eastwards towards their objective, then poured across Daba at deck-level in the face of fierce defensive gunfire. In the process Darwen's Hurricane was hit and he hit the ground and crashed after delivering his attack, to be picked up later by a patrol from the 11th Hussars and returned to his base. A few weeks later, following the start of the El Alamein battle, he led No 243 Wing, comprised of Nos 213 and 238 Squadrons, to LG125, an unoccupied landing strip some 140 miles *behind* the German front lines, arriving at the LG early in the morning of 13 November 1942

(*Left*) Group Captain John Darwen, DSO, DFC (*Right*) Flt Lt Neil Cameron who served with 213 Sqn at one period. He rose to become MRAF Lord Cameron, GCB, DSO, DFC

(*Left* Wg Cdr (later, Gp Capt) John Bisdee, DFC (*Right*) Flt Lt J.D. Rae, DFC (Bar), the New Zealand Malta fighter 'ace'

and leaving there on the 16th after destroying more than 300 German road vehicles, 15 enemy aircraft on the ground, and two more in the air.

On 18 February 1943 Darwen finally handed over the command of 244 Wing to the recently-arrived Wing Commander Ian 'Widge' Gleed, DSO, DFC*, but soon continued operations as Wing Leader of No 239 Wing from July 1943, being promoted to Group Captain in the following month. As ever, Darwen's conception of his appointment was to lead the Wing literally, from the cockpit of a fighter, while his unceasing urge to 'get at the Hun' (*sic*) led him to experiment with novel tactics for creating greater destruction of the Axis. One idea he tried was 'skip-bombing' i.e. attacking enemy ships from wave-height broadside-on, and skipping or ricocheting his bombs along the surface of the sea into the ship's side. A few experimental attacks by this method proved unsuccessful and he abandoned the ploy – much to the relief of the pilots who had to follow him, under whom their leader's bombs were prone to detonate!

By August 1943 Darwen's Wing was based in Sicily and on 4 August he tried out yet another tactical innovation. Throughout the day the Wing despatched a total of nine separate missions on various recce and strafing sorties in the Mount Etna region from the Wing base at Agnone. On the last of these Darwen split his eleven Kittyhawks into two parallel line-astern formations in a northerly course over Etna, then on his given command all turned sharply to starboard and, in two line-abreast waves, swooped down to strafe lines of enemy vehicles on the coastal roads, then swept out to sea before the flak defence gunners realised what was happening. At that period Darwen chose principally to fly with No 112 ('Shark') Squadron, selecting Kittyhawk III, FR868, as his personal aircraft and having it painted with his initials 'JD' as its coding. This 'honour' for the squadron, however, added no small measure of extra labours for the unit's Erks; to quote the unit historian:

His aircraft was always rather a problem for 112 Squadron's ground maintenance crews as after every mission they usually had

---

* Wing Commander Ian Richard Gleed, DSO, DFC, was killed in action on 16 April 1943.

to change the guns, as he tended to melt them with the long bursts he gave any German who happened to get into his sights … he invariably collected a bullet or two in return, and his aircraft was rarely undamaged. Once the tips of his propeller blades were bent back, having scraped the *roof* of an enemy truck!*

Nevertheless, Darwen was always concerned with the welfare of his crews, for whom nothing was too much trouble to organise. At the end of August 1943, for example, he gave 112 Squadron's pilots ready permission to go to Catania to 'liberate' three Caproni Ca100 two-seat light biplanes, formerly property of the Catania Flying Club – the Club, in fact, had eight of these aircraft and Darwen's actual words were 'Take the lot!' – with which the pilots amused themselves in off-duty hours, giving the ground crews plentiful joy-rides.

Throughout September 1943 No 239 Wing maintained its offensive against all forms of enemy transports and installations despite often appalling weather conditions. On 7 October 1943 torrential rain storms nullified all air operations during the morning, but in the afternoon No 260 Squadron managed to send off a sortie led by Darwen. As he was flying over Foggia at 8,000 feet a 'stray 80mm flak shell plucked him from the sky' (*sic*) and 'Jackie' Darwen died in the subsequent crash. Three days later all Wing operations were cancelled for the day as most 239 Wing crews and others attended a memorial service for Darwen. His epitaph might well be the words of one of his fellow pilots:

Jackie Darwen's name never appears on any of the published fighter 'aces' lists, yet he was without question one of the RAF's greatest fighter boys. His hatred of the Germans was a byword in Desert Air Force circles and he flew without consideration for personal safety, almost as if he had a death-wish. Yet to follow him was a privilege because he truly inspired his men to their greatest efforts purely by his own example. His death was perhaps inevitable considering his total disregard for danger, but was nevertheless a tragedy, and we deeply mourned his loss.

* *112 Squadron History* by R.A. Brown; Private pub'n, 1960.

A man whose name *is* prominent on any aces list of RAF fighter pilots during World War Two was one of the many hundreds of 'neutral' American citizens who flocked to Britain in the first year of the war to fly and fight in RAF uniform, Lance Wade. A Texan, born in Tucson in 1915, he was the son of a World War One pilot and showed an early interest in aviation by learning to fly in 1933 and then owning his own aircraft three years later. Thus, on arrival in England in December 1940, he could offer the RAF a certain amount of flying experience and, having declined an invitation to join his fellow Americans in forming the first Eagle squadron, Wade was enlisted and given full Service training as a fighter pilot before arriving in Middle East Command in September 1941 to join No 33 Squadron as a newly-commissioned Pilot Officer to fly long-range Hurricanes with this veteran unit.

He soon settled in to the unit's daily operations and first came into prominence on 18 November 1941, the first day of *Operation Crusader*, when 33 Squadron strafed an airfield at El Eng. The Hurricanes were jumped by three Fiat CR42s and Wade destroyed two of these in quick succession, while other pilots sent the third down flaming. Four days later the roles were reversed when 33 Squadron were scrambled to intercept nine Ju88s of II/KLG1 engaged in bombing an Allied landing ground. Diving on the bombers Wade again shot down two in two brief passes. Later the same day he destroyed an Italian SM79 bomber for good measure.

On November 24 he and one companion patrolled the Gialo area in search of Italian aircraft and intercepted an SM79 with several Fiat CR42 fighters in attendance. Tackling the fighters first Wade helped in damaging two Fiats, then dived on the SM79 and shot it into the earth as it attempted to escape at virtual ground-level. Another airfield strafe on 5 December was carried out against Agedabia by six Hurricanes from 33 Squadron, with two more Hurricanes above as top cover. The strike destroyed or damaged at least ten Italian fighters and bombers, including an SM79 attacked by Wade which exploded violently and damaged his Hurricane badly. Struggling to remain airborne, Wade finally accepted defeat and crashlanded some 20 miles east of the airfield, where a fellow squadron pilot, Sergeant (later, Flying Officer) Wooler landed alongside in the desert intending to give Wade a lift back to base. In doing so, however, Wooler's Hurricane broke its tail wheel. Both men set off walking eastwards and were eventually retrieved next day by a Blenheim.

Wade's achievements to date brought him a DFC award on 7 April 1942, its citation quoting a total of 54 operational sorties flown, and he re-opened his victory tally on 28 May by shooting down a Ju87 and a Macchi 202 near Acroma. On 9 June, as the battle around Bir Hackeim was reaching its peak, 33's pilots joined with those of 274 Squadron in scouring the fighting area and tangled with a batch of Macchi 202s and Messerschmitt Bf109s, with Wade destroying one of the latter. Two days later 274's Hurricanes provided the high cover for 33 Squadron on a fighter sweep and five miles north-west of El Adem found a large formation of Ju87s being escorted by 30 Bf109s from JGs 27 and 53, with a number of Italian fighters nearby. In the sprawling dogfight which followed 33 Squadron lost one pilot killed and two other Hurricanes severely damaged, one of the latter pair being piloted by Wade who forcelanded at El Adem and, again, walked home.

He gained another victory on 5 July by shooting down a Bf109 from JG27, and repeated this success by destroying another Bf109 on 14 July followed on 16 July by a Ju88. 33's casualty rate by then had grown alarmingly and the unit was reduced to flying less sorties, while its constant moving from base to base during the early months of 1942 exacerbated the situation. Promoted to Flight Lieutenant, and to all intents the deputy commander of 33 Squadron, Wade claimed a further victim on 2 September; a Bf109 from II/JG27, which thereby became Wade's twelfth – and 33 Squadron's 200th – claimed victory. His thirteenth kill came on 11 September – a Ju87 destroyed – but on a later sortie that day during a clash with enemy fighters south of Alamein his Hurricane was badly shot up and damaged and he regained base in a barely flyable machine. On 13 October he was awarded a Bar to his DFC, its citation crediting him with a total of 15 combat victories, and he left the Middle East temporarily for a spell of home leave in the USA.

On his return from leave Lance Wade joined No 145 Squadron on 12 January 1943 as a Flight commander, but two weeks later, on 26 January, he was promoted to Squadron Leader and succeeded Roy Marples, DFC, as unit commander. Flying Spitfire Vc aircraft,

(*Left*) Wg Cdr Lance Wade, DSO, DFC (*Right*) Lt-Col Lawrence Aubrey Wilmot, DSO, DFC, SAAF

Nose marking of Lance Wade's Hurricane

the squadron was based at Hamraiet, then Wadi Sirru in that month, but soon began moving westwards following the advancing Allied armies. On 1 March 1943 Wade led six of his men to cover some Kittyhawks on a sweep north of the Mareth Line and ran into nine Bf109s. Wade dived on four of these flying at 3,000 feet and shot pieces out of one Messerschmitt which fell away. Though he only claimed it as probably destroyed, later confirmation came that it had indeed crashed. Five days later, again providing top cover for Kittyhawks attacking German troops north of Medenine, Wade and his men tackled six Bf109s, claiming two of these as damaged.

On a second sortie that day Wade was leading eight Spitfires over the forward fighting zone and spotted eight to ten Macchi 202s below him plus a stray Bf109. Wade fastened on the 109's tail, fired, but had his cannons jam. Continuing to fire with his machine guns he saw the 109 belly-land in enemy-held territory and therefore merely claimed it as damaged. Two days later he added another 109 'scalp' to his 'belt', and on 21 March sent a Bf109 down into the sea. Next day Wade led six of his Spitfires into a whirling dogfight north of Mareth and promptly sent one Bf109 from II/JG77 down in flames into the earth.

By then 145 Squadron had begun receiving Spitfire IXs as the start of replacement of their battle-weary Mk Vcs, and on 29 March Wade led off ten Spitfires, including four Mk IXs, for a patrol north of Gabes. The quartet of Mk IXs maintained high cover for the Mk Vcs and destroyed a Ju88 south of Zitouna early in the patrol, while the lower section attacked a mixed gaggle of Bf109s and Macchi 202s some 25 miles north of Gabes. The higher section soon joined them and Wade sent one Bf109 down spinning from 7,000 feet, then dived on three others flying 2,000 feet lower. Getting behind one Bf109 he fired one short burst and the 109 exploded. Wade was later credited with both 109s as destroyed, and soon after received the award of a second Bar to his DFC.

Continuing his run of successes, Wade destroyed four more enemy fighters in April 1943, though the last of these, a Bf109 shot into the sea off Cap Bon, nearly proved to be his ultimate victory for shortly after Wade became embroiled with a pair of particularly determined 109s, one of which got on his tail and riddled his Spitfire IX before being driven off by another spitfire. Two weeks later the

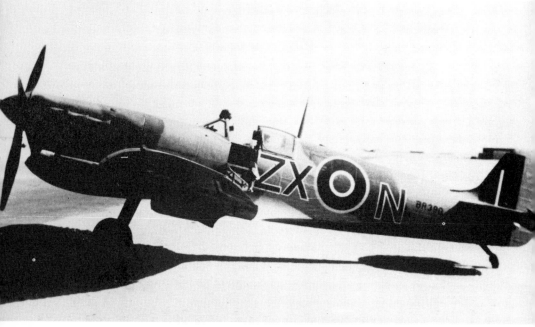

Spitfire Vb, BR390, of 145 Sqn

L-R: Flt Lt Ray Hudson, DFC; Sqn Ldr Ken Sands, DFC; Flt Lt Colin Robertson, DFC – all Australians of No. 450 Sqn RAAF (Kittyhawks)

Tunisian campaign ended with the surrender of the remaining Axis troops, and operations ground to a temporary halt. No 145 Squadron moved in June 1943 to Malta, at the same time receiving its first examples of Spitfire VIIIs – a Mark of superior performance to any previously flown – and by early July was part of No 244 Wing, alongside Nos 92, 417, 601, and 1 SAAF Squadrons, commanded by Group Captain Brian Kingcome, DSO, DFC, and ready to participate in the invasion of Sicily – *Operation Husky* – which got underway on the night of 9/10 July. Wade was in action as the first troops went ashore, damaging a Bf109, and on the 13th the Wing moved from Malta to Pachino, Sicily, and recommenced operations immediately.

With Sicily by then in Allied hands, the invasion of Italy commenced on 3 September, and within two weeks 145 Squadron was operating from Italian soil at Gioia. On 20 October Wade shot down two Focke Wulf Fw190s over the Trigno area, and on 3 November 1943 flew his ultimate operational sortie and, with his No 2, damaged at least three Fw190s during a running dogfight. Next day he was taken off operations and posted to an HQ staff job.

On 12 January 1944 Wade took off in an Auster light aircraft on a routine flight behind Allied lines but soon after the Auster was seen to spin down out of control and crash, killing Wade. His posthumously-announced award of a DSO credited him with a total of 25 combat victories – the highest scoring American pilot to serve in RAF uniform throughout the war.

*

If one facet of the desert air force could be singled out as epitomising its essential character it must be the truly international amalgam of its air crews. Men from every country of the British Commonwealth, and even a few neutral lands, intermingled with ease, combining readily in the common cause. Even units titled as belonging to the RAAF, RNZAF, SAAF, or RCAF were never wholly populated by men from those countries of origin, and every air crew mess tent echoed a dozen tongues and dialects, with only rare exceptions such as the Free French and, later, USAAF squadrons which were brought under the aegis of the desert air arms.

Virtually each of those countries produced outstanding pilots in every aspect of the air war over North Africa, men whose names were to all intents 'unknown' outside their own esoteric circles of acquaintances, yet men whose prowess and courage played not insignificant parts in ensuring ultimate victory over the Axis. Men like the Australian John William – 'Slim' – Yarra who was born on 24 August 1921 in Stanthorpe, Queensland, who joined the RAAF and served with Nos 232 and 64 Squadrons RAF in England before flying one of the first Spitfires off an aircraft carrier to deliver to 249 Squadron on Malta in early 1942. With his previous experience of flying Hurricanes he joined 185 Squadron on the island, though a few weeks later 185 also converted to Spitfires. On 12 May Yarra shot down a Bf109, followed by two Macchi 202s destroyed and a Bf109 damaged three days later.

On 18 May, accompanied only by a New Zealander, Sergeant Shaw, Yarra mixed it with four Bf109s to no avail, but was then told by the controller to protect a RAF rescue launch going out to retrieve a baled-out German pilot from the sea. Shaw's aircraft was badly damaged so he returned to base, leaving Yarra on his own. In the air near the launch were at least 13 Bf109s, but Yarra coolly took up an 'umbrella' position over the launch and waited. As one 109 dived to attack Yarra skidded sideways, recovered, then shot the 109 into the sea, its pilot baling out and being retrieved by the RAF launch crew. As they hauled the soaked 109 pilot on board another 109 attacked the launch, being forced away quickly by Yarra's fire. The Australian continued warding off individual diving attacks until his ammunition ran out, probably destroying a second Bf109, and then calmly continued making dummy attacks on each 109 to come within range of his launch 'charge'. This cat and mouse engagement lasted for 45 minutes but Yarra remained over the rescue launch until it was safely back in harbour, despite determined attacks by a section of four Bf109s during the return journey. He landed with dry petrol tanks, and was awarded a DFM and was commissioned shortly after.

By mid-July Yarra had brought his score up to twelve destroyed over Malta, and he was then posted to England where he joined No 453 Squadron RAAF on 14 September 1942 as 'B' Flight commander. On 10 December Yarra led six Spitfires down to strafe four enemy coastal vessels and a flak ship 10 miles north-west of

Flushing and was killed by flak as he made his first attack.

'Slim' Yarra was but one of Malta's 'Few' whose defiance of all odds ensured the island's retention by the Allies. These included fellow-Australian Sergeant (later, Pilot Officer) John – 'Tony' – Boyd from Brynestown, Queensland who served with 185 Squadron and claimed ten enemy aircraft destroyed or probably destroyed, apart from damaging at least seven others, in ten weeks of non-stop fighting, February to May 1942, was awarded a DFM, but died over Ta Kali attempting to fight eight Macchi 202 fighters on 14 May. Only five days before Boyd's death yet another Queenslander, Gordon Tweedale, DFM of 185 Squadron, who had claimed nine victories in a mere three weeks of intensive combat, had also been lost in action. New Zealand was well represented on Malta by pilots like John ('Jackie') Rae, DFC, who claimed a share in destroying or damaging at least 17 enemy aircraft between April and July 1942; or Gray Stenborg from Auckland who destroyed seven enemy aircraft over Malta, was awarded a DFC, but was killed in action on 24 September 1943 when flying with No 91 Squadron in England, having accumulated an overall tally of 14 combat kills.

From Rhodesia had come John Plagis (of Greek parentage) who was to claim the destruction of 13 enemy aircraft over the island, winning a DFC and Bar, and eventually finishing the war as Rhodesia's top fighter ace. Canada had provided such stalwarts as George Beurling, Henry ('Wally') McLeod, 'Buck' McNair, and 'Ted' Kopp; while its near-neighbour, the USA, had such men as Reade Tilley, 'Dick' McHan, 'Jimmy' Peck and Hiram Putnam (killed over Malta on 21 April 1942) to uphold the honour of Uncle Sam.

To almost every pilot allotted to defend or operate from Malta, the pace and intensity of the fighting came as a distinct shock, whether initiate or veteran in experience of aerial combat. One such veteran fighter pilot was John Derek Bisdee – the 'Bishop', or just 'Bish' to his intimate colleagues. A scholar of Marlborough and an exhibitioner of Corpus Christi, Cambridge, Bisdee had joined the RAFVR just prior to the war, and arrived on his first unit, 609 Squadron AAF on 26 December 1939, to fly Spitfires though he had never flown a monoplane before. He was to remain with 609 for the next 18 months and fought through the Battle of Britain, gaining five victories, then adding another five during early 1941 and being awarded a DFC on 11 July 1941.

Taken off ops that same month he became a Flight commander at 53 OTU, Heston, was promoted to Squadron Leader in December 1941 and posted to 61 Group HQ, then on 10 March 1942 returned to the sharp end when he was appointed OC No 601 Squadron AAF at Acaster Malbis. His squadron was equipped with the unorthodox American-designed Bell Airacobra tricycle-undercarriage fighter but Bisdee promptly 'arranged' for these to be exchanged for Spitfires, and shortly after he was ordered to prepare 601 Squadron for overseas 'somewhere in the Mediterranean'.

The unit's Spitfires and personnel were duly embarked aboard the USS *Wasp* at Glasgow and sailed for the Middle East. At dawn on 20 April the pilots bundled their personal kit aboard their Spitfires and, led by Wing Commander E.J. 'Jumbo' Gracie, DFC, flew off the carrier in waves of twelve – 47 in all took off shortly before 7 am – and set course 'red on blue' towards Algeria on a dog-leg to avoid reported heavy flak guns on Pantellaria. Bisdee, leading the second section of twelve, preferred to omit the dog-leg and led his dozen direct to Malta, arriving intact three hours later before the rest of the formations.

In the event only 41 of the 47 Spitfires reached Malta intact; one crashed on take-off into the sea, one forcelanded back on the carrier minus its long-range fuel tank, one landed in Algeria, one ran out of fuel en route, two others crashed at Hal Far and Grand Harbour respectively. The main bunch landed successively at Ta Kali, some while Bf109s were busy strafing the airfield. By evening three of those Spitfires had been lost in combat.* Bisdee and his men of 601 were billeted in the Naxxar Palace, near Ta Kali, and were quickly told that the Spitfires were now part of Malta's fighter pool, belonging to no particular unit or pilot.

The morning after his arrival Bisdee led off a section of four Spitfires southwards to climb around an incoming German raid of Ju88s accompanied by Bf109s. Attacking the Ju88s from above and out of the sun, Bisdee carefully selected one Ju88 and sent his first

---

* On the same day two Spitfires were totally destroyed and 15 more made unserviceable by the Luftwaffe's raids, leaving only 27 combat-fit next morning. By the following day this number was reduced to 17 due to technical problems.

shells into its starboard engine. The engine plumed black smoke, so Bisdee lined his sight onto its port engine, thumbed his firing button, but had no time to observe results as a pair of Bf109s riddled his Spitfire in a series of bangs and explosions. The Spitfire jumped crazily and when Bisdee tried the controls he realised he'd have to abandon the aircraft as it was out of control and by then down to 1,500 feet. Baling out smartly he pulled the parachute's D-ring, the canopy cracked open, and his harness webbing was torn off his shoulders. Reacting swiftly Bisdee managed to hook his right leg round one of the loops before he fell out of the harness, and seconds later plunged into the sea headfirst. Luckily for him he had been flying with his canopy hood pushed back, giving him those precious few extra seconds in his perilous descent. Surfacing again he inflated his dinghy and clambered in. The time was 10 am, and he was some four miles from the island.

Bisdee began the laborious job of paddling to shore on the heavy swell of the sea and it took him eight and a half hours before he finally reached the rocky shoreline of some towering cliffs. By then his strength was utterly spent and he was unable even to get out of the dinghy onto the rocks, while all around him – unbeknown to Bisdee – the sea was strewn with 'flower-pot' mines! By sheer chance he had been spotted by a naval airman from Hal Far named Monck, who made his way down the cliff and dragged the semi-conscious pilot ashore. As he did so a Ju88 appeared and released some bombs which covered both men with flying earth as they exploded nearby.

Helping Bisdee to his feet, Monck remarked lightly, 'You've had a busy day.'

'Yes', replied Bisdee in a croak, 'and it's only my first here ...'.

The Ju88 Bisdee had damaged was seen to crash and Bisdee added a Cant bomber to his score on 10 May, but on 23 June he led his twelve Spitfires off Malta and flew to LG07 in Egypt to join the North African war. On the squadron's first sortie on 5 July he claimed a Messerschmitt 210 recce aircraft as 'damaged', but was next promoted to Wing Commander, Day Fighters with a newly forming Anglo-American formation and planned the air cover for the assault convoys in the forthcoming invasion of Sicily. For obvious security reasons Bisdee was forbidden to fly actual operations and was next given the command of the RAF Wing on

(Above) The unpublicised and usually unhonoured labours of the ground crews played no small part in the overall Allied victory; epitomised here by Erks at work on Hurricane I, 'Alma Baker' 'Malaya'. Note 0.303-inch calibre Browning machine guns on wings awaiting installation

(Left) Propeller servicing – the hard way!

Lampedusa, an appointment which also entailed the duties of Military Governor of the island simultaneously. Subsequent appointments saw him command a fighter Wing of three French squadrons which took part in the capture of Corsica, then command of 323 Wing at Foggia comprised of anti-shipping strike, fighter, seaplane, and air-sea rescue units – the latter rescuing 550 Allied airmen out of the 'drink' in six months' operations. He eventually rose to Group Captain before leaving the RAF.

This United Nations complexion applied to almost every unit in North Africa with nominally British squadrons commonly commanded by South African, Australian, New Zealand, and Canadian veterans – leadership and experience were the criteria for such appointments, not the chance identity of a man's accident of birthplace. Even the DAF's top brass was a mix of nationalities; men like Ray Collishaw, the Canadian distinguished fighter ace from World War One, who was succeeded by Arthur 'Maori' Coningham, a New Zealander by birth and another with an outstanding fighting career. He was to be followed by Harry Broadhurst, a Briton who, at the age of 37, became the RAF's youngest Air Vice-Marshal with a personal combat tally of 16 enemy aircraft destroyed or probably destroyed before taking up the reins of command of the desert air arm.

Indeed, the Commonwealth participation in the RAF's North African (and, later, Italian) air war was well exemplified by the contribution of South Africa. It is seldom appreciated that the South African Air Force (SAAF) provided almost half of all the medium bomber forces and a large part of the fighter complement of the DAF during 1940-42 particularly. By May 1945 of the 61 squadrons (all roles) still in firstline operational areas commanded then by the Mediterranean Allied Air Forces HQ, no less than 23 were SAAF squadrons. Such willing support for the Allied cause was perhaps all the more remarkable when it is remembered that during the war years 1939-45, under South African law, no member of its armed Services could be *compelled* to serve outside the Union of South Africa – in the 'Outer World' as a contemporary phrase termed it – though any Serviceman was free to *volunteer* for such duty.

On 6 September 1939, the date on which South Africa legally entered the war on the side of Britain and her other allies, the SAAF comprised a total personnel strength of 173 officers and, 1,664 other ranks, while its equipment consisted of a motley collection of outmoded biplanes – Hartbeests, Wapities, Furies – plus one Blenheim I, one Fairey Battle, and four Hurricane Is. Hastily, conversion of some civil Junkers Ju86 airliners from South African Airways to become 'bombers' met technical problems in adapting British General Purpose (GP) bombs to the Junkers' 'bomb bays'. No material help from the RAF was available at that stage – the RAF had no aircraft to spare – but on 1 June 1940 a Joint Air Training Scheme agreement was signed to train RAF and SAAF airmen in the Union. By the close of the war this scheme had turned out a gross total of 33,347 air crew men of most categories, of which total 20,800 were for the RAF, 12,221 for the SAAF, and 326 were other Allied personnel.

The rapid expansion of the scheme can be judged by the fact that by December 1941 a total of 29 air training schools had been established with nearly 10,000 airmen undergoing instruction. In May 1940 units of the SAAF moved north to Kenya, ready to oppose the Italian forces in occupation in Abyssinia, and when at one minute past midnight on 10/11 June 1940 Italy declared war the SAAF strength in Kenya was 13 Ju86 'bombers', 24 Hartbeests, six Hurricanes, six Furies, and a single Fairey Battle.

At 0800 hours on 11 June four Ju86s from 12 Squadron SAAF left Eastleigh, refuelled at Bura, then bombed a concentration of Italian tanks and transports at Moyale; while on the same day No 14 Squadron RAF, based at Port Sudan, sent its Wellesleys to bomb Massawa, destroying a huge petrol dump estimated at containing 350,000 gallons and damaging aircraft and hangars.

The ensuing struggle to defeat Mussolini's forces in East Africa was to last until an eventual Italian surrender in November 1941, during which period the SAAF was truly blooded in modern aerial warfare and firmly established its overt superiority over Italy's Regia Aeronautica. From that little-publicised conflict emerged a host of South African air crew men who, having established outstanding fighting reputations over Somaliland and Eritrea, then joined the ranks of the desert air forces in North Africa and further embellished their records. The first South African unit to move north to Egypt was No 1 Squadron SAAF, equipped with

Hurricanes, which relieved No 274 Squadron RAF at Amriya for the defence of Alexandria on 16 April 1940, and next day flew its first – and the SAAF's first – operational sorties in the desert war.

Of the many doughty SAAF fighter pilots to participate in the East African campaign, the most successful to emerge was Captain John Everitt Frost, DFC, who accounted for three Caproni bombers and two Fiat fighters in a single combat on 2 February 1941. A Sword of Honour graduate from the South African Military College, Frost was serving with No 3 Squadron SAAF in that campaign and returned to South Africa in May, then with promotion to Major he was given command of No 5 Squadron SAAF on 23 July 1941 and, on 16 December, led his Tomahawks to join the North African war. During the first six months of 1942 Frost personally shot down eight enemy aircraft as destroyed and six others probably destroyed or damaged, bringing his war total to at least 15 destroyed, five probables, nine damaged, and a further 25 (at least) destroyed on the ground. On 16 June 1942 Frost led six Tomahawks from 5 Squadron in a 14-fighter escort for some Boston bombers west of El Adem. The formation was bounced by Bf109s and in the ensuing dogfight John Frost was killed. In 1943 came a tardy announcement of the award of a Bar to Frost's DFC, and he proved to be the SAAF's highest-scoring ace of the entire war.[*]

If a specific unit could be singled out as representative of all the desert squadrons' composition, exploits, and sacrifices, perhaps No 112 Squadron RAF exemplified those squadrons in a variety of ways. Certainly, its distinctive 'sharkmouth' markings on its Tomahawks, Kittyhawks, and Mustangs remain for many desert airmen a prime memory of those years under the African sun. From May 1939 until May 1945 an overall total of 312 pilots served with 112 Squadron at some period among whom were British, Australian, New Zealand, Canadian, Polish, and South African men – 35 of the SAAF in toto – while its toll of casualties amounted to 108 pilots killed, prisoner of war, or simply recorded as 'Missing' (fate unknown); almost exactly one in three of all pilots to serve with the squadron. In its pure fighter role i.e. in the context of aerial combat only the 'Sharks' claims for enemy aircraft, as detailed in *contemporary* unit records,

[*] Though not the highest-scoring South African-*born* fighter ace.

varies with the official summary issued by the Air Ministry Historical Branch later. The following tabulations may be compared accordingly:

	AM AHB	*Squadron records*
Destroyed	164	205
Probably destroyed	48	50
Damaged	81	97
Strafed on ground	?	62

It should be borne in mind, however, that 112 Squadron spent a large proportion of its operational work as low-level fighter-bombers from March 1942 and thereafter created an unrecorded tally of significant damage to the Axis forces by strafing, bombing, and wrecking enemy troops, transports, installations, airfields, and the like. The high turnover in aircraft used by the squadron was by no means uncommon among the desert fighter squadrons throughout the war. From 1939 to May 1945, No 112 Squadron had taken on charge a gross total of 599 operational aircraft. Of these, two were Gloster Gauntlets, 33 were Gloster Gladiators, 67 were Curtiss Tomahawks, 409 were Curtiss Kittyhawks, and 88 were North American Mustangs. Of the overall total, 163 aircraft (all types) were destroyed or severely damaged due directly to enemy action of some form (airborne or grounded), apart from no small number wrecked in non-operational flying accidents; such was the toll of 112's war.

Select Bibliography

The Desert Air Force, R. Owen; Hutchinson, 1948

Middle East, 1940-42, P. Guedalla; Hodder & Stoughton, 1944

Libyan Log, E.G. Ogilvie; Oliver & Boyd, 1943

They Flew Through Sand, G.W. Houghton, R. Schindler, Cairo, 1942

Wings over Olympus, T. Wisdom; Allen & Unwin, 1942

Triumph over Tunisia, T. Wisdom; Allen & Unwin, 1944

Near East, C. Beaton; Batsford, 1943

Tattered Battlements, H. Johnson; P. Davies, 1943

Spitfires over Malta, R. Hesselyn/P. Brennan; Jarrolds, 1944

Malta Spitfire, G. Beurling/L. Roberts; OUP, Toronto, 1943

Mediterranean Airpower, A.W.F. Glenn; Conrad Press, 1944

RAF Middle East Review, 1942-45, HMSO; Crown Copyright

The Air Battle of Malta, HMSO, 1944

RAF Middle East, HMSO, 1945

Imshi, A. Myers; W.H. Allen, 1943

Briefed to Attack, H.P. Lloyd; Hodder & Stoughton, 1949

Diary of a Canadian Fighter Pilot, W.S. Large; R. Saunders, Toronto, 1944

Gen, Vols 1-5, GHQ, Middle East, 1942-45

80 Squadron, J.H. Schultz; Private, 1945

112 Squadron History, R.A. Brown; Private, 1959

Desert Squadron (272), V. Houart; Souvenir Press, 1959

Camera at War, H. Hensser; Jarrolds, 1945

Paiforce, HMSO, 1948

Escape to Live, E. Howell; Longmans, Green & Co, 1947

Faith, Hope and Charity, K. Poolman; W. Kimber, 1954

Night Strike from Malta, K. Poolman; Jane's, 1980

One Man's Window, D. Barnham; W. Kimber, 1956

Pattle, E.C.R. Baker; W. Kimber, 1965

The Unseen Eye, G. Millington; Gibbs & Phillips, 1961

War in the Aegean, P. Smith/E. Walker; W. Kimber, 1974

We Find and Destroy, P. Alexander; 458 Sqn Council, 1959

Per Noctem per Diem, Tucker/MacGregor; 24 Sqn Committee, 1961

Theirs is the Glory, S. McCreath; Widdicombe & Ogden

3 Squadron RAAF at War, J. Watson/L. Jones; 3 Sqn Ass'n, 1959

Wellington Wings, R. Chappell; W. Kimber, 1980

Fighters over the Desert, C. Shores/H. Ring; N. Spearman, 1969

Fighters over Tunisia, C. Shores/H. Ring/W. Hess; N. Spearman, 1975

Pictorial History of the Mediterranean Air War, 3 Vols, C. Shores; Ian Allan, 1972-74

RAF 1939-45, 3 Vols, Richards/Saunders; HMSO, 1953-54

RCAF Overseas, 3 Vols, OUP, 1946-47

RNZAF Official History, 3 Vols, H. Thompson; WHB, NZ, 1953

RAAF Official History, 3 Vols, AWM, 1954

SAAF History, 3 Vols, Brown/Martin/Orpen; Purnell, 1970-77

Desert Air Force at War, C. Bowyer/C. Shores; Ian Allan, 1981

Spitfire Saga, R.H. White; W. Kimber, 1981

The Air Battle for Malta, Lord Douglas-Hamilton; Mainstream, 1981

Hero, B. Nolan; Lester & Orpen Dennys, 1981

Photo-Reconnaissance, A.J. Brookes; Ian Allan, 1975

Test Pilot, Duke/Mitchell; Wingate, 1953

In Full Flight, A. Spooner; Macdonald, 1965

Index

Place names